Room 101 Has WI-FI: How Digital Technology Turned Orwell's Warning Into Today's World

David G. Stone

Published by ELC Publishing, 2026.

ROOM 101 HAS WI-FI: HOW DIGITAL TECHNOLOGY TURNED ORWELL'S WARNING INTO TODAY'S WORLD

First edition. September 4, 2026.

ISBN: 979-8235975989

Written by David G. Stone.

Table of Contents

INTRODUCTION: THE SCREEN IS WATCHING YOU

The year 2025 marks 76 years since George Orwell penned *1984*, yet his dystopian warnings have never felt more prophetic. Today, the telescreens of Room 101 aren't forced upon us by totalitarian regimes—we carry them willingly in our pockets, invite them into our homes, and pay monthly subscriptions for the privilege of being watched. This introduction establishes how digital technology has transformed Orwell's fictional nightmare into our voluntary reality, exploring why we've traded privacy for convenience and freedom for connectivity.

THE VOLUNTARY PANOPTICON: HOW WE INVITED BIG BROTHER HOME

The Smartphone Telescreen

In Orwell's Oceania, Winston Smith lived in constant fear of the telescreen's watchful eye, that omnipresent device that could never be fully turned off. How quaint that fear seems now, when billions of people voluntarily carry devices far more invasive than Orwell ever imagined. Our smartphones don't merely watch and listen—they track our every movement, monitor our heartbeats, record our conversations even when we think they're off, and analyze our behavioral patterns with algorithmic precision that would make the Thought Police weep with envy.

The modern smartphone represents the ultimate achievement of surveillance capitalism. Unlike Orwell's crude telescreens, these devices have made surveillance seductive. They don't just monitor us; they serve us, entertain us, connect us to loved ones, and provide instant access to humanity's collective knowledge. We've willingly surrendered our privacy not through force or fear, but through the irresistible allure of convenience and connection. The genius of this system lies not in its oppression, but in its indispensability.

Smart Homes: The Connected Prison

Beyond our pockets, we've extended the surveillance network into our most intimate spaces. Smart speakers listen to our conversations, learning our voices, our routines, our secrets. Smart thermostats track when we're home and when we're away. Security cameras monitor our daily activities. Smart refrigerators know our eating habits. Even our televisions have become telescreens, watching us as we watch them, collecting data about our viewing preferences, our emotional responses, and our consumer desires.

This interconnected web of devices creates a comprehensive surveillance network that would make Orwell's Ministry of Love seem primitive by comparison. Yet we've embraced these technologies not as instruments of oppression, but as symbols of progress and sophistication. The modern home isn't just connected—it's surveilled, and we've paid handsomely for the privilege.

THE ARCHITECTURE OF DIGITAL OPPRESSION

Data as the New Currency of Control

In *1984*, the Party controlled Winston through fear, violence, and the constant threat of Room 101. Today's digital overlords have discovered something far more effective: voluntary surrender through value exchange. We don't give up our data because we're forced to—we trade it for services, convenience, and connection. Every Google search, every Facebook like, every Amazon purchase becomes a data point in an ever-expanding profile of our thoughts, desires, and behaviors.

This data doesn't just describe who we are—it predicts who we'll become. Algorithmic systems can forecast our purchasing decisions, our political leanings, our relationship status, even our mental health crises before we're fully aware of them ourselves. The result is a form of control more subtle and more complete than anything Orwell envisioned: predictive manipulation that shapes our choices while maintaining the illusion of free will.

The Algorithmic Thought Police

Orwell's Thought Police monitored citizens for signs of dissent and rebellion. Today's algorithms perform a similar function, but with infinitely greater sophistication. Social media platforms don't just track what we think—they shape how we think. Through carefully curated feeds, targeted advertising, and recommendation systems, these platforms create echo chambers that reinforce existing beliefs while gradually nudging users toward more profitable or politically useful positions.

The modern equivalent of thoughtcrime isn't the possession of forbidden ideas—it's the failure to engage with approved content. Platform algorithms reward conformity with visibility and punish deviation with shadow-banning and reduced reach. Dissent isn't crushed through violence; it's simply made invisible, filtered out of feeds and buried beneath mountains of algorithmic noise.

Social Credit and Digital Citizenship

While Western democracies haven't implemented formal social credit systems like those emerging in authoritarian regimes, informal versions already shape our digital lives. Credit scores determine our access to housing and employment. Online reputation systems affect our ability to participate in digital marketplaces. Social media algorithms evaluate our worthiness for visibility and engagement. Cancel culture serves as a distributed form of social policing, where violations of evolving social norms can result in digital exile and professional destruction.

This creates a form of self-censorship more effective than any government censorship program. When every statement, every association, every digital footprint can be weaponized against us, most people learn to police themselves. The result is a society where free expression exists in theory but withers in practice, replaced by careful performance of approved opinions and behaviors.

THE PSYCHOLOGY OF VOLUNTARY SUBMISSION

The Convenience Trap

Perhaps the most disturbing aspect of our digital surveillance state isn't its existence, but our eager participation in it. We've traded privacy for convenience so gradually and completely that most people can no longer imagine life without constant digital mediation. The idea of navigating without GPS, socializing without social media, or shopping without personalized recommendations seems not just inconvenient but almost barbaric.

This dependency isn't accidental—it's engineered. Tech companies have deliberately created systems that become more valuable the more data we provide, and more difficult to abandon the more integrated they become with our daily lives. The result is a form of technological addiction that makes privacy advocates seem like digital Luddites rather than defenders of fundamental human rights.

The Normalization of Surveillance

Orwell understood that the most effective oppression is invisible oppression—systems so thoroughly integrated into daily life that they become unnoticeable. Today's surveillance capitalism has achieved this invisibility through normalization. An entire generation has grown up assuming that privacy is dead, that surveillance is the price of participation in modern life, and that resistance is futile.

This normalization extends beyond individual acceptance to cultural celebration. We don't just tolerate surveillance—we embrace it as innovation. Privacy advocates are dismissed as paranoid or old-fashioned. Companies that collect more data are valued more highly. Politicians who promise more security through more surveillance are rewarded with votes. The very concept of privacy has been reframed from a fundamental right to a luxury good available only to those wealthy enough to opt out of the data economy.

The Illusion of Agency

The most insidious aspect of modern digital surveillance is its maintenance of the illusion of choice. Unlike Orwell's totalitarian state, which relied on obvious coercion, today's surveillance systems present themselves as voluntary. We can choose not to use Google, not to join Facebook, not to carry smartphones. Of course, these choices come with such severe social and economic penalties that they're not really choices at all—but the fiction of consent is maintained.

This illusion of agency serves a crucial psychological function. It allows us to maintain our self-image as free individuals while participating in systems of comprehensive surveillance and control. We tell ourselves we're making rational trade-offs, exchanging privacy for value, when in reality we're participating in a system designed to eliminate meaningful choice while preserving its appearance.

THE CORPORATE MINISTRY OF TRUTH

Information Control in the Digital Age

Orwell's Ministry of Truth controlled information by rewriting history and limiting access to alternative narratives. Today's information control operates through abundance rather than scarcity. Instead of limiting information, digital platforms overwhelm us with so much information that finding truth becomes nearly impossible. Search algorithms determine what information we see. Social media feeds curate reality based on engagement metrics rather than accuracy. Recommendation systems create filter bubbles that trap us in self-reinforcing information loops.

The result is a form of information control more effective than any government censorship program. Truth isn't suppressed—it's drowned in an ocean of misinformation, disinformation, and carefully crafted propaganda. Citizens aren't denied access to facts; they're overwhelmed with so many competing versions of reality that distinguishing truth from fiction becomes exhausting and ultimately futile.

The Weaponization of Attention

In *1984*, the Party controlled citizens by controlling their thoughts. Today's digital platforms have discovered something more valuable than thought control: attention control. By designing systems optimized for engagement rather than truth or wellbeing, these platforms have learned to capture and monetize human attention on an industrial scale. Our focus, our emotional energy, our cognitive resources become raw materials in an attention economy that profits from distraction, outrage, and addiction.

This attention capture isn't neutral—it shapes how we think, what we care about, and how we understand the world around us. When algorithms reward extreme content with greater reach, they gradually shift our collective discourse toward polarization and conflict. When recommendation systems prioritize engagement over accuracy, they create information environments where truth becomes secondary to emotional impact.

The Manufacture of Consent in Real-Time

Edward Bernays wrote about engineering consent through propaganda; today's digital systems engineer consent through personalization. Rather than broadcasting the same message to everyone, modern propaganda systems craft individualized messages designed to resonate with each person's unique psychological profile. Political campaigns use voter data to send different messages to different demographics. Advertisers use browsing history to create personalized desire. Social media platforms use behavioral data to surface content that confirms existing biases while introducing new ideas gradually and subtly.

This personalized propaganda is more effective than mass media because it feels organic rather than imposed. We don't experience it as manipulation because it aligns with our existing preferences and beliefs. The result is a form of consent manufacturing that operates below the threshold of conscious awareness, shaping our opinions while preserving the illusion of independent thought.

DIGITAL RESISTANCE AND THE LIMITS OF FREEDOM

The Impossibility of Digital Escape

In *1984*, Winston's greatest fear was Room 101—the place where the Party would force him to confront his worst nightmare and break his will to resist. Today's Room 101 isn't a place but a condition: the impossibility of digital escape. Opting out of digital surveillance isn't just inconvenient—it's increasingly impossible. Employment requires digital connectivity. Banking requires digital access. Healthcare requires digital records. Social relationships require digital mediation. Even basic civic participation requires digital engagement.

This digital dependency creates a form of soft totalitarianism where resistance becomes practically impossible. Unlike Orwell's regime, which needed to break dissidents through torture, today's surveillance systems simply make non-participation so costly that resistance withers naturally. The choice between privacy and participation isn't really a choice at all—it's an ultimatum disguised as consumer preference.

The Surveillance Entrepreneur and the Data Proletariat

Marx wrote about the exploitation of workers by owners of production capital. Today's surveillance capitalism creates a new form of exploitation: the appropriation of human experience as raw material for data production. We've become unpaid laborers in a vast data extraction operation, generating valuable behavioral surplus that's captured, analyzed, and sold without compensation or consent.

This creates a new class structure: surveillance entrepreneurs who own the platforms and algorithms that process human experience, and data proletariat who provide the raw material for this processing. Unlike traditional workers, data proletariat aren't paid for their labor—they're charged subscription fees for the privilege of being exploited. The result is an economic system where the primary source of value comes from unpaid human activity, creating unprecedented wealth concentration while impoverishing the very people who generate that wealth.

Technological Solutionism and the Myth of Innovation

The tech industry has successfully framed surveillance capitalism as innovation, data extraction as progress, and privacy erosion as inevitable technological evolution. This framing makes resistance seem backward-looking and futile. Why fight the future? Why resist progress? Why cling to outdated concepts like privacy when connectivity offers so many benefits?

This technological solutionism obscures the reality that these systems aren't natural evolutionary developments but deliberate design choices made by specific people for specific economic and political purposes. The surveillance economy isn't inevitable—it's engineered. The privacy erosion we're experiencing isn't the price of progress—it's the cost of allowing private corporations to commodify human experience without meaningful oversight or consent.

THE FUTURE OF FREEDOM IN A SURVEILLED WORLD

Artificial Intelligence and the Completion of Control

As artificial intelligence systems become more sophisticated, the gap between Orwell's dystopian vision and our digital reality continues to narrow. AI-powered surveillance can now identify individuals from their gait patterns, predict criminal behavior from facial features, and detect emotional states from voice patterns. Machine learning algorithms can discover patterns in human behavior that humans themselves don't recognize, creating possibilities for manipulation and control that exceed anything Orwell imagined.

The integration of AI with existing surveillance infrastructure creates the possibility of total social control without human intervention. Automated systems could monitor, evaluate, and respond to human behavior in real-time, creating a form of techno-totalitarianism that operates through code rather than ideology. The result would be a society where dissent becomes literally unthinkable, not because it's forbidden but because it's automatically detected and neutralized before it can fully form.

The Generational Divide and the Future of Privacy

Perhaps the most troubling aspect of our slide toward digital totalitarianism is the generational normalization of surveillance. Young people who have grown up with smartphones, social media, and constant connectivity don't experience privacy as a loss because they've never known its absence. For digital natives, privacy isn't a fundamental right but an abstract concept, like typewriters or rotary phones—interesting historical artifacts but irrelevant to modern life.

This generational shift suggests that resistance to surveillance capitalism may weaken over time rather than strengthen. As older generations who remember pre-digital privacy pass away, they'll be replaced by generations who view surveillance as natural and inevitable. The result could be the complete elimination of privacy as a social value, creating a world where Orwell's dystopian vision becomes not just acceptable but desirable.

Corporate Feudalism and Digital Serfdom

The concentration of digital power in the hands of a few tech corporations has created a new form of feudalism, where digital serfs depend on tech lords for access to information, communication, commerce, and social connection. Like medieval serfs who couldn't survive without their lord's protection, digital citizens can't function without access to corporate-controlled platforms and services.

This digital feudalism operates through terms of service rather than force, creating the illusion of voluntary participation while establishing comprehensive control over digital life. Users who violate platform rules can be exiled from digital society without trial or appeal. Entire communities can be eliminated through algorithmic changes. Alternative platforms can be destroyed through coordinated deplatforming campaigns. The result is a form of private tyranny that operates outside traditional legal and democratic constraints.

CONCLUSION: BEYOND ORWELL'S WORST NIGHTMARES

George Orwell's *1984* warned us about a future where totalitarian governments would use technology to create perfect systems of surveillance and control. What he couldn't have anticipated was that such systems would emerge not through government coercion but through corporate seduction, not by forcing surveillance upon us but by making us eager participants in our own digital enslavement.

The telescreens of Oceania seem primitive compared to the sophisticated surveillance apparatus we carry in our pockets and invite into our homes. Big Brother's crude propaganda pales beside the personalized manipulation of algorithmic feeds. The Ministry of Truth's ham-fisted information control can't compete with the elegant chaos of information abundance designed to obscure rather than reveal truth.

Yet perhaps the most chilling aspect of our current situation isn't the sophistication of modern surveillance but our willing participation in it. Orwell's dystopia required constant violence and terror to maintain control. Our digital dystopia maintains itself through convenience and connectivity, making resistance seem not just difficult but irrational. Why fight systems that serve us so well? Why resist technologies that connect us so completely? Why protect privacy that seems increasingly obsolete?

The answer lies in recognizing that convenience and connection aren't neutral goods—they're tools that can liberate or enslave depending on who controls them and how they're deployed. The same technologies that can enhance human freedom and creativity can also eliminate them entirely. The same systems that can democratize information can also weaponize it against democracy itself.

We stand at a crossroads that Orwell could never have imagined: a world where dystopia presents itself as utopia, where oppression markets itself as empowerment, where surveillance sells itself as service. The screens are watching us not because they have to, but because we've asked them to. The question isn't whether we can resist this surveillance—it's whether we still want to, and whether we'll recognize the need for resistance before it's too late.

The future of human freedom depends not on our ability to build better technologies, but on our willingness to build better relationships with the technologies we've already created. In 2025, 76 years after Orwell's warning, the screen is indeed watching us. The only question that remains is whether we're still watching back, and what we're willing to do about what we see.

Chapter 1: From Telescreens to Smartphones

The Evolution from Orwell's Static Surveillance to Mobile, Personalized Monitoring

When George Orwell penned "1984" in 1948, his vision of the telescreen seemed like the ultimate instrument of totalitarian control—a device that could both broadcast propaganda and monitor citizens, mounted on walls like electronic sentinels that never slept. These fictional devices were crude by today's standards: static, obvious, and limited to fixed locations. Citizens in Oceania knew they were being watched; the telescreen's presence was deliberately intimidating, a constant reminder of Big Brother's watchful eye. The surveillance was external, imposed, and inescapable within certain spaces, yet paradoxically limited by its very obviousness and immobility.

Fast-forward to the 21st century, and we find ourselves living in a reality that would have astounded even Orwell's dystopian imagination. The evolution from telescreens to smartphones represents not merely a technological advancement, but a fundamental transformation in the nature of surveillance itself. Where Orwell's devices were stationary monuments to authoritarian power, modern smartphones are intimate companions that accompany us everywhere—into our bedrooms, our bathrooms, our most private moments and sacred spaces. The surveillance has become mobile, personalized, and infinitely more sophisticated than anything the Party in "1984" could have conceived.

This transformation represents a paradigm shift from external coercion to internal compliance, from obvious monitoring to invisible tracking, from state-imposed surveillance to citizen-embraced connectivity. The smartphone has evolved into something far more powerful than Orwell's telescreen precisely because it doesn't feel like surveillance at all—it feels like freedom, convenience, and empowerment. We carry these devices not because we must, but because we cannot imagine life without them.

The Technological Leap: From Broadcasting to Data Harvesting

The fundamental difference between telescreens and smartphones lies not just in their technological capabilities, but in their entire operational philosophy. Orwell's telescreens were primarily broadcasting devices that could monitor—they pushed information out and pulled limited information in. Today's smartphones represent a quantum leap in surveillance capability, functioning as sophisticated data harvesting machines that collect, process, and transmit vast amounts of personal information in real-time.

Modern smartphones are equipped with an array of sensors that would make Orwell's Thought Police envious: accelerometers that detect movement patterns, gyroscopes that track orientation, magnetometers that serve as digital compasses, proximity sensors, ambient light sensors, and multiple cameras capable of facial recognition. The microphones are always listening for wake words, the GPS chips track location with pinpoint accuracy, and the wireless radios constantly ping nearby networks, creating a digital footprint that follows us everywhere we go.

But perhaps most significantly, where telescreens were limited to observing behavior, smartphones actively shape it. Through push notifications, app interfaces, and algorithmic recommendations, these devices don't merely watch—they influence, suggest, and gradually modify our thoughts, preferences, and actions. They have evolved from passive monitoring tools into active agents of behavioral modification, making them far more sophisticated than anything Orwell imagined.

How Smartphones Became the Perfect Panopticon: Always On, Always Listening, Always Tracking

Jeremy Bentham's concept of the panopticon—a theoretical prison where all inmates could be observed by a single guard without the prisoners knowing whether they were being watched—has found its perfect expression in the modern smartphone. Unlike Bentham's architectural design or Orwell's static telescreens, the smartphone panopticon is both more pervasive and more insidious because it operates under the guise of convenience and connectivity.

The genius of the smartphone surveillance system lies in its omnipresence and its invisibility. These devices are quite literally always on, even when they appear to be off. The "power" button on most modern smartphones doesn't actually turn the device off—it merely puts it into a low-power state where essential systems continue running. Location services, wireless scanning, and various background processes continue operating, ensuring that the device remains connected to networks and continues collecting data even when users believe they've achieved privacy by "turning off" their phones.

The Always-Listening Reality

The microphones in smartphones are perhaps the most unsettling example of constant surveillance. While companies insist that devices only "actively" listen after wake words are detected, the reality is more complex and concerning. To detect wake words like "Hey Siri" or "OK Google," the device must constantly process audio input. This means sophisticated audio processing systems are perpetually analyzing ambient sounds, conversations, and environmental audio cues. Even when not explicitly activated, smartphones are calibrated to detect patterns, voices, and contextual audio information.

Recent studies have revealed that smartphone microphones can pick up ultrasonic beacons—high-frequency sounds inaudible to human ears—that are embedded in advertisements, retail environments, and even television shows. These beacons can trigger specific app behaviors, track user movements between physical and digital spaces, and create detailed profiles of consumer behavior without any visible indication to users that such tracking is occurring.

The implications extend beyond simple advertising. Voice pattern recognition can identify emotional states, health conditions, and psychological profiles. Changes in speech rhythm, tone, and frequency can indicate everything from emerging depression to early-stage neurological disorders. The smartphone's always-listening capability transforms every conversation, every phone call, every moment of vocalization into potential data points for analysis.

Location Tracking: The Invisible Leash

GPS tracking represents perhaps the most comprehensive surveillance capability of modern smartphones. These devices don't simply track where we are—they track where we've been, where we're going, how fast we're traveling, and how long we stay in each location. The location data creates detailed behavioral profiles that reveal intimate details about users' lives: their work schedules, shopping habits, relationship patterns, and even political affiliations based on the locations they frequent.

But GPS is only one component of location tracking. Smartphones also use WiFi network scanning, Bluetooth beacons, cell tower triangulation, and even ambient sound analysis to determine location. This multi-layered approach means that location tracking continues even when GPS is disabled, creating a redundant system that ensures continuous monitoring regardless of user privacy settings.

The precision of modern location tracking is extraordinary. Smartphones can determine not just which building users are in, but which floor, which room, and even which section of a room. This level of precision enables surveillance that extends far beyond simple geography—it reveals social patterns, professional relationships, and intimate behaviors that users never explicitly agreed to share.

The Psychology of Voluntary Submission to Surveillance

The most remarkable aspect of smartphone surveillance is not its technical sophistication, but the psychological mechanisms that make users willing participants in their own monitoring. Unlike Orwell's overtly authoritarian system, smartphone surveillance operates through what might be called "surveillance capitalism"—a system where personal data becomes the primary commodity, and users voluntarily provide this commodity in exchange for convenience, connectivity, and social acceptance.

The Convenience Trap

The psychology of voluntary submission begins with convenience. Smartphones offer genuine utility—communication, navigation, entertainment, and access to information—that significantly improves users' daily lives. This utility creates what psychologists call a "reciprocity bias," where users feel obligated to provide personal data in return for the services they receive. The more convenient and valuable the service becomes, the more willing users are to sacrifice privacy for functionality.

Navigation apps exemplify this dynamic perfectly. GPS navigation is genuinely useful—it saves time, reduces stress, and helps users discover new places. However, to provide this service, navigation apps must continuously track user location, movement patterns, and destination preferences. Users willingly accept this trade-off because the immediate benefit feels more tangible than the abstract privacy cost. Over time, this creates a dependency where users cannot imagine navigating without constant location tracking, making the surveillance feel not just acceptable but necessary.

Social Validation and Fear of Missing Out

Social media integration has created powerful psychological incentives for voluntary surveillance participation. Smartphones enable constant connection to social networks, where users receive validation through likes, comments, and social engagement. This creates what researchers call "intermittent variable reward schedules"—the same psychological mechanism that makes gambling addictive.

To maintain these social connections, users must accept extensive data collection. Social media apps track not just posts and interactions, but reading patterns, scroll speeds, pause durations, and even typing behaviors. Users accept this comprehensive monitoring because disconnecting from social media feels like social isolation. The fear of missing out (FOMO) becomes a powerful driver of surveillance acceptance.

The Illusion of Control

Perhaps most insidiously, smartphone interfaces are designed to create an illusion of privacy control while actually facilitating more comprehensive data collection. Privacy settings menus give users the impression they can control their data, but these settings are often confusing, incomplete, or ineffective. Users who take the time to adjust privacy settings often discover that they've only modified the most obvious tracking mechanisms while deeper, less visible surveillance continues unabated.

The complexity of modern privacy settings serves to discourage meaningful privacy protection. With dozens of apps, each with multiple permission categories and sub-settings, achieving genuine privacy requires expertise and persistent effort that most users cannot or will not invest. This creates what researchers call "privacy fatigue"—a state where users become so overwhelmed by privacy decisions that they simply accept default settings that maximize data collection.

Cognitive Dissonance and Rationalization

Many users who understand the privacy implications of smartphone surveillance continue using these devices anyway, creating cognitive dissonance that they resolve through rationalization. Common rationalizations include: "I have nothing to hide," "The convenience is worth it," "Everyone else is doing it," and "The data is anonymized anyway." These rationalizations allow users to maintain their smartphone usage while minimizing psychological discomfort about privacy loss.

The "nothing to hide" argument is particularly problematic because it assumes that current social and political norms will remain stable indefinitely. Users who feel comfortable sharing location data, browsing habits, and communication patterns with current governments and corporations may find this information problematic if social norms shift, political regimes change, or data security is compromised.

Case Studies: Location Tracking, App Permissions, and the Illusion of Choice

Case Study 1: The Google Location Timeline Revelation

In 2018, an Associated Press investigation revealed that Google continued tracking Android users' locations even when they had explicitly disabled "Location History" in their privacy settings. The investigation found that Google was collecting location data through other services like Google Maps, weather updates, and automated searches. This revelation demonstrated how privacy settings can create an illusion of control while actual data collection continues through alternative channels.

The psychological impact of this discovery was significant. Users who had believed they were controlling their privacy discovered that their explicit preferences had been effectively ignored. However, rather than abandoning Google services, most users simply accepted this reality and continued using their smartphones with the understanding that comprehensive location tracking was unavoidable. This response illustrates how privacy violations can actually reinforce surveillance acceptance through learned helplessness.

Google's response to the controversy was equally revealing. Rather than significantly changing their data collection practices, they primarily focused on improving their privacy communication—making the language clearer while maintaining the same fundamental surveillance capabilities. This approach demonstrated that the primary concern was user perception of privacy rather than actual privacy protection.

Case Study 2: The Cambridge Analytica Facebook Scandal

The Cambridge Analytica scandal revealed how smartphone apps could harvest vast amounts of personal data not just from users, but from their entire social networks. The scandal demonstrated that Facebook's smartphone app was collecting data from users' contacts, their friends' contacts, and even from people who had never used Facebook at all through shadow profiling techniques.

What made this case particularly significant was the revelation that users who had never explicitly agreed to data collection were nonetheless being monitored through their association with smartphone users who had granted app permissions. This demonstrated how individual privacy decisions could compromise the privacy of entire social networks, making personal privacy protection nearly impossible even for users who tried to opt out.

The psychological response to the Cambridge Analytica revelation followed a predictable pattern: initial outrage, followed by resignation, followed by continued usage with minor modifications to privacy settings. Despite widespread media coverage and public concern, Facebook's user numbers continued growing, and smartphone usage patterns remained largely unchanged. This response illustrated how privacy scandals often serve as temporary disruptions rather than fundamental changes to surveillance acceptance.

Case Study 3: The iOS App Tracking Transparency Paradox

Apple's introduction of App Tracking Transparency (ATT) in iOS 14.5 appeared to give users meaningful control over cross-app tracking. However, detailed analysis revealed that this feature primarily addressed third-party tracking while leaving Apple's own comprehensive data collection largely unchanged. Users who opted out of tracking by third-party apps were still subject to extensive data collection by Apple itself.

This case study illustrates the "illusion of choice" problem in smartphone privacy. Users were given highly visible controls over some aspects of tracking while other, potentially more significant surveillance continued invisibly. The ATT feature served primarily as a competitive weapon against companies like Facebook and Google while reinforcing user trust in Apple's surveillance ecosystem.

The psychological impact was particularly interesting. Users who enabled ATT felt more secure about their privacy, even though their overall exposure to surveillance had decreased only marginally. This demonstrates how visible privacy controls can create psychological satisfaction even when they provide limited actual protection.

Case Study 4: Fitness Tracker Integration and Health Surveillance

The integration of fitness tracking with smartphones has created new categories of surveillance that users actively seek out. Health and fitness apps collect extraordinarily intimate data—heart rate patterns, sleep cycles, menstrual cycles, step counts, and even bathroom habits. This data reveals information about users' physical condition, stress levels, sexual activity, and potential health conditions.

Users typically embrace this surveillance because it provides immediate feedback and helps them achieve health and fitness goals. However, this health data is often shared with insurance companies, employers, and government agencies in ways that users don't fully understand. The surveillance feels beneficial and voluntary, making users more likely to accept comprehensive monitoring of their most private biological functions.

The psychological mechanism here is particularly powerful because health surveillance feels like self-improvement rather than privacy violation. Users who would be outraged by government access to their medical records willingly provide the same information to smartphone apps, creating a surveillance system that feels empowering rather than invasive.

Expanding Surveillance: The Internet of Things Integration

Modern smartphones serve as central hubs for expanding surveillance networks through Internet of Things (IoT) device integration. Smart home devices, connected cars, wearable technology, and even smart city infrastructure all connect through smartphone apps, creating surveillance networks that extend far beyond the phone itself. Each connected device adds new data collection points and new opportunities for behavioral monitoring.

Smart home integration represents a particularly comprehensive surveillance expansion. Smartphones control smart thermostats that track occupancy patterns, smart locks that monitor entry and exit times, smart cameras that record activities, and smart speakers that listen to conversations. The smartphone becomes the command center for a comprehensive home surveillance system that users install and maintain themselves.

The psychological appeal of smart home integration demonstrates how surveillance can be marketed as empowerment and control. Users feel that they are taking charge of their environment and improving their lives through technology, while actually creating comprehensive monitoring systems that track their most intimate behaviors and routines.

Conclusion: The Perfection of Voluntary Surveillance

The evolution from Orwell's telescreens to modern smartphones represents more than technological advancement—it represents the perfection of surveillance through voluntary participation. Where Orwell imagined a system of obvious, external coercion, we have created something far more sophisticated: a surveillance apparatus that feels like freedom, empowerment, and social connection.

The smartphone surveillance system succeeds where Orwell's telescreen would have failed because it operates through psychological manipulation rather than physical coercion. Users choose to carry these devices, choose to install surveillance apps, and choose to accept privacy-invasive terms of service because the immediate benefits feel more valuable than the abstract privacy costs. This voluntary participation creates a surveillance system that is more comprehensive, more intimate, and more psychologically sustainable than anything Orwell imagined.

The implications of this transformation extend far beyond individual privacy concerns. A society where comprehensive surveillance feels voluntary and beneficial is a society that has fundamentally altered the relationship between individuals and authority. When citizens actively participate in their own monitoring, when they compete to provide more personal data, when they defend surveillance systems against criticism, the traditional concepts of freedom and autonomy require complete reexamination.

Perhaps most concerning is how this voluntary surveillance system creates its own psychological defenses. Users who have invested significant time, money, and social identity in smartphone ecosystems become psychologically invested in defending these systems against privacy criticism.

The surveillance becomes part of their identity rather than an external imposition, making resistance feel like self-denial rather than liberation.

The smartphone represents the ultimate realization of Bentham's panopticon—not because it enables perfect observation, but because it makes perfect observation feel like perfect freedom. In creating surveillance systems that users love, we have achieved something far more powerful than Orwell's crude telescreens: we have made surveillance irresistible, making it the foundation of modern social, economic, and personal life.

As we move forward into an increasingly connected world, the smartphone surveillance model is expanding into every aspect of human experience—our homes, our cars, our workplaces, our cities, and our bodies. The question is no longer whether we can escape surveillance, but whether we can maintain any meaningful concept of privacy and autonomy in a world where comprehensive monitoring has become the price of participation in modern society.

The transition from telescreens to smartphones marks not just a technological evolution, but a fundamental transformation in human civilization—from a world where surveillance was imposed to a world where surveillance is embraced, from a world where privacy was assumed to a world where privacy must be actively defended against our own desires for convenience and connection.

Chapter 2: Big Tech is Big Brother

The consolidation of power among tech giants: Google, Apple, Amazon, Meta, Microsoft

The modern digital landscape has witnessed an unprecedented concentration of power within the hands of five technological behemoths, creating what can only be described as a digital oligarchy that would make the fictional Big Brother envious. Google, Apple, Amazon, Meta, and Microsoft—collectively commanding market capitalizations that exceed the GDP of most nations—have systematically consolidated control over virtually every aspect of our digital existence. This consolidation didn't happen overnight; it represents decades of strategic acquisitions, aggressive market expansion, and the methodical elimination of competition through practices that would have been deemed monopolistic in any previous era.

Google's dominance extends far beyond search, encompassing advertising networks that reach billions, mobile operating systems that power the majority of smartphones worldwide, cloud infrastructure that hosts countless websites and applications, and video platforms that have become the primary source of information for entire generations. When a single company controls how information is discovered, consumed, and monetized across the globe, the implications for free thought and open discourse become staggering. Apple's ecosystem creates a walled garden so complete that users become trapped within its confines, with the company exercising unprecedented control over what applications can exist, what content can be accessed, and how users interact with their own devices. The App Store's rejection policies have effectively created a corporate censorship apparatus that decides what ideas can reach millions of users.

Amazon's tentacles reach into every corner of commerce, from the books we read to the servers that power the internet itself through Amazon Web Services. The company's ability to simultaneously compete with merchants on its platform while controlling the infrastructure they depend upon represents a conflict of interest so fundamental that it mirrors the oppressive control mechanisms Orwell imagined. Meta's stranglehold on social connectivity means that for billions of people worldwide, Facebook, Instagram, and WhatsApp aren't just social media platforms—they are the internet itself, the primary means through which human connection and information sharing occur in the digital age.

Microsoft's influence permeates the corporate world through its operating systems, productivity software, and cloud services, creating dependencies so deep that entire industries cannot function without the company's blessing. The collective power of these five entities extends beyond mere market dominance; they have become the architects of reality itself, determining what information we see, whom we connect with, and how we understand the world around us. Their algorithms don't just reflect our preferences—they shape them, creating feedback loops that gradually mold human behavior and thought patterns in ways that serve corporate interests rather than human flourishing.

The Infrastructure of Control

The true power of Big Tech lies not merely in the services they provide, but in the infrastructure they control. Cloud computing has become the backbone of the modern internet, with Amazon Web Services, Microsoft Azure, and Google Cloud Platform hosting everything from small business websites to critical government services. This infrastructure control means that these companies can effectively switch off large portions of the internet at will, as demonstrated when Amazon Web Services removed Parler from its servers, causing the entire platform to disappear overnight. The implications of this power extend far beyond individual platforms—entire economic sectors now depend on the continued goodwill of these technological overlords.

The consolidation extends into hardware as well, with Apple's control over the iPhone ecosystem, Google's Android operating system, and Microsoft's dominance in desktop computing creating chokepoints that no information or service can bypass. These companies don't just compete in markets—they create and control the markets themselves, setting the rules by which all other players must operate. This vertical integration across multiple layers of technology creates a form of control that is both more subtle and more comprehensive than traditional monopolies ever achieved.

The Revolving Door with Government

The relationship between Big Tech and government has evolved into a sophisticated revolving door system that would make Orwell's Party proud. Former government officials regularly transition into high-paying positions at tech companies, while tech executives move into regulatory positions with concerning frequency. This interchange of personnel ensures that the interests of Big Tech remain aligned with government policy, creating a fusion of corporate and state power that eliminates the traditional checks and balances that might limit either form of control.

The COVID-19 pandemic provided a perfect example of this collaboration, as tech platforms worked hand-in-hand with government agencies to control information flow, suppress dissenting opinions, and track population movements with an efficiency that exceeded the wildest dreams of previous authoritarian regimes. The fact that this collaboration was largely voluntary, driven by shared ideological goals rather than explicit legal mandates, makes it even more insidious than direct government censorship.

How algorithmic control mirrors thought-crime policing

The algorithms that govern our digital lives have evolved into something far more sophisticated and dangerous than simple content recommendation systems—they have become instruments of thought control that operate with a precision and subtlety that makes Orwell's Thought Police seem crude by comparison. These algorithmic systems don't merely respond to our existing preferences; they actively shape and manipulate our thoughts, creating artificial realities tailored to influence behavior in ways that serve the interests of their corporate masters.

Consider the search algorithm that determines what information billions of people can access when seeking answers to their questions. Google's PageRank algorithm and its successors don't simply return the most relevant or accurate information—they return information that has been filtered through layers of corporate bias, advertising interests, and ideological preferences. When someone searches for information about a controversial topic, the algorithm doesn't present a neutral set of results; it presents a curated reality designed to guide the searcher toward predetermined conclusions. This process is so seamless and appears so natural that users rarely question whether they're receiving complete or accurate information.

Social media algorithms take this manipulation to even more sophisticated levels, creating personalized echo chambers that reinforce existing beliefs while gradually introducing new ideas that align with platform objectives. Facebook's News Feed algorithm doesn't show users what their friends are actually posting; it shows them a carefully curated selection designed to maximize engagement, which often means promoting content that generates strong emotional responses—anger, fear, outrage, or validation. Over time, these algorithms train users to expect and crave certain types of content, creating addiction-like dependencies that make users more susceptible to further manipulation.

The concept of "shadow banning" represents perhaps the most Orwellian aspect of algorithmic control. Users continue posting content believing they're participating in normal social discourse, while algorithms silently limit the reach of their messages. They experience the illusion of free speech while being effectively silenced, creating a form of gaslighting that makes traditional censorship seem almost honest by comparison. The user may never know their reach has been limited, continuing to participate in what they believe is open dialogue while being systematically excluded from meaningful conversation.

The Automation of Bias

These algorithms don't operate in a political vacuum—they reflect and amplify the biases of their creators while presenting themselves as neutral and objective. When YouTube's recommendation algorithm consistently guides users toward certain political perspectives, or when Twitter's trending topics consistently exclude certain viewpoints, these platforms claim their algorithms are simply responding to user engagement patterns. However, the parameters used to measure engagement, the weights assigned to different types of interactions, and the underlying assumptions built into these systems all reflect deliberate choices that shape public discourse in predictable directions.

The machine learning systems that power these algorithms are trained on data sets that inherently reflect the biases and preferences of their creators. When engineers at these companies make decisions about what constitutes "quality" content, "reliable" sources, or "harmful" speech, they're embedding their own worldview into systems that will influence billions of people. The result is a form of ideological colonization that spreads certain ways of thinking while suppressing alternatives, all under the guise of technological neutrality.

Predictive Punishment and Pre-Crime

Perhaps most disturbing is the emergence of predictive algorithms that attempt to identify and neutralize potential "problems" before they manifest. These systems analyze user behavior patterns, social connections, content consumption habits, and communication patterns to flag individuals who might be likely to engage in "problematic" behavior. The definition of "problematic" is, of course, determined by the platforms themselves, creating a system where punishment precedes crime and guilt is determined by algorithmic prediction rather than actual behavior.

This predictive punishment system operates through reduced reach, limited functionality, increased scrutiny, or outright suspension based on the algorithm's assessment of future risk rather than past behavior. Users find themselves punished for crimes they haven't committed, based on patterns that algorithms have identified as potentially dangerous. The opacity of these systems means that users cannot understand why they're being punished or how to avoid future punishment, creating a climate of uncertainty and self-censorship that achieves the goals of authoritarian control without the need for explicit rules or transparent enforcement.

The role of AI in behavioral prediction and modification

Artificial Intelligence has evolved beyond a mere technological tool to become the primary mechanism through which human behavior is analyzed, predicted, and systematically modified on a global scale. The AI systems deployed by Big Tech companies represent the most sophisticated behavioral modification apparatus ever created, operating with a level of precision and scale that makes previous attempts at mass persuasion look primitive by comparison. These systems don't simply observe human behavior—they actively reshape it, creating feedback loops that gradually alter how people think, feel, and act in ways that serve corporate and ideological objectives.

The foundation of this system lies in the unprecedented data collection capabilities of modern technology platforms. Every click, scroll, pause, like, share, and purchase is recorded and analyzed, creating detailed behavioral profiles that capture not just what people do, but how they think and what motivates them. This data goes far beyond simple demographic information or stated preferences; it includes subtle behavioral patterns that reveal psychological states, emotional vulnerabilities, cognitive biases, and decision-making processes that users themselves may not be consciously aware of.

Machine learning algorithms process this behavioral data to create predictive models that can forecast with remarkable accuracy what content will capture attention, what messages will be most persuasive, what timing will maximize engagement, and what emotional triggers will drive specific behaviors. These models operate at a level of granularity that allows for individualized manipulation strategies tailored to each user's unique psychological profile. The result is a form of personalized persuasion that adapts in real-time based on the user's responses, continuously refining its approach to maximize influence.

The Psychology of Algorithmic Manipulation

The AI systems powering social media feeds, search results, and content recommendations exploit fundamental aspects of human psychology that evolved long before digital technology existed. These algorithms leverage cognitive biases such as confirmation bias, availability heuristic, and social proof to guide user behavior in predictable directions. They understand that humans are more likely to engage with content that confirms their existing beliefs, that creates emotional arousal, or that appears to be popular among their peer groups.

The sophistication of this manipulation extends to the timing and sequencing of content delivery. AI systems analyze when users are most susceptible to different types of influence, adjusting their strategies based on factors such as time of day, emotional state, recent activity patterns, and social context. A user who appears stressed or anxious might receive content designed to exploit those emotional states, while someone experiencing positive emotions might be targeted with different types of persuasive messaging.

Perhaps most insidiously, these systems create artificial social environments that feel natural and organic while being carefully orchestrated to produce specific behavioral outcomes. The AI doesn't just show users content—it creates entire social realities populated with carefully selected posts, comments, reactions, and interactions designed to guide the user toward predetermined conclusions or behaviors. Users experience what feels like authentic social discourse while actually participating in an elaborately staged performance designed to influence their thoughts and actions.

Behavioral Modification Through Intermittent Reinforcement

The addictive properties of social media platforms aren't accidental byproducts of engaging design—they're the result of deliberate behavioral modification techniques implemented through AI systems. These platforms employ intermittent reinforcement schedules similar to those used in gambling, providing unpredictable rewards (likes, comments, shares, notifications) that create compulsive usage patterns. The AI systems optimize these reward schedules for each individual user, adjusting the timing and intensity of positive feedback to maximize addiction potential.

This addiction serves a dual purpose: it ensures continued engagement with the platform, providing more opportunities for data collection and influence, while simultaneously creating psychological dependencies that make users more susceptible to manipulation. Addicted users are less likely to critically evaluate the content they consume or to seek alternative sources of information, making them ideal subjects for behavioral modification programs.

The AI systems also implement what behavioral psychologists call "variable ratio reinforcement," where rewards are delivered after an unpredictable number of actions. This creates the strongest form of behavioral conditioning, leading to persistent behavior even when rewards become rare. Users continue scrolling, clicking, and engaging even when the content becomes less satisfying, driven by the psychological conditioning created by these AI-optimized reward systems.

The Erosion of Human Agency

The ultimate goal of these AI-driven behavioral modification systems isn't simply to influence individual decisions—it's to gradually erode human agency itself, creating populations that respond predictably to algorithmic stimuli without conscious awareness of being manipulated. This process operates through subtle shifts in attention patterns, emotional responses, and decision-making processes that accumulate over time to create fundamental changes in personality and behavior.

Users begin to lose the ability to focus on content that doesn't provide immediate gratification, as their attention spans are gradually trained to expect constant stimulation and reward. They develop dependencies on external validation through social media metrics, losing confidence in their own judgment and increasingly relying on algorithmic suggestions for entertainment, information, and even life decisions. Critical thinking skills atrophy as AI systems provide increasingly personalized and easily digestible content that requires minimal cognitive effort to consume.

The end result is a population that has been systematically trained to be passive consumers of algorithmically-generated reality, rather than active participants in creating and shaping their own understanding of the world. This represents perhaps the most successful program of mass behavioral modification in human history, achieved not through force or explicit coercion, but through the subtle manipulation of psychological reward systems and the gradual erosion of human agency.

Corporate surveillance vs. government surveillance: a false distinction

The traditional framework for understanding surveillance—which positions government monitoring as the primary threat to privacy and freedom while treating corporate data collection as a separate, lesser concern—has become not only outdated but dangerously misleading. This false distinction obscures the reality of how surveillance actually operates in the modern world: as an integrated system where corporate and government interests have merged into a seamless apparatus of social control that exceeds the wildest ambitions of any historical authoritarian regime.

The notion that corporate surveillance is somehow more benign than government surveillance rests on several flawed assumptions. First is the idea that corporations are primarily motivated by profit rather than control, making them less dangerous than power-seeking governments. However, the scale and sophistication of corporate data collection has reached levels where the distinction between profit and control becomes meaningless. When companies possess detailed psychological profiles on billions of people, the ability to influence behavior, shape public opinion, and determine social outcomes becomes indistinguishable from political power.

Second is the assumption that users consent to corporate surveillance through terms of service agreements and privacy policies, making it fundamentally different from government surveillance conducted without consent. This assumption ignores the coercive nature of these agreements in a world where digital participation has become essential for economic and social survival. When the choice is between accepting comprehensive surveillance or being excluded from modern society, the concept of meaningful consent becomes illusory.

Third is the belief that corporate surveillance is limited by market forces and competition, while government surveillance is limited only by political constraints. In reality, the consolidation of the tech industry has eliminated meaningful competition in most sectors, while the integration between corporate and government surveillance has removed many traditional political constraints on state power. The result is a system that combines the worst aspects of both forms of surveillance while being constrained by neither market forces nor democratic oversight.

The Intelligence-Industrial Complex

The relationship between Big Tech companies and intelligence agencies represents one of the most significant developments in modern surveillance, yet it operates largely outside public awareness and democratic accountability. Programs like PRISM, revealed through Edward Snowden's disclosures, demonstrated that tech companies were directly providing user data to government agencies. However, focusing on these formal programs misses the broader reality of how corporate and government surveillance have become integrated at a fundamental level.

Tech companies employ thousands of former intelligence agency personnel, while former tech executives regularly move into government positions. This revolving door ensures that corporate surveillance capabilities are developed with government needs in mind, while government surveillance programs are designed to leverage corporate data collection infrastructure. The result is a system where the distinction between corporate and government surveillance becomes largely academic—they represent different components of a single surveillance apparatus rather than separate systems with different objectives.

The Five Eyes intelligence alliance—comprising the United States, United Kingdom, Canada, Australia, and New Zealand—has developed sophisticated methods for circumventing domestic surveillance restrictions by sharing intelligence gathered by partner nations. Similarly, the corporate-government surveillance partnership allows both sectors to access capabilities and data that would be restricted if they acted independently. Governments can access detailed behavioral data collected by corporations, while corporations can benefit from government intelligence gathering and analysis capabilities.

Data Sharing and Fusion

The flow of information between corporate and government surveillance systems operates through multiple channels that extend far beyond formal intelligence sharing agreements. Location data collected by smartphone apps is regularly purchased by government agencies from data brokers, providing law enforcement and intelligence services with detailed tracking information on millions of citizens without the need for warrants or legal oversight. Social media monitoring tools used by corporations to track brand sentiment and consumer behavior are identical to those used by government agencies for social media surveillance and protest monitoring.

Credit card companies, telecommunications providers, and other corporations routinely provide data to government agencies through legal mechanisms that operate with minimal oversight or public awareness. The Patriot Act and similar legislation in other countries created frameworks that essentially deputized corporations as extensions of the surveillance state, requiring them to provide data and services while prohibiting them from disclosing their cooperation with government agencies.

Perhaps most significantly, the development of artificial intelligence and machine learning capabilities is increasingly coordinated between corporate and government sectors. The same AI systems used by social media companies to identify and suppress "misinformation" are used by government agencies for propaganda analysis and opinion monitoring. The behavioral prediction models developed by advertising companies are adapted for law enforcement predictive policing programs and national security threat assessment systems.

The Elimination of Privacy as a Conceptual Framework

The merger of corporate and government surveillance has effectively eliminated privacy as a meaningful concept in modern society. Traditional privacy frameworks were built around the assumption that individuals could maintain control over personal information by choosing what to share and with whom. However, the pervasive nature of modern surveillance means that virtually all human activity generates data that is collected, analyzed, and shared across corporate and government systems regardless of individual preferences or choices.

The Internet of Things has extended surveillance into previously private spaces, with smart home devices, connected cars, and wearable technology creating comprehensive monitoring systems that track behavior, conversations, and activities within homes and personal spaces. This data is collected by corporations and shared with government agencies through mechanisms that operate outside traditional privacy protections and legal frameworks.

Even more fundamentally, the behavioral modification capabilities of modern surveillance systems mean that the concept of autonomous choice—which underlies traditional privacy frameworks—has become problematic. If individuals' preferences, decisions, and behaviors are being continuously shaped by algorithmic manipulation, then the notion of voluntary consent to surveillance becomes circular and meaningless. People may consent to surveillance systems that have already modified their ability to make independent decisions about that consent.

The Totalitarian Synthesis

The ultimate result of merged corporate and government surveillance is the emergence of what can only be described as a totalitarian system that operates through voluntary participation rather than explicit coercion. This system combines the efficiency and innovation of corporate technology with the authority and resources of government power, creating a form of social control that exceeds the capabilities of any historical authoritarian regime while maintaining the appearance of freedom and choice.

Citizens volunteer for comprehensive surveillance by using social media, carrying smartphones, making digital payments, and participating in the digital economy. They provide detailed information about their thoughts, relationships, behaviors, and preferences while believing they are simply using convenient technologies. The surveillance system appears benign because it operates through market mechanisms and user choice rather than government mandate, yet it achieves levels of social monitoring and behavioral control that would be impossible through traditional authoritarian methods.

This synthesis represents the realization of Orwell's vision through means he could never have anticipated. The telescreens of 1984 have been replaced by devices that people carry voluntarily and use enthusiastically. The Thought Police have been replaced by algorithms that monitor and influence thinking patterns through social media manipulation. The Ministry of Truth has been replaced by search engines and recommendation systems that control access to information while maintaining the illusion of comprehensive and neutral access to knowledge.

Conclusion

The emergence of Big Tech as a modern incarnation of Big Brother represents perhaps the most significant threat to human freedom and autonomy in our time, yet it operates through mechanisms so subtle and seemingly benevolent that its victims often become its most enthusiastic advocates. The five technological giants that dominate our digital landscape have achieved something that traditional authoritarian regimes could only dream of: comprehensive control over human thought and behavior achieved through voluntary participation and market mechanisms rather than explicit coercion.

The consolidation of power within these corporations has created an oligarchy that controls not just markets, but the very infrastructure of modern communication, commerce, and social interaction. Their algorithms don't merely respond to our preferences—they shape them, creating artificial realities tailored to influence behavior in ways that serve corporate and ideological interests rather than human flourishing. The AI systems they deploy represent the most sophisticated behavioral modification apparatus ever created, operating with a precision that makes traditional propaganda look crude by comparison.

Perhaps most insidiously, the merger of corporate and government surveillance has created a totalitarian system that operates through the illusion of choice and freedom. Users voluntarily carry tracking devices, eagerly share personal information, and submit to comprehensive behavioral monitoring while believing they are simply using convenient technologies. The traditional frameworks for understanding privacy, consent, and autonomy have become obsolete in a world where human agency itself is being systematically eroded through algorithmic manipulation.

The false distinction between corporate and government surveillance has allowed this system to develop largely outside democratic oversight and public awareness. By treating corporate data collection as a market phenomenon rather than a political one, society has failed to recognize the emergence of a form of power that transcends traditional categories of political and economic control. The result is a system that combines the efficiency of corporate innovation with the authority of state power, creating a form of social control that operates through voluntary participation while achieving totalitarian outcomes.

The implications extend far beyond individual privacy concerns to fundamental questions about human agency, democratic governance, and the future of free thought. If algorithms can predict and manipulate human behavior with increasing precision, what happens to the concept of free will? If a small number of corporations can control access to information and shape public discourse, what happens to democratic deliberation? If AI systems can modify human preferences and decision-making processes, what happens to the notion of autonomous choice that underlies both market economics and democratic politics?

These questions demand urgent attention because the trajectory of technological development suggests that the current system represents only the beginning of what artificial intelligence and behavioral modification technologies might achieve. The consolidation of power, the sophistication of manipulation techniques, and the integration of corporate and government surveillance are all accelerating, creating a window of opportunity for resistance that may not remain open indefinitely.

The challenge lies not just in understanding these systems, but in developing new frameworks for thinking about freedom, privacy, and autonomy in an age of algorithmic control. Traditional liberal concepts of individual rights and market choice appear increasingly inadequate for addressing forms of power that operate through the manipulation of choice itself. New forms of resistance, regulation, and social organization may be necessary to preserve human agency in an age of machine intelligence and corporate-state fusion.

The stakes could not be higher. We stand at a historical inflection point where the choices made about technology governance, corporate power, and surveillance systems will determine whether future generations live as free agents capable of independent thought and autonomous action, or as managed populations whose beliefs, behaviors, and life choices are determined by algorithmic systems designed to serve interests other than their own. The emergence of Big Tech as Big Brother is not an inevitable result of technological progress—it represents specific choices about how technology is developed, deployed, and governed. Different choices remain possible, but only if we can recognize the true nature and scope of the system that has already begun to reshape human consciousness itself.

Chapter 3: The Ministry of Truth Goes Digital

In *1984*, Orwell's Ministry of Truth stood as a towering monument to authoritarian control over information, where an army of workers rewrote history daily to align with the Party's ever-changing narrative. Today, that ministry has been replaced by something far more sophisticated and infinitely more pervasive: a network of digital platforms that don't merely control information—they create it, curate it, and weaponize it on a scale that would have made Big Brother himself dizzy with admiration. The modern Ministry of Truth doesn't operate from a single imposing building in the heart of London; it operates from server farms scattered across the globe, its algorithms working tirelessly to shape reality one click, one like, one share at a time.

SOCIAL MEDIA PLATFORMS AS MODERN INFORMATION MINISTRIES

The New Gatekeepers of Truth

Where once newspaper editors and television producers served as the primary gatekeepers of information, today's social media platforms have assumed this role with unprecedented power and reach. Facebook's News Feed algorithm doesn't just deliver news—it determines what millions of people will consider newsworthy. Twitter's trending topics don't merely reflect public interest—they shape it, elevating certain stories to viral status while others disappear into digital obscurity. YouTube's recommendation engine doesn't simply suggest videos—it creates pathways of thought that guide viewers down increasingly narrow corridors of belief and understanding.

These platforms have achieved something Orwell's Ministry of Truth could only dream of: the ability to customize reality for each individual citizen. Unlike the crude, one-size-fits-all propaganda of traditional totalitarian regimes, modern digital platforms create personalized realities tailored to each user's psychological profile, political leanings, and behavioral patterns. The result is not a single, monolithic truth imposed from above, but millions of individual truths, each carefully crafted to maximize engagement, compliance, and profitability.

The Algorithmic Editing of Reality

The most insidious aspect of platform-controlled information isn't what it includes, but what it excludes. Every social media feed represents thousands of editorial decisions made not by human judgment but by algorithmic systems optimized for engagement rather than truth, profit rather than public good. These algorithms don't just filter information—they actively reshape it, promoting content that generates strong emotional responses while suppressing material that might encourage critical thinking or nuanced understanding.

The result is a form of reality editing that operates below the threshold of conscious awareness. Users experience their feeds as natural reflections of what's happening in the world, unaware that every piece of content has been selected, ranked, and positioned according to complex algorithmic calculations designed to maximize platform revenue. This creates a feedback loop where algorithmic choices shape public opinion, which in turn influences algorithmic training, creating ever-more-sophisticated systems of reality manipulation.

Platform Consolidation and Information Monopolization

The concentration of information control in the hands of a few tech giants represents an unprecedented threat to intellectual diversity and democratic discourse. When Facebook, Google, Twitter, and a handful of other platforms control the vast majority of information distribution, they effectively control the boundaries of acceptable thought and discussion. Unlike traditional media monopolies, which were constrained by geography and technology, digital platform monopolies operate on a global scale with the ability to shape information flows for billions of users simultaneously.

This consolidation creates what economists call "network effects"—the more people use a platform, the more valuable it becomes, making it increasingly difficult for alternatives to compete. The result is a form of intellectual monoculture where diversity of thought is gradually eliminated not through direct censorship but through the inexorable logic of algorithmic optimization and market concentration. Alternative perspectives don't disappear overnight; they simply become increasingly invisible, buried beneath the weight of algorithmic indifference and economic pressure.

CONTENT MODERATION, FACT-CHECKING, AND THE CONTROL OF NARRATIVE

The Rise of the Digital Thought Police

Orwell's Thought Police monitored citizens for signs of ideological deviation and punished thoughtcrime with imprisonment and torture. Today's content moderators perform a similar function, but with greater efficiency and less obvious brutality. Instead of breaking dissidents in Room 101, modern platforms simply delete their posts, suspend their accounts, or reduce their visibility through shadow-banning and algorithmic suppression. The result is the same—the elimination of unwanted thoughts from public discourse—but the method is so clean and clinical that it barely registers as censorship.

Content moderation operates under the guise of protecting users from "harmful" content, but the definition of harm has expanded far beyond direct threats or illegal activities to include anything that challenges approved narratives or disrupts platform profitability. Medical information that contradicts official health authorities becomes "dangerous misinformation." Political opinions that deviate from mainstream positions become "extremist content." Scientific debates about controversial topics become "conspiracy theories." The gradual expansion of what constitutes prohibited content creates a chilling effect where users self-censor to avoid punishment, leading to the voluntary surrender of intellectual freedom that Orwell's regime could only achieve through violence.

The Fact-Checking Industrial Complex

Perhaps no development better illustrates the transformation of information control than the emergence of professional fact-checking as a tool of narrative management. What began as a legitimate journalistic practice—verifying the accuracy of factual claims—has evolved into a sophisticated system for legitimizing approved viewpoints while delegitimizing dissent. Fact-checkers don't merely evaluate the accuracy of specific claims; they determine which questions are acceptable to ask, which sources are credible to cite, and which conclusions are reasonable to draw.

The genius of the fact-checking system lies in its apparent objectivity. Unlike traditional censorship, which openly suppresses information, fact-checking creates the illusion of rational, evidence-based evaluation while actually serving to reinforce existing power structures and approved narratives. When fact-checkers declare certain claims "false" or "misleading," they're not just evaluating evidence—they're establishing the boundaries of acceptable discourse and marking certain ideas as socially unacceptable to hold or express.

The Weaponization of Community Standards

Platform community standards represent one of the most effective tools of modern information control, combining the appearance of democratic participation with the reality of algorithmic enforcement. These standards are presented as collective agreements about appropriate behavior, but they're actually unilateral impositions by platform owners designed to eliminate content that threatens their business model or political interests. The language of community standards—emphasizing safety, respect, and inclusion—makes opposition seem antisocial and unreasonable.

The enforcement of community standards operates through a combination of automated systems and human moderators, creating a form of distributed censorship that's both comprehensive and deniable. When content is removed for violating community standards, platforms can claim they're simply enforcing rules that users agreed to follow, deflecting responsibility for censorship decisions while maintaining complete control over information flows. This system is particularly effective because it makes resistance seem like a violation of social norms rather than a defense of fundamental rights.

The Outsourcing of Censorship to Private Companies

One of the most troubling developments in modern information control is the outsourcing of censorship functions from government agencies to private companies. Governments can maintain their constitutional commitments to free speech while achieving effective censorship through pressure on platforms to voluntarily remove unwanted content. This public-private censorship partnership allows democratic governments to achieve levels of information control that would be politically impossible through direct government action.

The beauty of this system, from an authoritarian perspective, is its deniability. When platforms remove content at government request or under government pressure, both parties can claim that the decision was voluntary and based on community standards rather than government coercion. This creates a form of laundered censorship where government suppression of speech is disguised as private business decisions, making legal challenges extremely difficult and public opposition seemingly misguided.

ECHO CHAMBERS AND FILTER BUBBLES AS FORMS OF REALITY MANIPULATION

The Architecture of Intellectual Isolation

Orwell's dystopia achieved thought control through the elimination of alternative perspectives—citizens of Oceania literally couldn't access information that contradicted Party doctrine. Modern digital platforms achieve a similar result through abundance rather than scarcity, creating personalized information environments that expose users to vast amounts of content while carefully filtering out perspectives that might challenge their existing beliefs. These echo chambers don't prevent access to alternative viewpoints; they make such access increasingly unlikely through algorithmic curation designed to maximize engagement and minimize cognitive dissonance.

The sophistication of modern filter bubbles far exceeds anything Orwell imagined. Rather than simply blocking access to forbidden information, algorithmic systems analyze user behavior patterns to predict what content will generate the strongest emotional response, then deliver increasingly extreme versions of that content to maintain engagement. This creates a form of intellectual radicalization where users are gradually led toward more extreme positions not through explicit persuasion but through the subtle manipulation of information exposure.

The Psychology of Confirmation Bias Exploitation

Digital platforms have become expert at exploiting fundamental human psychological weaknesses, particularly our tendency toward confirmation bias—the inclination to seek out information that confirms our existing beliefs while avoiding information that challenges them. Platform algorithms don't create confirmation bias, but they weaponize it, using sophisticated behavioral analysis to deliver content that provides the dopamine hit of intellectual validation while avoiding the discomfort of cognitive challenge.

This exploitation of confirmation bias creates a form of intellectual addiction where users become dependent on platforms for regular doses of belief confirmation. Just as drug dealers create dependency by providing increasingly potent doses of their product, platform algorithms create intellectual dependency by providing increasingly concentrated doses of ideological validation. The result is user behavior that becomes more predictable and more profitable over time, as users retreat into ever-narrower information silos that generate consistent engagement and advertising revenue.

The Fragmentation of Shared Reality

One of the most profound consequences of algorithmic information curation is the fragmentation of shared reality into competing, incompatible worldviews that have little common ground for productive dialogue. When different groups of citizens receive completely different information about the same events, they develop fundamentally different understandings of reality that make democratic discourse increasingly impossible. This fragmentation serves the interests of those who benefit from social division and political paralysis, creating conditions where effective resistance to existing power structures becomes extremely difficult.

The fragmentation of reality operates through what researchers call "epistemic closure"—the creation of self-reinforcing information systems where all sources of information confirm each other while systematically excluding contradictory evidence. Users trapped within these closed epistemic systems don't experience their worldview as narrow or biased; they experience it as obviously correct, supported by overwhelming evidence from multiple credible sources. This creates a form of intellectual imprisonment that's particularly effective because prisoners don't realize they're confined.

The Gamification of Belief

Modern platforms have transformed belief formation from a private, contemplative process into a public, gamified experience where ideas compete for attention based on their ability to generate engagement rather than their correspondence to reality. The metrics of social media success—likes, shares, comments, followers—create powerful incentives for users to adopt and express beliefs that maximize social validation rather than seek truth or understanding.

This gamification of belief creates what researchers call "performative epistemology," where users adopt positions not because they believe them to be true but because they generate social rewards within their chosen communities. The result is a form of intellectual theater where genuine belief becomes secondary to social performance, creating information environments where truth becomes increasingly irrelevant compared to tribal loyalty and social signaling.

THE WEAPONIZATION OF "MISINFORMATION" AS A TOOL OF CONTROL

The Elastic Definition of Truth

The concept of "misinformation" has become one of the most powerful tools of modern information control, precisely because it appears to serve the objective goal of promoting truth while actually serving the subjective goal of eliminating dissent. The definition of misinformation has proven remarkably elastic, expanding from clearly false factual claims to include accurate information presented without proper context, legitimate scientific debates about unsettled questions, and even accurate predictions about future events that contradict official forecasts.

This elasticity allows authorities to label almost any unwanted information as "misinformation" while maintaining the appearance of objective truth-seeking. When scientific studies produce results that contradict official policies, they become "misinformation." When journalists report facts that undermine approved narratives, they become "purveyors of misinformation." When citizens share personal experiences that contradict official accounts, they become "spreaders of misinformation." The result is a system where truth becomes whatever those in power say it is, while maintaining the fiction that truth is objective and discoverable.

The Preemptive Strike Against Future Dissent

One of the most insidious applications of misinformation rhetoric is its use to delegitimize dissent before it can fully form. By establishing certain topics as inherently susceptible to misinformation, authorities can create presumptions against any information that challenges official narratives, regardless of its accuracy or the credibility of its sources. This creates a form of preemptive censorship where entire categories of information become suspect simply because they contradict approved viewpoints.

The power of this approach lies in its ability to make critical thinking itself seem dangerous and irresponsible. When citizens are repeatedly told that questioning official narratives makes them vulnerable to misinformation, many learn to suppress their own critical instincts and defer to approved authorities rather than risk being labeled as conspiracy theorists or misinformation spreaders. This creates a population that's not just compliant but actively self-policing, reporting and suppressing dissent within their own communities.

The Militarization of Information

The transformation of information from a public good into a battlefield represents one of the most significant developments in modern warfare. Military and intelligence agencies now openly discuss "information warfare," "narrative control," and "cognitive security" as essential elements of national defense. This militarization of information has profound implications for civilian discourse, as techniques developed for warfare against foreign enemies are increasingly applied to domestic populations under the guise of protecting them from misinformation.

The military approach to information treats civilian populations as potential targets for enemy propaganda who must be protected through careful control of information flows. This creates a justification for comprehensive surveillance, algorithmic manipulation, and content suppression that would be politically impossible if presented as censorship but becomes acceptable when framed as national security. The result is the application of military-grade information control techniques to civilian populations, transforming democratic discourse into a form of cognitive warfare.

The Privatization of Truth Determination

The outsourcing of truth determination to private companies represents one of the most dangerous developments in modern information control. When platforms claim the authority to determine what information is true or false, they assume a function that democratic societies have traditionally reserved for courts, scientific institutions, and democratic deliberation. This privatization of truth determination creates enormous potential for abuse, as companies can suppress information that threatens their business interests while claiming to protect the public from misinformation.

The danger of privatized truth determination is compounded by the lack of accountability and transparency in platform decision-making. Unlike government censorship, which is subject to legal challenge and democratic oversight, platform censorship operates according to opaque algorithms and secret deliberation processes that are largely immune from public scrutiny or legal challenge. This creates a form of private authoritarianism that combines the efficiency of corporate decision-making with the unaccountability of private power.

THE TECHNOLOGY OF NARRATIVE CONTROL

Artificial Intelligence and the Automation of Persuasion

The integration of artificial intelligence into information systems has created possibilities for narrative control that exceed even Orwell's most paranoid imaginings. AI systems can now generate convincing fake content at scale, create personalized propaganda tailored to individual psychological profiles, and respond to emerging narratives in real-time with counter-narratives designed to confuse and deflect public attention. This automation of persuasion creates the possibility of comprehensive narrative control without human intervention, where AI systems automatically adjust information flows to maintain desired public attitudes and behaviors.

The sophistication of AI-powered persuasion is particularly troubling because it operates below the threshold of conscious awareness. While humans can often recognize and resist obvious propaganda, AI systems can craft messages that bypass critical thinking by targeting emotional triggers and cognitive biases that operate at a subconscious level. This creates a form of subliminal programming that shapes attitudes and behaviors without users realizing they're being manipulated.

Deep Fakes and the Destruction of Epistemological Certainty

The development of deep fake technology represents a fundamental threat to shared reality by making it increasingly difficult to distinguish authentic information from sophisticated fabrications. When any video, audio recording, or photograph can be convincingly faked, the foundations of evidence-based reasoning begin to crumble. This creates what researchers call "epistemic apocalypse"—a condition where truth becomes unknowable not because information is scarce but because authentic and inauthentic information become indistinguishable.

The mere existence of deep fake technology has already begun to undermine public trust in authentic evidence, creating what researchers call the "liar's dividend"—the benefit that liars receive when the public becomes skeptical of all evidence. When every piece of damaging evidence can be dismissed as potentially fake, accountability becomes impossible and truth becomes whatever those with the most power say it is.

Predictive Algorithms and the Shaping of Future Reality

Perhaps the most sophisticated form of modern narrative control operates through predictive algorithms that don't just respond to existing attitudes and behaviors but actively shape them. These systems use vast databases of behavioral information to predict how individuals and groups will respond to specific messages, then craft information environments designed to produce desired outcomes. This creates a form of probabilistic mind control where human behavior becomes increasingly predictable and manipulable through carefully orchestrated information exposure.

The power of predictive narrative control lies in its ability to make manipulation feel like natural choice. When algorithms present users with information carefully selected to nudge them toward predetermined conclusions, users experience their resulting decisions as authentic expressions of free will rather than products of systematic manipulation. This creates a form of cognitive control that's particularly effective because it preserves the illusion of autonomy while eliminating its substance.

THE GLOBAL EXPANSION OF DIGITAL AUTHORITARIANISM

The Export of Surveillance Capitalism

The surveillance capitalism model pioneered by American tech companies has become a global standard, with governments and corporations around the world adopting similar approaches to information control and behavioral manipulation. This creates a form of digital colonialism where surveillance techniques developed in Silicon Valley are imposed on populations worldwide, often with even fewer legal protections and democratic safeguards than exist in their countries of origin.

The global expansion of digital authoritarianism is facilitated by the network effects of platform monopolies, which make it economically rational for smaller countries to adopt the surveillance infrastructure developed by dominant platforms rather than develop their own alternatives. This creates a form of technological dependency where entire nations surrender information sovereignty to foreign corporations, making democratic resistance to surveillance capitalism increasingly difficult on a global scale.

The Social Credit Revolution

China's social credit system represents the logical endpoint of digital information control, where every citizen's access to services, employment, travel, and social participation depends on their compliance with government-approved behaviors and beliefs. While Western democracies have not yet implemented formal social credit systems, informal versions already operate through credit scoring, background checks, and social media screening that increasingly determine access to economic and social opportunities.

The genius of social credit systems lies in their apparent objectivity and fairness. Rather than punishing people for their beliefs or associations, these systems punish them for their behaviors, creating the illusion that compliance is voluntary and punishment is deserved. This makes resistance seem irrational and self-destructive, encouraging voluntary compliance through rational self-interest rather than ideological commitment.

The Standardization of Global Censorship

The development of international content moderation standards has created a form of global censorship that operates across national boundaries and legal systems. When platforms develop unified standards for content removal that apply worldwide, they effectively impose the most restrictive national standards on global populations, creating a lowest-common-denominator approach to free expression that serves authoritarian interests while undermining democratic values.

This standardization of censorship is particularly dangerous because it operates through private corporate decisions rather than democratic lawmaking, making it largely immune from democratic oversight or legal challenge. When the same content policies apply in liberal democracies and authoritarian regimes, democratic values become subordinated to corporate convenience and authoritarian pressure, creating a form of global thought control that undermines the diversity of human expression and political organization.

CONCLUSION: THE COMPLETE TRANSFORMATION OF TRUTH

George Orwell's Ministry of Truth was a crude instrument compared to the sophisticated information control systems that operate in our digital age. Where Orwell's regime relied on obvious propaganda and brutal suppression of dissent, modern digital platforms have achieved something far more elegant and effective: the transformation of information control from an external imposition into an internal desire. We don't just tolerate the surveillance and manipulation of our information environment—we demand it, paying subscription fees for the privilege of having our reality carefully curated and our thoughts gently guided toward profitable and politically useful directions.

The digital Ministry of Truth doesn't need to rewrite history because it can simply make alternative histories invisible, buried beneath algorithmic indifference and social disapproval. It doesn't need to suppress dissent through violence because it can eliminate dissent through distraction, fragmentation, and the careful cultivation of intellectual helplessness. It doesn't need to impose truth from above because it can manufacture consent from below, using sophisticated psychological manipulation to make people want to believe what they're supposed to believe.

Perhaps most troubling of all, the digital Ministry of Truth has achieved what Orwell's regime could never accomplish: the elimination of the very concept of objective truth. In *1984*, Winston Smith's final defeat came when he genuinely believed that two plus two equals five. Today's information systems have made such crude reality distortion unnecessary by creating a world where mathematical truth becomes the only form of certainty, while everything else—history, science, politics, morality—becomes matter of opinion, preference, and tribal affiliation.

The result is not the monolithic totalitarianism that Orwell feared but something potentially more dangerous: a fragmented authoritarianism where truth becomes whatever generates the most engagement, profit, and political advantage for those who control the algorithms. In this world, the Ministry of Truth doesn't need to convince everyone to believe the same lies—it just needs to convince everyone that truth is unknowable, that all perspectives are equally valid, and that resistance is futile because there's nothing coherent enough to resist.

We have willingly constructed a world where truth is not discovered but manufactured, not shared but customized, not defended but monetized. The screens that watch us don't just monitor our behavior—they shape our understanding of what behavior means, what reality contains, and what truth itself could possibly be. In this completely mediated world, the question is not whether the Ministry of Truth has gone digital, but whether we can still remember what truth looked like before it became just another data point in the algorithm of control.

Chapter 4: Newspeak in 140 Characters

How Social Media Has Compressed and Degraded Language

When Orwell conceived Newspeak in "1984," he envisioned a deliberately constructed language designed to diminish the range of thought by systematically reducing vocabulary and eliminating words that could express dissent or complex ideas. The Party's philologists worked methodically to strip away nuance, ambiguity, and the very capacity for heretical thinking by making such thoughts literally inexpressible. What Orwell presented as a dystopian nightmare imposed by totalitarian decree has, in many ways, been achieved organically through the character limitations and behavioral incentives of social media platforms.

The transformation of human communication in the digital age represents perhaps the most profound linguistic shift since the invention of writing itself. Where previous communication revolutions expanded our capacity for expression—the printing press democratized knowledge, telegraph enabled long-distance communication, telephone brought voice across continents—social media has uniquely constrained and compressed our linguistic capabilities. The arbitrary character limits that began with SMS texting and were institutionalized by Twitter's original 140-character constraint have fundamentally altered not just how we communicate, but how we think and conceptualize ideas.

This compression hasn't occurred through government mandate or academic design, but through the seemingly innocent requirements of digital communication platforms. Each platform has shaped language in its own way: Twitter's character limits favor brevity over depth, Instagram's visual focus reduces complex ideas to simple captions, TikTok's short video format encourages immediate emotional impact over sustained argumentation, and Facebook's engagement algorithms reward inflammatory content over thoughtful discourse. The cumulative effect has been a systematic degradation of public discourse that would have impressed Orwell's fictional Ministry of Truth.

The Tyranny of the Character Count

The character limit represents more than a technical constraint—it functions as a cognitive straitjacket that forces complex thoughts into oversimplified formulations. When Twitter launched with its 140-character limit, it claimed to encourage conciseness and accessibility. In practice, however, this constraint has trained millions of users to think in soundbites, to reduce nuanced arguments to binary positions, and to favor emotional reactions over analytical thinking.

The psychological impact of character limits extends far beyond the platforms themselves. Users who spend significant time crafting thoughts within these constraints begin to internalize these limitations in their offline thinking. Educators report that students increasingly struggle with extended argumentation, preferring to express ideas in bullet points or brief statements rather than developing sustained logical arguments. The character limit doesn't just constrain online expression—it reshapes cognitive patterns, making users less capable of complex thought even when artificial constraints are removed.

Perhaps most insidiously, character limits create an illusion of democratic participation while actually favoring certain types of expression over others. Simple, emotional statements fit easily within character constraints, while complex, nuanced arguments require either oversimplification or fragmented "thread" formats that few users have the patience to follow. This creates a systematic bias toward reductive thinking and against sophisticated analysis.

Platform-Specific Linguistic Evolution

Each social media platform has evolved its own dialect of compressed communication, creating what linguists call "platform vernaculars" that reflect the specific constraints and incentives of different digital environments. Twitter's character limit has produced a culture of aggressive abbreviation, where complex political positions are reduced to hashtag slogans and policy debates become tribal declarations of allegiance. The platform's retweet function further encourages linguistic laziness by making it easier to share others' compressed thoughts than to develop original, extended arguments.

Instagram's visual-first design has created a peculiar form of linguistic-visual compression where complex ideas must be expressed through combinations of images and brief captions. This has led to the rise of "infographic activism"—complex social and political issues reduced to colorful, shareable graphics with minimal text. While visually appealing, these formats systematically exclude nuance, context, and contradiction in favor of simplified, easily digestible messages that support predetermined conclusions.

TikTok represents perhaps the most extreme example of linguistic compression, where ideas must be expressed not just briefly, but in formats designed for immediate emotional impact and viral transmission. The platform's algorithm rewards content that generates immediate engagement, creating powerful incentives for creators to abandon nuanced discussion in favor of provocative oversimplification. Complex social issues become dance trends, political arguments become comedy sketches, and serious discourse becomes performative entertainment.

The Fragmentation of Extended Thought

Social media platforms have not merely compressed language—they have fragmented it, breaking complex ideas into disconnected fragments that users encounter in isolation. The "timeline" or "feed" format presents information as a stream of disconnected posts, each competing for attention within a rapidly scrolling environment. This fragmentation makes sustained argumentation nearly impossible and encourages users to respond to individual fragments rather than engaging with complete arguments.

The psychological impact of fragmented communication extends beyond individual posts to entire conversations. Social media discussions rarely follow logical progression from premise to conclusion. Instead, they become collections of loosely related statements, reactions, and tangential observations that never coalesce into coherent discourse. Participants enter and exit conversations at random points, responding to fragments without understanding context, creating what resembles debate but lacks the logical structure necessary for productive disagreement.

This fragmentation has particularly devastating effects on political discourse, where complex policy issues are broken down into competing soundbites that users encounter in isolation. Voters may see dozens of fragments about healthcare policy, immigration reform, or economic strategy without ever encountering a complete, coherent argument about any of these issues. The result is a form of political understanding that resembles a jigsaw puzzle with most pieces missing—users develop strong opinions based on fragments while lacking the comprehensive understanding necessary for informed democratic participation.

The Rise of Emoji, Abbreviations, and Simplified Communication

The linguistic compression imposed by social media has given rise to entirely new forms of expression that prioritize efficiency and emotional immediacy over precision and nuance. Emoji, abbreviations, and simplified communication formats represent more than convenient shortcuts—they constitute a fundamental transformation in how humans encode and transmit meaning. While these innovations have made digital communication more accessible and emotionally expressive, they have simultaneously reduced the precision and complexity of human thought expression.

Emoji represent perhaps the most significant linguistic innovation of the digital age, creating a form of universal pictographic communication that transcends language barriers while simultaneously constraining expressive possibilities. These small, standardized images allow users to convey emotions and concepts quickly and efficiently, but they do so by reducing complex feelings and ideas to predetermined categories. The limited emoji vocabulary—even with thousands of available symbols—cannot capture the full range of human emotion and experience, forcing users to approximate their feelings using available options.

The Emoji as Emotional Straightjacket

The apparent democracy of emoji usage masks a more troubling reality: these symbols don't expand emotional expression but constrain it to predetermined categories created by corporate committees. The Unicode Consortium, which standardizes emoji across platforms, essentially determines which emotions, objects, and concepts are deemed worthy of symbolic representation. This process of standardization inevitably excludes experiences, cultures, and emotional states that don't fit neatly into universally marketable symbols.

The psychological impact of emoji usage is particularly significant among younger users who have grown up with these symbolic systems. Research indicates that heavy emoji users show decreased ability to articulate emotions using traditional language, suggesting that the convenience of pictographic communication comes at the cost of linguistic sophistication. When complex feelings can be "expressed" with a single symbol, users may lose the motivation and ability to explore and articulate the nuances of their emotional experiences.

Furthermore, emoji create the illusion of emotional communication while actually flattening the complexity of human feeling. A "sad face" emoji cannot distinguish between disappointment, grief, frustration, melancholy, or despair—emotions that require different responses and represent fundamentally different experiences. By reducing emotional expression to standardized symbols, emoji may actually decrease emotional intelligence and empathy by encouraging users to think of feelings in simplified, categorical terms rather than as complex, multifaceted experiences.

The Abbreviation Economy

The evolution of digital abbreviations represents a fascinating case study in linguistic adaptation under constraint. What began as practical shortcuts for mobile device keyboards has evolved into a comprehensive alternative language that prioritizes speed and efficiency over precision and clarity. Abbreviations like "LOL," "IMHO," "FOMO," and countless others have become so embedded in digital communication that many users employ them unconsciously, even when character limits are not a factor.

This abbreviation economy has created interesting generational and cultural divides in communication. Older users often struggle to decode abbreviations, while younger users may struggle to communicate without them. More problematically, abbreviations often carry implicit cultural assumptions and values that become embedded in communication patterns. "SMH" (shaking my head) doesn't just abbreviate a physical gesture—it encodes a particular attitude toward disagreement that emphasizes dismissal over engagement.

The proliferation of abbreviations has also created new forms of linguistic exclusion and in-group signaling. Knowing the current abbreviations becomes a marker of cultural relevance, while using outdated or incorrect abbreviations signals outsider status. This creates communication barriers that can exclude older users, non-native speakers, or anyone who hasn't kept up with rapidly evolving digital vernaculars.

Algorithmic Amplification of Simplification

Social media algorithms play a crucial role in promoting simplified communication by systematically rewarding content that generates immediate engagement while penalizing complex, nuanced posts that require extended attention. These algorithms don't explicitly prefer simple language, but their optimization for engagement metrics inevitably favors content that can be quickly consumed, emotionally processed, and immediately shared.

The result is a feedback loop where users learn to communicate in ways that satisfy algorithmic preferences rather than human needs for meaningful discourse. Content creators discover that posts using simple language, emotional triggers, and controversial statements receive more visibility and engagement than thoughtful, nuanced content. Over time, this shapes not just what users post, but how they think about issues—the pressure to create "engaging" content encourages users to adopt more extreme, simplified positions that can be easily communicated and quickly consumed.

This algorithmic preference for simplification has particularly dramatic effects on political and social discourse. Complex policy issues that require sustained attention and careful analysis receive less visibility than simplified, emotionally charged statements that confirm existing beliefs. The algorithm becomes a form of automated editor that systematically removes nuance from public discourse in favor of content that generates immediate reactions.

The Degradation of Written Literacy

Perhaps most concerning is how compressed digital communication has affected users' ability to engage with traditional written language. Educators across all levels report declining ability among students to read extended texts, follow complex arguments, and produce coherent written work. Students who are fluent in social media communication often struggle with academic writing, not because they lack intelligence, but because they have been trained to think and communicate in formats that are incompatible with sustained analysis.

This degradation affects not just academic performance but civic participation. Democratic societies require citizens capable of engaging with complex policy documents, following sustained arguments, and making decisions based on comprehensive information. When citizens can only process information in social media formats, they become vulnerable to manipulation and incapable of the thoughtful deliberation that democracy requires.

The problem extends beyond individual capability to collective discourse. When most participants in public conversations can only engage with simplified, compressed information, the entire conversation becomes simplified. Complex issues are reduced to competing soundbites, nuanced positions are abandoned in favor of tribal allegiances, and democratic discourse degrades into what resembles sporting events more than serious deliberation about shared challenges.

Cancel Culture as a Form of Thoughtcrime Enforcement

Perhaps nowhere is the parallel between Orwell's dystopian vision and contemporary digital culture more evident than in the phenomenon of cancel culture—a form of social enforcement that bears striking resemblance to the thoughtcrime policing described in "1984." While cancel culture lacks the formal institutional structure of Orwell's Thought Police, it operates through similar mechanisms: the identification of ideological deviation, public accusation, social isolation, and punishment that extends far beyond the original transgression.

The term "cancel culture" itself has become politically charged, with different groups using it to describe everything from legitimate accountability for harmful behavior to authoritarian suppression of free expression. However, beneath these political interpretations lies a more fundamental phenomenon: social media has created new mechanisms for enforcing ideological conformity that operate with unprecedented speed, scope, and severity. These mechanisms don't require government authority or formal institutional power—they emerge from the collective behavior of users operating within systems designed to amplify outrage and punishment.

The Mechanics of Digital Thoughtcrime

Cancel culture operates through several key mechanisms that parallel Orwell's thoughtcrime enforcement. First, the identification phase involves social media users monitoring each other's expressions for signs of ideological deviation. This monitoring is not centralized or coordinated—it emerges naturally from the structure of social media platforms where users' thoughts and opinions are constantly visible to vast audiences. Users develop sensitivity to detecting statements that violate current orthodoxies, much like Orwell's citizens became expert at recognizing thoughtcrime in their neighbors' expressions and behaviors.

The accusation phase involves public denunciation, often beginning with viral posts that frame the target's statements as evidence of moral or political failing. These accusations typically employ specific linguistic formulas—"This is literally violence," "This is not okay," "We need to talk about..."—that signal moral urgency and demand immediate response. The language of accusation has become standardized across platforms, creating recognizable patterns that trained users can deploy effectively against targets.

The amplification phase leverages social media's sharing mechanisms to spread accusations rapidly across networks. Retweets, shares, and comments create exponential visibility for accusations, often reaching audiences far larger than the original audience for the offending statement. This amplification typically occurs faster than fact-checking or context-gathering, creating situations where millions of users are responding to accusations before understanding what actually happened.

The Permanent Record Problem

Social media creates what might be called a "permanent record problem" where past statements can be retrieved and weaponized years or decades after they were made. Unlike Orwell's memory holes, which disappeared inconvenient information, social media preserves everything, creating extensive records of users' evolving thoughts, opinions, and expressions that can be mined for evidence of thoughtcrime. This permanence creates a retroactive enforcement mechanism where users can be punished for statements that were acceptable when made but violate current standards.

The permanent record problem has created a chilling effect on authentic expression, as users become aware that anything they post might someday be used against them. This awareness encourages self-censorship and performative conformity, as users learn to express only opinions that seem likely to remain socially acceptable indefinitely. The result is a form of temporal thoughtcrime enforcement where users must not only conform to current orthodoxies but anticipate future ones.

Perhaps most troubling is how the permanent record problem prevents genuine intellectual growth and evolution. When users know that changed opinions might be used as evidence of past thoughtcrime, they become reluctant to acknowledge previous mistakes or demonstrate intellectual development. This creates incentives for rigid ideological consistency rather than thoughtful evolution, effectively punishing the kind of intellectual humility and growth that healthy societies should encourage.

Algorithmic Amplification of Outrage

Social media algorithms play a crucial role in cancel culture by systematically amplifying content that generates strong emotional responses, particularly outrage and indignation. These algorithms don't distinguish between productive anger that might lead to positive social change and destructive mob behavior that silences legitimate discourse. They simply optimize for engagement, and outrage reliably generates engagement.

This algorithmic amplification creates powerful incentives for users to participate in cancel culture, even when they might prefer more measured responses. Users who post inflammatory accusations against targets receive more visibility, followers, and social validation than users who advocate for proportional responses or due process. The algorithm rewards participation in mob behavior while penalizing calls for moderation or context.

The result is a feedback system that encourages increasingly extreme responses to increasingly minor transgressions. Users compete for visibility and validation by demonstrating greater outrage than their peers, leading to escalating cycles of denunciation that bear little relationship to the severity of original offenses. The algorithm becomes a machine for manufacturing moral panic, automatically amplifying accusations and suppressing more measured responses.

The Destruction of Proportionality

Traditional justice systems incorporate concepts of proportionality—the idea that punishments should be commensurate with offenses. Cancel culture operates without such constraints, often imposing severe social and professional consequences for minor transgressions or even for statements that are taken out of context or misunderstood. A poorly worded tweet can result in job loss, death threats, and permanent social ostracism, creating a system where the punishment rarely fits the crime.

This lack of proportionality creates a climate of fear that extends far beyond direct targets of cancel culture. Users who witness disproportionate punishment of others learn to self-censor aggressively, avoiding not just obviously problematic statements but any expression that might possibly be misunderstood or weaponized. This creates what researchers call "preference falsification," where users publicly express opinions they don't actually hold while hiding their genuine thoughts and feelings.

The absence of proportionality also prevents the kind of good-faith disagreement that healthy societies require. When any expression of dissent might result in severe punishment, users avoid engaging with challenging ideas or questioning popular assumptions. This creates intellectual monocultures where dominant opinions go unchallenged, not because they are necessarily correct, but because the costs of disagreement have become prohibitively high.

The Ideological Enforcement Mechanism

Cancel culture functions as a decentralized ideological enforcement mechanism that maintains orthodoxy without requiring formal authority or explicit coordination. Users police each other's expressions, competing to demonstrate their own ideological purity by identifying and punishing deviation in others. This creates what sociologists call "pluralistic ignorance," where individual users may have private doubts about dominant ideologies but assume they are alone in their skepticism because public expression is so uniform.

The enforcement mechanism is particularly effective because it operates through social proof and tribal loyalty rather than rational argument. Users don't need to be convinced that targets deserve punishment—they simply need to see that punishment is occurring and that participation demonstrates tribal loyalty while non-participation risks being seen as complicit with thoughtcrime. This creates powerful incentives for bandwagon behavior that can mobilize thousands of users against targets without any individual user necessarily believing that such mobilization is justified or productive.

Perhaps most concerning is how this enforcement mechanism has begun extending beyond social media into offline institutions. Employers, schools, and other organizations increasingly monitor their members' social media activity and impose real-world consequences for online thoughtcrimes. This creates a seamless system of ideological enforcement that encompasses both digital and physical spaces, making ideological conformity a practical requirement for social and economic participation.

The Death of Nuanced Discourse in the Digital Age

The convergence of compressed communication, algorithmic amplification, and social enforcement mechanisms has created what may be the most significant threat to intelligent discourse in human history. Nuanced thinking—the ability to hold multiple perspectives simultaneously, to recognize complexity and ambiguity, to engage with ideas without immediately categorizing them as wholly good or evil—has become increasingly rare in digital spaces and, consequently, in offline discourse as well.

Nuance requires cognitive resources that social media systematically depletes. Thoughtful analysis demands sustained attention, tolerance for ambiguity, and willingness to consider perspectives that challenge existing beliefs. These cognitive requirements are incompatible with social media environments designed to capture and monetize attention through rapid-fire stimulation and emotional manipulation. Users trained to process information in social media formats become less capable of the patient, sustained thinking that nuanced discourse requires.

The Binary Trap

Digital communication has created what might be called a "binary trap"—a systematic bias toward reducing complex issues to simple either/or choices that admit no middle ground or alternative perspectives. This binary thinking emerges from several aspects of digital communication: character limits that prevent complex argumentation, engagement algorithms that reward controversial content, and social enforcement mechanisms that punish ambiguity or equivocation.

The binary trap is particularly evident in political discourse, where complex policy issues are reduced to tribal markers of identity rather than subjects for thoughtful analysis. Healthcare policy becomes a simple choice between government control and free market solutions, ignoring dozens of hybrid approaches used successfully around the world. Climate change becomes a binary choice between economic growth and environmental protection, ignoring innovations that might reconcile these goals.

Immigration becomes a choice between open borders and xenophobic exclusion, ignoring nuanced approaches to managing migration flows while protecting both immigrants and communities.

This binary reduction doesn't just simplify complex issues—it makes them harder to solve by eliminating the middle ground where compromise and innovation typically occur. When every issue is framed as a zero-sum battle between opposing sides, collaborative problem-solving becomes impossible. Users learn to see disagreement as evidence of moral failure rather than as an opportunity for learning and growth.

The Collapse of Intellectual Humility

Intellectual humility—the recognition that one's own knowledge and perspective are limited and that other perspectives might contain valuable insights—has become increasingly rare in digital discourse. Social media creates powerful incentives for displays of confidence and certainty while penalizing admission of uncertainty or complexity. Users who acknowledge the limitations of their knowledge or express uncertainty about complex issues receive less engagement and validation than users who express absolute confidence in their positions.

This erosion of intellectual humility has devastating effects on collective learning and problem-solving. Complex challenges like climate change, economic inequality, or technological governance require collaborative approaches that draw on diverse expertise and perspectives. When participants in these discussions are unable to acknowledge the limitations of their own understanding or the potential value of alternative approaches, productive collaboration becomes impossible.

The collapse of intellectual humility is particularly evident in how users respond to expertise and specialized knowledge. Rather than deferring to genuine expertise in complex technical fields, users increasingly treat all opinions as equally valid and dismiss expert knowledge as elitist bias. This creates a form of epistemic populism where popular opinion is valued over careful analysis, making evidence-based policy-making increasingly difficult.

The Echo Chamber Effect

Social media algorithms create what researchers call "echo chambers"—information environments where users primarily encounter information that confirms their existing beliefs while being shielded from challenging perspectives. These echo chambers aren't just about political bias—they shape how users understand the nature of knowledge and discourse itself. Users who spend most of their time in echo chambers may genuinely believe that their perspectives are universally shared and that disagreement represents ignorance or malice rather than legitimate difference of opinion.

Echo chambers make nuanced discourse nearly impossible by depriving users of the diverse perspectives necessary for sophisticated thinking. When users only encounter simplified versions of opposing viewpoints—often presented as strawman arguments designed to be easily dismissed—they never develop the ability to engage seriously with alternative perspectives. This creates a form of intellectual isolation that masquerades as informed engagement.

The echo chamber effect is particularly problematic because it's invisible to users experiencing it. People trapped in echo chambers typically believe they are well-informed and exposed to diverse perspectives because they consume large quantities of information. However, this information diversity is often superficial, covering many topics while providing little genuine perspective diversity on any of them.

The Attention Economy's War on Deep Thinking

The fundamental business model of social media platforms is the monetization of human attention, creating what researchers call the "attention economy." This economy systematically undermines the conditions necessary for nuanced thinking by training users to seek constant stimulation and immediate gratification while avoiding the sustained focus that complex analysis requires.

Deep thinking requires what psychologists call "sustained attention"—the ability to focus on challenging material for extended periods without seeking distraction or stimulation. Social media platforms are designed to prevent sustained attention by providing constant streams of new, stimulating content that creates addiction-like patterns of compulsive checking and scrolling. Users trained in these patterns become physiologically incapable of the sustained focus that reading, analysis, and reflection require.

The attention economy also creates economic incentives that systematically undervalue nuanced content. Writers, journalists, and content creators quickly discover that thoughtful, complex analysis generates less engagement and revenue than simplified, emotionally charged content. This creates a race to the bottom where content creators abandon nuanced analysis in favor of inflammatory oversimplification, not because they prefer such content, but because economic survival requires it.

The Expertise Crisis

The death of nuanced discourse has contributed to a broader crisis of expertise where specialized knowledge is increasingly dismissed as elitist bias while popular opinion is elevated as democratic wisdom. This crisis emerges partly from social media's flattening effect, where expert analysis and uninformed opinion appear in the same feeds with equal visual weight and algorithmic treatment.

Social media has democratized information access in many positive ways, but it has also created confusion about the difference between access to information and understanding of complex subjects. Users who can quickly Google information about climate science, epidemiology, or economic policy may believe they are as qualified as experts who have spent decades studying these fields. This creates a form of false equivalence where expertise is treated as just another opinion rather than as a form of knowledge that deserves special consideration.

The expertise crisis is particularly dangerous in areas where specialized knowledge is essential for good decision-making. When public health officials' recommendations are treated as equivalent to social media speculation, when climate scientists' research is dismissed as politically motivated opinion, when economists' analysis is ignored in favor of intuitive but incorrect assumptions, societies lose their capacity for evidence-based governance.

The Polarization Spiral

The combination of compressed communication, algorithmic amplification, and social enforcement has created what researchers call a "polarization spiral"—a self-reinforcing process where moderate positions become increasingly rare and extreme positions become increasingly common. This spiral operates through several mechanisms: algorithms that reward controversial content, social enforcement that punishes moderation, and compression that eliminates the space for nuanced positions.

The polarization spiral makes compromise and collaboration increasingly difficult by eliminating the shared middle ground where productive negotiation typically occurs. When most participants in public discourse hold extreme positions and view moderation as evidence of moral failure, finding common ground becomes nearly impossible. This creates gridlock in democratic institutions and makes collective problem-solving increasingly difficult.

Perhaps most troubling is how the polarization spiral creates its own momentum. As moderate voices are silenced or driven away, the remaining discourse becomes more extreme, which further alienates moderates and makes extreme positions seem normal. This creates a feedback loop where polarization feeds on itself, making return to nuanced discourse increasingly unlikely without significant changes to the underlying systems that created the spiral.

Conclusion: The Linguistic Dystopia We Created

The transformation of human communication in the digital age represents a profound shift that extends far beyond mere technological convenience. What began as innocent character limits and user-friendly interfaces has evolved into a comprehensive system that constrains thought, enforces conformity, and systematically degrades the quality of human discourse. We have created, without intending to, something remarkably similar to Orwell's

Newspeak—a form of communication that makes complex thought increasingly difficult and dissent increasingly dangerous.

The parallels to Orwell's dystopian vision are striking, but the reality is in many ways more troubling than the fiction. Where Orwell imagined a centralized authority deliberately constraining language to control thought, we have created a decentralized system that achieves similar results through market mechanisms and user behavior. The Ministry of Truth has been replaced by algorithmic optimization, the Thought Police by viral mob enforcement, and deliberate language manipulation by emergent linguistic degradation.

Perhaps most concerning is how voluntary this linguistic dystopia has become. Users choose to communicate in compressed formats, choose to participate in cancel culture, choose to consume simplified content over nuanced analysis. This voluntary participation makes the system more resilient and more psychologically sustainable than Orwell's explicitly coercive regime. When people actively defend the systems that constrain their thinking, reform becomes extraordinarily difficult.

The implications extend far beyond individual communication preferences to the foundations of democratic society itself. Democracy requires citizens capable of engaging with complex information, considering multiple perspectives, and participating in good-faith deliberation about shared challenges. When the primary systems of public communication systematically undermine these capabilities, democracy itself becomes unsustainable.

Yet understanding these challenges also points toward potential solutions. Just as the current system emerged from specific technological and economic choices, alternative systems could emerge from different choices. Platforms could be designed to reward nuanced thinking rather than inflammatory simplification. Algorithms could be modified to promote diverse perspectives rather than confirming existing beliefs. Educational systems could teach digital literacy and critical thinking skills that help users resist linguistic manipulation.

The question is whether we have the collective wisdom and political will to make such changes before the degradation of discourse becomes irreversible. The longer we allow current systems to shape how entire generations think and communicate, the more difficult it becomes to imagine alternatives. We stand at a crucial moment where we must choose between accepting the linguistic dystopia we have inadvertently created or working deliberately to construct systems that enhance rather than constrain human thought and communication.

The choice is ours, but the window for making it may be closing rapidly. Each day that passes sees millions more users trained in compressed thinking, algorithmic manipulation, and mob enforcement. Each day makes nuanced discourse seem more foreign, more difficult, more unnecessary. We have created Newspeak in 140 characters, and unless we act deliberately to reverse this transformation, we may find ourselves trapped in a linguistic prison of our own construction, unable to think our way to freedom because we have forgotten how to think complex thoughts at all.

PART II: THE MECHANICS OF MODERN CONTROL

Chapter 5: Your Data Doppelganger

How tech companies create digital twins from our data

In the shadowy databases of Silicon Valley's most powerful corporations exists a version of you that may know you better than you know yourself—a digital doppelganger constructed from the countless fragments of data you unknowingly surrender with every click, swipe, purchase, and pause. This algorithmic avatar represents one of the most profound violations of human autonomy ever conceived, yet it operates entirely within the boundaries of what we've been conditioned to accept as normal technological convenience. Your data doppelganger doesn't merely record your past behaviors; it predicts your future actions, influences your present decisions, and gradually shapes the very person you believe yourself to be.

The construction of these digital twins begins with the seemingly innocent act of creating online accounts and accepting terms of service that few people read and fewer understand. From the moment you first interact with any connected device or digital service, the data collection apparatus begins its meticulous work of documentation and analysis. Every search query reveals something about your curiosities, fears, desires, and knowledge gaps. Every pause before clicking indicates hesitation or consideration. Every abandoned shopping cart suggests financial constraints or changing preferences. Every social media interaction exposes your relationships, opinions, emotional states, and social dynamics.

This data collection extends far beyond the obvious digital touch-points into the physical world through location tracking, purchase histories, biometric data from wearable devices, smart home interactions, and increasingly sophisticated sensors embedded in vehicles, appliances, and urban infrastructure. The result is a comprehensive surveillance system that monitors not just what you do online, but how you move through physical space, what you buy, whom you meet, where you sleep, and even physiological indicators like heart rate, sleep patterns, and stress levels. This biological data adds layers of intimate knowledge to your digital profile, creating predictions about health conditions, emotional states, and behavioral patterns that you may not even be conscious of yourself.

The true sophistication of these digital twins lies not in the individual data points they collect, but in the complex relationships and patterns that emerge from analyzing vast datasets across millions of users. Machine learning algorithms identify correlations between seemingly unrelated behaviors, creating predictive models that can infer intimate details about your life from seemingly innocuous digital breadcrumbs. Your digital doppelganger might know you're pregnant before you do, predict your likelihood of divorce based on your music streaming patterns, or determine your political affiliations from your shopping habits and travel routes.

The Architecture of Digital Identity

The technical infrastructure supporting these digital twins represents a marvel of engineering dedicated to the systematic commodification of human experience. Data warehouses store petabytes of information about billions of individuals, while sophisticated machine learning pipelines continuously process this information to refine and update behavioral models. Real-time analytics systems monitor ongoing activity streams, updating predictions and recommendations instantaneously as new data becomes available. The sheer computational power dedicated to understanding and predicting human behavior rivals that used for scientific research into fundamental questions about the universe itself.

Cloud computing platforms have made it economically feasible to store and analyze unprecedented amounts of personal data, while advances in artificial intelligence have made it possible to extract meaningful insights from this data at scale. Neural networks trained on massive datasets can identify subtle patterns in human behavior that would be invisible to human analysts, creating predictive capabilities that seem almost supernatural in their accuracy. These systems don't just learn what you've done; they learn how you think, what motivates you, and how you're likely to respond to different stimuli.

The integration of data from multiple sources creates a phenomenon known as data fusion, where individual pieces of information combine to reveal insights that none of them could provide alone. Your location data combined with your search history and social media activity might reveal not just where you've been, but why you went there, whom you met, and how you felt about the experience. Purchase data combined with biometric information might reveal not just what you bought, but your emotional state while making the purchase and the likelihood that you'll be satisfied with your decision.

Psychometric Profiling and Personality Prediction

Perhaps the most invasive aspect of digital twin construction is the development of psychometric profiles that attempt to map the fundamental aspects of human personality onto algorithmic models. These systems go beyond simple behavioral prediction to create comprehensive psychological assessments based on digital footprints. Companies like Cambridge Analytica demonstrated the political applications of such profiling, but the techniques they pioneered have become standard practice across the technology industry, deployed not just for political manipulation but for commercial influence and social control.

Digital psychometric profiling operates by analyzing patterns in language use, social interactions, content consumption, timing of activities, and response patterns to create assessments of personality traits, emotional stability, risk tolerance, susceptibility to influence, and cognitive biases. These assessments are often more accurate than traditional psychological testing because they're based on actual behavior over extended periods rather than self-reported responses to hypothetical scenarios. Your digital doppelganger might know that you're prone to impulse purchases when stressed, that you're more likely to believe conspiracy theories when isolated from friends, or that you become politically radical when exposed to certain types of content.

The implications of this psychological modeling extend far beyond targeted advertising into realms that touch the core of human autonomy and dignity. When corporations can predict not just what you might buy, but how you might vote, whom you might date, what career decisions you might make, and how you might respond to various forms of persuasion, the line between prediction and control becomes dangerously thin. These models don't just forecast behavior; they identify the psychological vulnerabilities and emotional triggers that can be exploited to influence behavior in desired directions.

The Commodification of Human Experience

The creation of digital twins represents the ultimate commodification of human experience, transforming the most intimate aspects of human life into raw material for corporate profit and social control. Every emotion, relationship, struggle, and triumph becomes data to be harvested, analyzed, and monetized. The concept of private inner life begins to lose meaning when algorithms can infer thoughts and feelings from external behaviors with increasing accuracy. Even acts of resistance or attempts to maintain privacy become additional data points that reveal personality traits and behavioral patterns.

This commodification operates through what economists call "surveillance capitalism," where human experience becomes the free raw material for manufacturing behavioral predictions that are sold to third parties seeking to influence human behavior. Your digital doppelganger doesn't exist primarily to serve you; it exists to serve the interests of advertisers, employers, insurers, political operatives, and other entities seeking to profit from or control your behavior. The more accurately your digital twin can predict and influence your actions, the more valuable it becomes in this marketplace of human behavioral control.

The psychological impact of living under such comprehensive surveillance and prediction creates what researchers call "anticipatory conformity," where individuals begin modifying their behavior based on how they think it might be interpreted by algorithmic systems. People start choosing music, books, and social interactions not based on their genuine preferences, but based on how these choices might affect their digital profiles. This creates a feedback loop where digital twins don't just predict behavior but actively shape it, gradually transforming people into conforming versions of their algorithmic assessments.

Behavioral prediction and pre-crime in the digital age

The evolution of digital surveillance systems has ushered in an era of predictive enforcement that makes the "pre-crime" concepts of science fiction seem quaint by comparison. Modern algorithmic systems don't merely wait for deviant behavior to occur; they actively identify individuals likely to engage in non-conformist activities and implement preemptive measures designed to prevent such behavior from manifesting. This represents a fundamental shift from reactive to predictive social control, where punishment precedes crime and guilt is determined by algorithmic probability rather than actual actions.

Law enforcement agencies across the globe have embraced predictive policing systems that analyze vast datasets to identify individuals at high risk for criminal activity. These systems combine traditional criminal justice data with information gleaned from social media monitoring, financial transaction analysis, location tracking, and behavioral pattern recognition to create risk assessment scores for entire populations. Police departments deploy resources based on these algorithmic predictions, concentrating surveillance and enforcement activities on individuals flagged by the system as likely future criminals, regardless of whether they have actually committed any crimes.

The sophistication of these predictive systems extends far beyond simple recidivism analysis to encompass comprehensive behavioral modeling that attempts to identify criminal intent before it translates into action. Natural language processing algorithms analyze social media posts, text messages, and online communications for indicators of violent ideation, criminal planning, or anti-social attitudes. Sentiment analysis tools monitor emotional states across digital platforms, flagging individuals who exhibit patterns associated with criminal behavior. Location tracking systems identify suspicious movement patterns that might indicate planning for illegal activities.

Corporate applications of predictive behavioral analysis operate with even less oversight than law enforcement systems, creating a parallel infrastructure of social control that influences access to employment, credit, housing, and other essential services based on algorithmic assessments of future behavior. Insurance companies use predictive models to identify customers likely to file claims, adjusting premiums or denying coverage based on behavioral predictions rather than actual risk history. Employers use similar systems to screen job applicants, rejecting candidates who exhibit digital behavior patterns associated with poor job performance, workplace conflict, or early resignation.

The Mathematics of Social Control

The algorithmic systems powering predictive behavioral analysis represent some of the most sophisticated applications of machine learning and artificial intelligence ever deployed, utilizing neural networks trained on massive datasets to identify subtle patterns in human behavior that correlate with future actions. These systems don't rely on simple rule-based logic but on complex mathematical models that can identify non-obvious relationships between seemingly unrelated variables. A person's music streaming patterns might correlate with their likelihood of defaulting on loans. Their social media posting times might predict their susceptibility to substance abuse. Their online shopping behavior might indicate their risk of engaging in domestic violence.

The black box nature of these machine learning systems means that even their creators often don't understand exactly how they arrive at their predictions. Neural networks with millions of parameters process information in ways that resist human interpretation, creating systems that can make accurate predictions without providing explanations for their decisions. This opacity becomes particularly problematic when these systems are used to make consequential decisions about people's lives, as individuals find themselves subject to algorithmic judgments that they cannot understand, challenge, or appeal.

The feedback loops built into these systems create self-reinforcing cycles that can amplify existing biases and create new forms of discrimination. When predictive policing systems consistently flag individuals from certain neighborhoods or demographic groups as high-risk, increased police attention in those areas generates more arrest data that reinforces the algorithm's initial bias. When employment screening systems reject candidates based on algorithmic assessments, the lack of opportunity for those individuals to prove themselves creates conditions that may actually increase the likelihood of the negative outcomes the system was designed to prevent.

Digital Panopticon and Behavioral Modification

The awareness of comprehensive behavioral monitoring creates what sociologists call a "panopticon effect," where the possibility of observation modifies behavior even when actual surveillance cannot be detected. In the digital age, this effect operates at unprecedented scale, as billions of people modify their behavior based on the knowledge that their actions are being monitored, recorded, and analyzed by algorithmic systems. The result is a form of social control that operates through self-censorship and anticipatory conformity rather than direct coercion.

Social media users begin crafting their online presence not as authentic self-expression but as strategic performance designed to optimize their algorithmic assessments. They avoid controversial topics, associate with socially approved individuals, and engage with content that signals conformity to algorithmic expectations. This behavioral modification extends beyond online activities into the physical world, as people become aware that their location data, purchase histories, and social interactions all contribute to their digital profiles and predictive scores.

The gamification elements built into many digital platforms amplify these behavioral modification effects by providing immediate feedback on actions and their algorithmic consequences. Social media metrics like likes, shares, and follower counts train users to optimize their behavior for algorithmic approval. Credit monitoring services that provide real-time updates on score changes create similar feedback loops in financial behavior. Dating apps that use algorithmic matching systems encourage users to modify their profiles and behavior to maximize their attractiveness to the algorithm rather than to potential partners.

The Weaponization of Mental Health Data

One of the most disturbing developments in predictive behavioral analysis is the incorporation of mental health data into risk assessment systems. Digital platforms routinely monitor user behavior for signs of depression, anxiety, suicidal ideation, and other mental health conditions, ostensibly to provide support and resources. However, this same data can be used to make predictions about behavioral reliability, social stability, and risk of non-conformist behavior that affect access to employment, insurance, and other services.

The stigmatization of mental health conditions through algorithmic assessment creates perverse incentives for individuals to hide signs of psychological distress, potentially worsening mental health outcomes in order to avoid algorithmic discrimination. People may avoid seeking help for depression because they fear it will affect their employment prospects. They may modify their social media behavior to hide signs of anxiety because they worry about insurance implications. The result is a system that punishes vulnerability and incentivizes deception about psychological well-being.

The predictive models used in these systems often conflate mental health conditions with behavioral risk in ways that reflect societal prejudices rather than scientific evidence. Algorithms trained on biased datasets may learn to associate depression with unreliability, anxiety with unpredictability, or trauma history with violence risk, creating systematic discrimination against individuals with mental health conditions. The opacity of these systems makes it difficult to identify and correct such biases, while the scale of their deployment amplifies discriminatory effects across entire populations.

The credit score model extended to social behavior

The credit scoring system, originally designed to assess financial risk, has evolved into a comprehensive model for evaluating human worth that extends far beyond economic transactions into every aspect of social behavior and personal conduct. This expansion represents one of the most insidious developments in modern social control, as the seemingly objective mathematics of credit assessment provides a veneer of scientific legitimacy to what amounts to a comprehensive system of social ranking and behavioral control that would make Orwell's fictional hierarchies seem primitive by comparison.

Traditional credit scores purported to measure only financial responsibility, evaluating an individual's history of borrowing and repayment to predict future creditworthiness. However, the data sources feeding into modern credit assessment have expanded dramatically to include social media activity, online behavior, shopping patterns, employment history, educational background, geographic location, social associations, and countless other factors that have little direct relationship to financial risk. The result is a system that effectively scores individuals on their overall social conformity and lifestyle choices rather than their ability to repay debts.

The algorithmic models powering these expanded scoring systems analyze correlations between seemingly unrelated behaviors and financial outcomes, creating credit assessments based on factors that individuals may not even realize are being monitored. The types of websites you visit, the time of day you make online purchases, the social media connections you maintain, the neighborhoods you frequent, and even the language patterns in your text messages all contribute to algorithmic assessments of your financial reliability and social standing. These models don't just evaluate what you've done; they judge who you are and whom you associate with.

The implications of this expansion extend far beyond access to credit into fundamental questions about social mobility and equality of opportunity. When credit scores based on social behavior determine access to housing, employment, insurance, and other essential services, they create rigid social hierarchies that are difficult to escape. Individuals from disadvantaged backgrounds find themselves trapped by algorithmic assessments that penalize them not just for past financial mistakes, but for their social environment, cultural background, and lifestyle choices that may be beyond their control.

The Algorithmic Caste System

The expansion of credit-style scoring into social behavior has created what amounts to an algorithmic caste system that assigns individuals numerical values representing their worth to society and their eligibility for various opportunities and services. These scores operate as modern versions of social hierarchies that historically determined life chances based on birth, race, or class, but with the added authority of mathematical precision and technological sophistication. The algorithms generating these scores claim objectivity while embedding the biases and value judgments of their creators into seemingly neutral mathematical formulas.

Employment screening systems use credit score models to evaluate job candidates, creating situations where past financial difficulties can permanently exclude individuals from economic opportunities needed to improve their situations. Housing algorithms assess rental applicants using expanded credit models that consider social media activity and online behavior, making it possible to be denied housing based on political opinions, lifestyle choices, or social associations. Insurance companies deploy similar models to adjust premiums or deny coverage based on behavioral predictions derived from digital surveillance and social analysis.

The recursive nature of these scoring systems creates self-reinforcing cycles of advantage and disadvantage that become increasingly difficult to escape over time. Individuals with high scores receive better opportunities that further improve their scores, while those with low scores find themselves excluded from opportunities that might help them improve their situations. The algorithmic nature of these systems makes them appear natural and inevitable rather than the result of specific policy choices about how society should be organized and opportunities distributed.

Social Media as Character Assessment

Social media platforms have become primary sources of data for expanded credit and behavioral scoring systems, transforming every post, like, share, and connection into potential evidence for algorithmic character assessment. These platforms encourage users to share personal information and opinions while quietly analyzing this content to generate insights about personality traits, reliability, social stability, and conformity to social norms that feed into scoring algorithms used by employers, insurers, lenders, and other institutions.

The analysis of social media data for scoring purposes operates through sophisticated natural language processing and behavioral analysis techniques that can extract insights about individuals' psychological states, political opinions, social relationships, lifestyle choices, and value systems. Algorithms evaluate not just what people post, but how they write, when they post, whom they interact with, what content they engage with, and how others respond to their contributions. This creates a comprehensive assessment of social behavior that extends far beyond traditional notions of creditworthiness or job qualifications.

The pressure to optimize social media presence for algorithmic assessment creates new forms of self-censorship and performance anxiety as individuals become aware that their online behavior affects their access to real-world opportunities. People begin curating their social media presence not for authentic self-expression or genuine social connection, but as strategic career management and score optimization. This transforms social media from platforms for communication and creativity into elaborate performance spaces designed to demonstrate algorithmic acceptability.

The Quantified Self Movement and Voluntary Surveillance

The expansion of scoring systems into social behavior has been facilitated by the "quantified self" movement, which encourages individuals to voluntarily monitor and measure various aspects of their lives through wearable devices, smartphone apps, and other tracking technologies. This movement, originally focused on personal health and productivity optimization, has created vast streams of intimate behavioral data that feed into expanded scoring systems used by insurance companies, employers, and other institutions to make decisions about individuals' access to opportunities and services.

Fitness trackers, sleep monitors, meditation apps, diet tracking systems, and other quantified self technologies collect detailed information about physical activity, health habits, stress levels, sleep patterns, and lifestyle choices that insurance companies and employers increasingly use to assess risk and determine eligibility for various benefits. The voluntary nature of this data sharing provides legal cover for discrimination based on personal health and lifestyle choices while creating pressure for individuals to participate in comprehensive self-monitoring to avoid being penalized for non-participation.

The gamification elements built into quantified self technologies create addiction-like dependencies on external validation and measurement that make individuals more susceptible to manipulation through scoring systems. Users become obsessed with optimizing their metrics rather than improving their actual health or well-being, creating behaviors designed to game the measurement systems rather than achieve genuine personal improvement. This metric fixation extends the logic of credit scoring into intimate aspects of personal life, transforming health, relationships, and personal growth into algorithmic optimization problems.

Financial Inclusion as Social Control

The expansion of credit scoring models is often justified as promoting "financial inclusion" by using alternative data sources to assess the creditworthiness of individuals who lack traditional credit histories. However, this apparent democratization of credit access masks a more sinister expansion of social control that brings previously unbanked populations under the surveillance and behavioral management systems of the financial industry. Alternative credit scoring systems monitor and evaluate behaviors that have nothing to do with financial risk but everything to do with social conformity and political reliability.

Microfinance and alternative lending platforms use social network analysis to assess loan applications, making individuals' friends and family members unwitting participants in credit evaluation processes. These systems evaluate not just an individual's behavior, but the behavior and creditworthiness of their social connections, creating pressure for social groups to police each other's financial behavior and maintain conformity to credit scoring algorithms. The result is the extension of financial surveillance and control into communities and social relationships that previously operated outside the formal banking system.

The mobile payment systems increasingly common in developing countries create comprehensive digital payment trails that feed into expanded credit scoring systems, making it difficult for individuals to engage in economic activity without subjecting themselves to comprehensive behavioral monitoring and assessment. Cash transactions become increasingly difficult or impossible, forcing participation in digital payment systems that track every purchase, transfer, and financial interaction for incorporation into behavioral scoring algorithms.

China's social credit system as the Western future

The People's Republic of China's Social Credit System represents the most comprehensive and explicit implementation of behavioral scoring and social control through algorithmic surveillance ever attempted, yet it would be a profound mistake to view this system as uniquely Chinese or fundamentally different from the trajectories already well underway in Western democracies. The Chinese system simply makes explicit and centralized what Western nations accomplish through a more diffuse network of corporate and government surveillance systems that achieve similar outcomes while maintaining the illusion of voluntary participation and market-driven efficiency.

China's Social Credit System, launched nationally in 2014 with full implementation targeted for 2020, aims to create a unified scoring system that evaluates the trustworthiness of individuals, businesses, and organizations based on their social behavior, financial conduct, legal compliance, and political reliability. The system integrates data from government agencies, financial institutions, technology companies, and social organizations to create comprehensive behavioral profiles that determine access to travel, employment, education, housing, and other essential services. Citizens with high social credit scores receive benefits and privileges, while those with low scores face restrictions and penalties that can effectively exclude them from modern society.

The sophistication of China's system lies not just in its comprehensive data collection, but in its integration of behavioral modification techniques designed to create self-reinforcing cycles of social conformity. The system doesn't merely punish non-conformist behavior after it occurs; it creates incentive structures that encourage individuals to modify their behavior preemptively to maintain or improve their scores. Citizens monitor their own social credit ratings through smartphone apps, adjust their behavior based on score changes, and pressure friends and family members to conform to system expectations to avoid guilt-by-association penalties that can affect their own ratings.

The Western response to China's Social Credit System has been largely characterized by horror and condemnation, with politicians and commentators expressing outrage at the authoritarian implications of comprehensive behavioral monitoring and control. However, this response conveniently ignores the reality that Western nations have implemented remarkably similar systems through different mechanisms that achieve comparable levels of social control while maintaining plausible deniability about their authoritarian implications. The primary difference lies not in the degree of surveillance or behavioral control, but in the institutional arrangements through which such control is exercised.

The Distributed Western Model

While China's Social Credit System operates through explicit government coordination and centralized scoring, Western nations achieve similar outcomes through a distributed network of corporate surveillance systems, financial institutions, government agencies, and technology platforms that share information and coordinate behavioral assessments without formal centralization. This distributed model provides several advantages over the Chinese approach: it maintains the appearance of market-driven efficiency rather than government coercion, it allows for plausible deniability about surveillance and control objectives, and it makes the system more difficult to understand, challenge, or reform.

Credit reporting agencies like Experian, Equifax, and TransUnion already operate comprehensive behavioral scoring systems that affect access to housing, employment, insurance, and other essential services based on assessments that extend far beyond financial behavior. Technology companies like Google, Facebook, Apple, Amazon, and Microsoft collect and analyze behavioral data that feeds into scoring systems used by employers, insurers, and government agencies. Data brokers aggregate information from hundreds of sources to create detailed behavioral profiles sold to anyone willing to pay for access.

The integration between these systems creates a de facto social credit system that operates through market mechanisms rather than government mandate. An individual flagged by one system finds themselves penalized across multiple platforms and institutions as information flows between corporate databases, government watchlists, and algorithmic assessment systems. The result is comprehensive behavioral control that rivals the Chinese system in scope and effectiveness while maintaining the fiction that such control emerges from voluntary market transactions rather than deliberate social engineering.

Technological Infrastructure and Implementation

The technological infrastructure supporting comprehensive behavioral monitoring and control has already been deployed across Western nations through the same digital platforms and surveillance systems that citizens use for entertainment, communication, and commerce. Smartphones equipped with location tracking, biometric sensors, and behavioral monitoring capabilities provide real-time surveillance data to corporate and government databases. Social media platforms analyze communication patterns, social relationships, and opinion expression for insights into political reliability and social conformity. Internet of Things devices embedded in homes, vehicles, and urban infrastructure create comprehensive monitoring networks that track behavior across all aspects of daily life.

The integration of artificial intelligence and machine learning into these surveillance systems provides analytical capabilities that exceed those available to traditional authoritarian regimes, enabling behavioral prediction, influence, and control at scales previously impossible to achieve. These systems don't just monitor what people do; they predict what they might do and implement interventions designed to guide behavior in desired directions. The sophistication of these technological systems makes the enforcement mechanisms of historical dictatorships seem crude by comparison.

Cloud computing platforms controlled by major technology companies provide the infrastructure for storing and analyzing the massive datasets required for comprehensive behavioral monitoring and control. The same systems used for entertainment streaming, social networking, and e-commerce also serve as the backbone for surveillance and behavioral management systems that affect access to employment, housing, credit, and other essential services. This dual-use infrastructure makes it difficult to reform surveillance systems without disrupting the digital services that modern society depends upon.

Corporate-Government Integration

The integration between corporate surveillance systems and government security apparatus in Western nations creates a hybrid model of social control that combines the efficiency of private enterprise with the authority of state power. Technology companies regularly share user data with government agencies through formal intelligence programs and informal cooperation agreements. Government agencies purchase behavioral data from corporate data brokers to supplement their own surveillance capabilities. Former government officials move into executive positions at technology companies, while tech executives transition into government roles, creating a revolving door that ensures alignment between corporate and state interests.

This integration operates largely outside democratic oversight and public accountability, as commercial data sharing agreements and national security classifications shield the cooperation from public scrutiny. Citizens remain unaware of how their data flows between corporate and government systems, making it impossible to understand the full scope of surveillance and behavioral control systems affecting their lives. The distributed nature of this surveillance network makes it more resilient and harder to reform than centralized systems like China's Social Credit System.

The COVID-19 pandemic provided a preview of how quickly Western nations can implement comprehensive behavioral monitoring and control systems when circumstances permit. Contact tracing programs, vaccine passport systems, and mobility restrictions demonstrated the technical feasibility and political acceptance of using digital surveillance systems to monitor and control population behavior in real-time. Many of these emergency measures have been normalized or expanded beyond their original public health justifications, creating precedents for future expansions of surveillance and control systems.

The Inevitability Narrative

Perhaps the most dangerous aspect of the trajectory toward comprehensive behavioral monitoring and control is the development of an "inevitability narrative" that presents such systems as natural consequences of technological progress rather than deliberate policy choices. This narrative suggests that privacy, anonymity, and behavioral autonomy are obsolete concepts incompatible with modern technological society, making resistance to surveillance systems seem futile and anti-progressive. The Chinese Social Credit System is presented as an extreme example of where such technologies might lead, allowing Western nations to implement similar capabilities while claiming they represent more moderate and democratic approaches to the same underlying technological possibilities.

The normalization of comprehensive surveillance through consumer technology platforms has created populations that are psychologically prepared for and even welcoming of more explicit behavioral monitoring and control systems. Citizens who willingly share intimate details of their lives on social media, carry tracking devices disguised as conveniences, and submit to comprehensive behavioral analysis for modest discounts on consumer goods have been conditioned to accept surveillance as a normal part of modern life. The transition from voluntary surveillance for commercial purposes to mandatory surveillance for social control becomes a small step rather than a fundamental change in social organization.

The competitive pressures of global capitalism create incentives for Western nations to match the efficiency and control capabilities of China's Social Credit System through their own technological and institutional innovations. Countries that fail to implement comprehensive behavioral monitoring and control systems may find themselves disadvantaged in economic competition, security threats, and social management challenges.

This creates a race toward maximum surveillance and control that makes the expansion of such systems seem inevitable rather than chosen.

Democratic Resistance and Authoritarian Drift

The expansion of behavioral monitoring and control systems poses fundamental challenges to democratic governance and individual liberty that Western political institutions appear ill-equipped to address. Traditional privacy rights and civil liberties frameworks were designed for an era of limited surveillance capabilities and clear distinctions between public and private spheres. These frameworks become inadequate when surveillance is comprehensive, behavioral modification is subtle and continuous, and the boundaries between voluntary and coercive participation become blurred.

The corporate mediation of surveillance and control systems provides a layer of legal protection that makes democratic oversight and reform more difficult to achieve. When behavioral monitoring is conducted by private companies rather than government agencies, traditional constitutional protections and democratic accountability mechanisms don't apply. Citizens have no vote in corporate boardrooms and no constitutional rights against private surveillance, making corporate-mediated social control systems more resistant to democratic pressure than government-operated systems.

The global nature of technology platforms and data systems creates additional challenges for democratic governance, as national regulations can be circumvented through data processing in jurisdictions with weaker privacy protections. The scale and complexity of modern surveillance systems make them difficult for democratic institutions to understand and regulate, while the technical expertise required to oversee such systems concentrates power in the hands of technology companies and security agencies that may not share democratic values or priorities.

Conclusion

The emergence of comprehensive digital surveillance and behavioral control systems represents perhaps the most significant threat to human autonomy and democratic governance in our time, yet it unfolds through mechanisms so subtle and apparently beneficial that its implications remain largely invisible to those being monitored and controlled. Your data doppelganger exists not as science fiction but as present reality, constructed from the intimate details of your digital life and used to predict, influence, and control your behavior in ways that extend far beyond simple commercial advertising into the fundamental structures of social organization and political power.

The creation of digital twins from our personal data represents the ultimate commodification of human experience, transforming every aspect of individual life into raw material for corporate profit and social control. These algorithmic avatars don't merely observe and record human behavior; they actively shape it through feedback mechanisms, prediction systems, and behavioral modification techniques that operate below the threshold of conscious awareness. The result is a form of control that achieves the objectives of authoritarian governance while maintaining the appearance of voluntary participation and personal choice.

The expansion of predictive behavioral analysis into pre-crime enforcement represents a fundamental shift from reactive to proactive social control that abandons traditional notions of individual rights and due process in favor of algorithmic efficiency and risk management. When punishment precedes crime and guilt is determined by mathematical probability rather than actual behavior, the foundations of justice and human dignity begin to erode. The sophistication of modern machine learning systems makes these predictions accurate enough to be practically useful while remaining opaque enough to resist meaningful challenge or accountability.

The extension of credit scoring models into comprehensive social behavior assessment creates rigid hierarchical systems that determine access to essential services, economic opportunities, and social participation based on algorithmic judgments about personal worth and social conformity. These systems operate as modern versions of historical caste structures, but with the added authority of mathematical precision and technological sophistication. The recursive nature of these scoring systems creates self-reinforcing cycles of advantage and disadvantage that become increasingly difficult to escape over time.

China's Social Credit System provides an explicit template for comprehensive behavioral control that Western nations are implementing through more distributed and market-mediated mechanisms. The technological infrastructure, data collection capabilities, and analytical systems required for such comprehensive social control already exist in Western democracies, deployed through consumer technology platforms and justified as commercial convenience rather than social engineering. The primary difference between Chinese and Western approaches lies not in their capabilities or objectives, but in their institutional arrangements and public presentation.

The trajectory toward comprehensive behavioral monitoring and control represents a choice about the kind of society we want to live in, not an inevitable consequence of technological progress. The same technologies that enable unprecedented surveillance and control could be deployed in ways that enhance human freedom, creativity, and authentic choice rather than constraining them. However, the window of opportunity for democratic resistance to these systems may be closing as the infrastructure of control becomes embedded in the essential services and institutional arrangements that modern society depends upon.

The challenge lies not merely in understanding these systems, but in developing new frameworks for thinking about autonomy, privacy, and human dignity in an age of algorithmic control. Traditional liberal concepts of individual rights and democratic governance appear increasingly inadequate for addressing forms of power that operate through the manipulation of choice itself and the gradual erosion of the cognitive and emotional capacities required for autonomous decision-making. New forms of resistance, regulation, and social organization may be necessary to preserve human agency in an age where the boundaries between prediction and control, convenience and coercion, voluntary participation and systematic manipulation have become impossibly blurred.

The stakes extend beyond individual privacy concerns to fundamental questions about the future of human freedom and democratic governance. If comprehensive behavioral monitoring and control systems become normalized and embedded in the basic structures of social organization, future generations may lose not just privacy but the very capacity for independent thought and autonomous action that makes meaningful democracy possible. The construction of digital doppelgangers represents more than a violation of privacy; it represents the systematic reconstruction of human identity itself according to algorithmic logic and corporate priorities rather than human values and individual choice.

The resistance to these systems requires not just policy reforms or technological solutions, but a fundamental recommitment to human dignity and autonomous choice as organizing principles for social organization. This may require accepting less efficiency, convenience, and security in exchange for preserving the conditions that make authentic human flourishing possible. The alternative is a future where human beings become optimized components in algorithmic systems designed to serve interests other than their own, where the concept of authentic choice becomes meaningless because the cognitive and emotional capabilities required for such choice have been systematically eroded through comprehensive behavioral modification programs masquerading as consumer convenience and social progress.

Chapter 6: The Dopamine Panopticon

Jeremy Bentham's panopticon was designed as a prison where inmates could be watched at all times without knowing when they were being observed, creating a state of perpetual self-surveillance through uncertainty and fear. Today's digital landscape has achieved something far more insidious: a panopticon powered not by fear but by pleasure, where we eagerly place ourselves under constant observation in exchange for intermittent rewards of social validation and digital dopamine. This is the dopamine panopticon—a surveillance system so addictive, so perfectly calibrated to our neurochemical reward pathways, that we don't just accept our imprisonment; we compete for better cells, pay premium prices for enhanced monitoring, and panic at the thought of being disconnected from our digital captors even temporarily.

Unlike Bentham's architectural prison or Orwell's oppressive telescreen, the dopamine panopticon operates through pleasure rather than pain, seduction rather than coercion. It transforms surveillance from something done to us into something we actively perform, turning every citizen into both prisoner and guard, subject and collaborator in an endless spectacle of self-revelation and mutual observation. The genius of this system lies not in its ability to watch us, but in its capacity to make us want to be watched, to crave the digital attention that validates our existence while simultaneously commodifying our consciousness and weaponizing our most basic human needs for connection and recognition.

SOCIAL MEDIA ADDICTION AND THE GAMIFICATION OF SURVEILLANCE

The Neurochemistry of Digital Dependency

The dopamine panopticon operates by exploiting fundamental features of human neurobiology, particularly the brain's reward prediction system that evolved to help our ancestors survive in environments of scarcity and uncertainty. Social media platforms have reverse-engineered these ancient neural pathways, creating digital experiences that trigger dopamine release with the precision of pharmaceutical interventions. Every notification, every like, every comment creates a small neurochemical reward that reinforces the behavior that produced it, gradually training users to seek validation through increased self-surveillance and digital performance.

The sophistication of this neurochemical manipulation cannot be overstated. Platform designers employ teams of neuroscientists, behavioral economists, and addiction specialists to create what they euphemistically call "engaging experiences" but what more accurately represents a form of digital drug dealing. Variable ratio reinforcement schedules—the same psychological principle that makes gambling addictive—ensure that users never know when the next reward will come, creating a state of constant anticipation and compulsive checking behavior that generates reliable engagement and advertising revenue.

The addiction to social media validation operates through the same neural pathways as substance addiction, creating measurable changes in brain structure and function that persist even when users are offline. Neuroimaging studies reveal that heavy social media users develop increased activity in the brain's reward centers when receiving social feedback, while simultaneously showing decreased sensitivity to real-world pleasures and rewards. This creates a form of digital tolerance where users require increasingly intense levels of online validation to achieve the same neurochemical satisfaction, leading to escalating patterns of self-revelation and attention-seeking behavior.

The Gamification of Self-Surveillance

Social media platforms have transformed the act of sharing personal information from an occasional social behavior into a competitive game where users compete for attention, validation, and social status through increasingly intimate forms of self-revelation. This gamification operates through elaborate scoring systems—followers, likes, shares, comments, views—that create quantified hierarchies of social value and encourage users to optimize their behavior for algorithmic rewards rather than authentic human connection.

The genius of gamified surveillance lies in its ability to make monitoring feel like play rather than work, achievement rather than submission. Users don't experience themselves as subjects of surveillance; they experience themselves as players in a social game where success requires strategic self-presentation and careful attention to platform metrics. This transforms privacy violations from impositions into opportunities, making users eager to share increasingly personal information in pursuit of higher scores and better performance in the attention economy.

The competitive dynamics of gamified surveillance create what researchers call "surveillance capitalism competition," where users compete not just for attention but for the privilege of being more thoroughly monitored and analyzed. Premium features often provide enhanced surveillance capabilities—more detailed analytics about who viewed your content, when they engaged with it, and how their engagement patterns compare to other users. This creates a perverse market where consumers pay for the privilege of more comprehensive self-surveillance, turning privacy invasion into a luxury good.

The Addiction Economy and Platform Profitability

The transformation of human attention into a commodity requires the creation and maintenance of addictive user behaviors that generate predictable engagement patterns and advertising revenue. This has given rise to what researchers call the "addiction economy"—a business model based explicitly on creating and exploiting psychological dependency to maximize platform profitability. Unlike traditional media businesses that sold content to consumers, social media platforms sell consumers' attention to advertisers, creating incentives to maximize time spent on platform regardless of the consequences for user wellbeing or mental health.

The addiction economy operates through what behavioral economists call "dark patterns"—design features intentionally created to manipulate user behavior in ways that serve platform interests while often conflicting with user intentions and values. Infinite scroll features eliminate natural stopping points that might allow users to disengage. Push notifications create artificial urgency that interrupts other activities. Algorithmic feeds provide unpredictable rewards that maintain compulsive checking behavior. Read receipts and activity indicators create social pressure to respond immediately to communications.

The profitability of addiction-based business models has created a form of "race to the bottom of the brain stem," where platforms compete to create ever-more-addictive features that bypass rational decision-making and exploit unconscious psychological vulnerabilities. This competition has produced increasingly sophisticated manipulation techniques that would be regulated or banned in other industries but operate freely in the largely unregulated digital attention market.

Variable Reinforcement and Behavioral Control

The most powerful tool in the dopamine panopticon's arsenal is the strategic application of variable reinforcement schedules—patterns of reward delivery that create maximum psychological dependency while minimizing platform costs. Unlike fixed reinforcement schedules, where rewards arrive predictably, variable schedules create unpredictable reward delivery that maintains high levels of engagement even when rewards become less frequent or less satisfying.

Social media platforms employ sophisticated algorithms to optimize reward delivery timing, ensuring that users receive just enough positive feedback to maintain engagement while preventing the satisfaction that might lead to voluntary disengagement. This creates what psychologists call "extinction resistance"—the tendency for behaviors maintained by variable reinforcement to persist even when rewards become rare or stop entirely. Users continue checking their feeds, posting content, and engaging with platforms even during periods when they receive little or no positive feedback.

The application of variable reinforcement to social media creates a form of behavioral control that's both comprehensive and invisible. Users experience their compulsive platform usage as personal choice rather than psychological manipulation, making them unlikely to seek treatment or support for what is increasingly recognized as a form of behavioral addiction.

This creates a population of willing surveillance subjects who actively resist efforts to limit their own digital monitoring and manipulation.

HOW LIKES, SHARES, AND COMMENTS CREATE BEHAVIORAL CONDITIONING

The Quantification of Human Worth

The dopamine panopticon operates by reducing complex human experiences and relationships to simple numerical metrics that can be easily measured, compared, and optimized. Likes, shares, comments, and other engagement metrics create a quantified system of social value that transforms every human interaction into a performance measured by its ability to generate algorithmic approval. This quantification doesn't just measure social success; it defines it, creating new forms of social hierarchy based on platform performance rather than traditional markers of achievement or character.

The psychological impact of quantified social feedback cannot be overstated. When human worth becomes measurable through digital metrics, users inevitably begin to optimize their behavior for metric improvement rather than authentic self-expression or meaningful relationship building. This creates what researchers call "metric fixation"—an obsessive focus on improving quantified measures of success that often undermines the very goals those metrics were supposed to represent.

The quantification of social interaction creates a feedback loop where users internalize platform values and begin to evaluate their own worth through algorithmic metrics. Self-esteem becomes tied to follower counts, personal relationships get measured by engagement rates, and life experiences get evaluated by their potential for viral content creation. This represents a fundamental shift in how humans understand themselves and their relationships, transforming inner-directed individuals into other-directed performers constantly seeking external validation through digital applause.

Intermittent Reinforcement and Compulsive Behavior

The strategic withholding and delivery of social rewards through platform algorithms creates patterns of intermittent reinforcement that are particularly effective at generating compulsive behavior. Unlike consistent reinforcement, which quickly leads to satiation and reduced engagement, intermittent reinforcement creates a state of perpetual anticipation where users never know when the next reward will arrive. This uncertainty makes each potential reward more valuable and each checking behavior more likely to be repeated.

Platform algorithms deliberately vary the timing and intensity of social feedback to maximize addictive potential. A post that initially receives no engagement might suddenly generate multiple likes and comments, creating a powerful reward experience that reinforces both the posting behavior and the checking behavior required to discover the reward. This variability ensures that users develop compulsive checking habits while simultaneously making them more likely to continue creating content even when rewards are scarce.

The intermittent nature of social media rewards creates what psychologists call "partial reinforcement extinction effect"—the tendency for behaviors learned through variable reward schedules to persist much longer than behaviors learned through consistent rewards. This explains why social media addiction is particularly difficult to overcome and why users continue engaging with platforms even when they consciously recognize the negative impacts on their wellbeing and productivity.

Social Comparison and Competitive Validation

The dopamine panopticon amplifies natural human tendencies toward social comparison by providing constant access to carefully curated representations of other people's lives and achievements. This creates a form of "compare and despair" cycle where users experience their own lives as inadequate compared to the highlight reels presented by others on social media. The psychological impact is compounded by the fact that platform algorithms preferentially surface content that generates strong emotional responses, meaning that users are disproportionately exposed to content that makes them feel envious, inadequate, or left out.

The competitive nature of social media metrics transforms social interaction from cooperative relationship building into zero-sum competition for finite attention and validation. When likes and shares become scarce resources, users begin competing rather than collaborating, leading to the breakdown of community bonds and the rise of performative rather than authentic social behavior. This competition is particularly intense because it operates continuously—there are no time-outs, no off-seasons, no breaks from the constant pressure to perform and compete for social validation.

The gamification of social comparison creates what researchers call "compare addiction," where users become compulsively focused on measuring their own success against others rather than pursuing intrinsically meaningful goals and relationships. This comparison addiction is particularly damaging because it shifts attention from personal growth and authentic relationship building toward external metrics that are largely outside individual control and often manipulated by algorithmic systems designed to maximize engagement rather than user satisfaction.

The Conditioning of Authentic Expression

Perhaps the most insidious aspect of behavioral conditioning through social media metrics is its impact on authentic self-expression. When every form of communication gets evaluated through engagement metrics, users gradually learn to suppress thoughts, feelings, and experiences that don't generate positive feedback while amplifying those that do. This creates a form of "algorithmic self-censorship" where individuals modify their authentic expression to optimize for platform performance rather than personal truth or genuine communication.

The conditioning process operates so gradually that users rarely notice their authentic expression being replaced by performed expression designed to generate engagement. Over time, the performance becomes habitual, and users may lose touch with their authentic thoughts and feelings, replacing them with algorithmically optimized versions that generate better social media metrics. This represents a profound form of identity distortion where individual personality becomes subordinated to platform performance requirements.

The impact on authentic expression is particularly severe for young people who develop their sense of self within social media environments where every aspect of identity must be optimized for digital performance. This generation grows up believing that authentic expression naturally includes strategic self-presentation designed to generate social media engagement, making it difficult for them to distinguish between genuine self-expression and performance for algorithmic rewards.

THE ATTENTION ECONOMY AND HUMAN CONSCIOUSNESS AS COMMODITY

The Commodification of Consciousness

The attention economy represents a fundamental transformation in how human consciousness gets understood and valued in economic systems. Rather than treating attention as a personal resource that individuals control and direct according to their own interests and values, the attention economy treats consciousness as a raw material to be extracted, processed, and sold to third parties for profit. This commodification turns the most intimate aspect of human experience—our moment-to-moment awareness and focus—into a product optimized for economic extraction rather than personal flourishing.

The process of consciousness commodification operates through sophisticated systems of behavioral analysis that track not just what users do online, but how they think, feel, and respond to different types of stimuli. Eye-tracking technology monitors where users look and for how long. Engagement metrics measure emotional responses to different types of content. Behavioral analytics track patterns of attention and distraction to optimize content delivery for maximum psychological impact. This creates comprehensive profiles of individual consciousness that are more detailed and accurate than most people's understanding of their own minds.

The economic value of commodified consciousness lies in its predictability and manipulability. When platforms understand how individual minds respond to different stimuli, they can engineer experiences that reliably produce desired behaviors—clicking on advertisements, making purchases, sharing content, or spending more time on platform. This transforms human consciousness from a tool for individual navigation of the world into a resource for corporate profit generation, creating a fundamental conflict between individual wellbeing and economic optimization.

The Industrialization of Attention Capture

The attention economy has given rise to an entire industry dedicated to the systematic capture and manipulation of human attention on an industrial scale. This industry employs thousands of engineers, designers, psychologists, and data scientists whose primary job is to make digital products more addictive and attention-consuming. The techniques developed by this industry draw from decades of research in behavioral psychology, neuroscience, and addiction medicine to create products designed to override rational decision-making and conscious intention.

The industrialization of attention capture operates through what researchers call "persuasive design"—the application of psychological manipulation techniques to digital interface design. Colors, sounds, animations, and layout patterns are all carefully chosen to trigger specific neurochemical responses that increase engagement and reduce users' ability to disengage voluntarily. A/B testing allows companies to rapidly iterate and optimize these manipulation techniques, creating increasingly effective methods of attention capture and behavioral control.

The industrial scale of attention capture means that billions of people are simultaneously exposed to sophisticated psychological manipulation designed to override their conscious intentions and values. This creates a form of mass cognitive exploitation where individual autonomy becomes subordinated to corporate profit motives, fundamentally altering the relationship between human agency and technological systems.

The Economics of Cognitive Exploitation

The business model of the attention economy requires the systematic exploitation of cognitive vulnerabilities and psychological weaknesses that evolved for entirely different purposes than resisting corporate manipulation. Companies profit by identifying and exploiting the gap between what users consciously want and what their unconscious psychological systems can be manipulated to desire. This creates a form of cognitive arbitrage where companies extract value by manipulating users into behaviors that serve corporate interests while conflicting with user values and intentions.

The economics of cognitive exploitation operate through what behavioral economists call "exploitation of cognitive biases"—the systematic use of psychological shortcuts and mental blind spots to influence decision-making in ways that users don't recognize or intend. Loss aversion makes users reluctant to delete apps or cancel subscriptions. Social proof manipulates users into behaviors they observe others performing. Scarcity creates artificial urgency around digital experiences and purchases.

The profitability of cognitive exploitation has created a market where companies compete to discover and exploit new psychological vulnerabilities, leading to an escalating arms race in manipulation techniques. As users develop resistance to existing manipulation methods, companies invest in more sophisticated approaches that operate at deeper psychological levels, creating an ongoing cycle of exploitation and resistance that generally favors those with more resources and technological sophistication.

The Transformation of Time and Temporal Experience

The attention economy has fundamentally altered how humans experience time, transforming it from a natural rhythm of activity and rest into a commodity to be maximized and optimized for platform engagement. Social media platforms use sophisticated techniques to manipulate users' perception of time passage, making sessions feel shorter than they actually are while maximizing the actual time spent on platform. This creates a form of "temporal hijacking" where users lose control over their own time allocation and scheduling.

The fragmentation of attention into micro-moments of engagement creates what researchers call "time confetti"—the breakdown of sustained attention spans into brief fragments that are individually less satisfying but collectively more addictive. Users find themselves unable to engage in activities requiring sustained attention, such as reading books, having deep conversations, or pursuing complex creative projects, because their attention has been conditioned to expect constant stimulation and immediate rewards.

The temporal manipulation of the attention economy has profound implications for human development and achievement. When time gets fragmented into advertising-optimized micro-moments, users lose the ability to engage in the sustained, focused work required for skill development, creative achievement, and meaningful relationship building. This creates a population that's highly responsive to digital stimulation but increasingly incapable of the deep work and sustained attention that characterize human flourishing.

The Psychological Infrastructure of Surveillance Capitalism

The attention economy serves as the psychological infrastructure for surveillance capitalism, creating the behavioral conditioning necessary to make comprehensive surveillance feel natural and desirable rather than invasive and oppressive. By making users addicted to digital validation and social feedback, platforms create psychological dependency that overrides privacy concerns and resistance to monitoring. Users become willing to trade increasing amounts of personal information and behavioral data for access to the dopamine rewards provided by social media engagement.

This psychological infrastructure operates through what researchers call "surveillance bargaining," where users gradually trade privacy for convenience in a series of small exchanges that individually seem reasonable but collectively result in comprehensive life monitoring. Each app permission, each data sharing agreement, each personalization feature represents a small surrender of privacy in exchange for enhanced user experience, creating a ratcheting effect where privacy erosion becomes irreversible and surveillance becomes normalized.

The effectiveness of this psychological infrastructure lies in its ability to make surveillance feel like service rather than monitoring. When platforms use personal data to provide more relevant content, better recommendations, and more personalized experiences, users experience surveillance as value rather than violation. This transforms the relationship between monitor and monitored from adversarial to collaborative, making users active participants in their own comprehensive surveillance.

MENTAL HEALTH IMPACTS OF CONSTANT DIGITAL SURVEILLANCE

Anxiety and the Performance of Self

The constant awareness of being watched, measured, and evaluated through digital platforms creates a state of chronic performance anxiety that affects users both online and offline. When every social interaction might be screenshotted, every statement might be taken out of context, and every behavior might be recorded and analyzed, users develop what researchers call "social media anxiety disorder"—a persistent fear of digital judgment that affects their ability to behave authentically and spontaneously in both digital and physical environments.

The performance anxiety created by digital surveillance operates through anticipatory fear of negative evaluation, rejection, or social punishment based on online behavior. Users become hyper-vigilant about their digital self-presentation, constantly monitoring and editing their thoughts, expressions, and behaviors to avoid potential negative consequences. This hyper-vigilance is exhausting and prevents the relaxed, authentic interactions that are necessary for mental health and genuine relationship building.

The anxiety-inducing effects of digital surveillance are particularly severe for young people who develop their sense of self within surveilled environments where every aspect of identity formation is potentially subject to public evaluation and judgment. This creates what developmental psychologists call "surveillance identity disorder," where individuals never develop a stable sense of self because their identity remains constantly subject to external validation and social media metrics.

Depression and Social Comparison

The dopamine panopticon's emphasis on quantified social comparison creates ideal conditions for the development and exacerbation of depression, particularly among users who struggle to achieve the social media success that the platforms present as normal and achievable. When users compare their internal experiences of struggle, boredom, and difficulty with the carefully curated highlight reels presented by others on social media, they inevitably conclude that their own lives are inadequate, boring, or unsuccessful by comparison.

The social comparison facilitated by social media operates through what psychologists call "compare and despair" cycles, where users seek social media validation to relieve feelings of inadequacy, only to encounter more evidence of their relative social failure, leading to deeper depression and more compulsive social media use. This creates a negative feedback loop where the behavior intended to relieve depression actually exacerbates it, leading to increasing social media dependency and worsening mental health outcomes.

The depression-inducing effects of social media comparison are compounded by algorithmic systems that preferentially surface content designed to generate strong emotional responses, including envy, inadequacy, and social exclusion. Users don't encounter representative samples of other people's experiences; they encounter algorithmically optimized content designed to maximize engagement through emotional manipulation, creating distorted impressions of social reality that make their own lives seem inadequate by comparison.

Attention Deficit and Cognitive Fragmentation

The constant interruption and stimulation provided by social media platforms creates what researchers call "digital attention deficit disorder"—a condition characterized by difficulty maintaining sustained focus on any single task or thought process. This condition develops through the repeated conditioning of attention toward brief, highly stimulating experiences that provide immediate gratification while requiring minimal cognitive effort or sustained engagement.

The fragmentation of attention created by social media use affects not just digital behavior but cognitive function in all areas of life. Users find themselves unable to read books, have deep conversations, or engage in complex problem-solving without experiencing boredom, anxiety, or compulsive urges to check their devices. This represents a fundamental alteration in cognitive capacity that affects academic performance, professional achievement, and personal relationship quality.

The attention fragmentation caused by social media creates what neuroscientists call "continuous partial attention"—a state where individuals are always partially engaged with multiple streams of information but never fully focused on any single activity. This condition prevents the deep cognitive processing necessary for learning, creativity, and complex problem-solving, creating a population that's highly responsive to digital stimulation but increasingly incapable of sustained intellectual work.

Sleep Disruption and Circadian Dysregulation

The dopamine panopticon operates 24 hours a day, creating artificial light exposure and psychological stimulation that disrupts natural circadian rhythms and sleep patterns. The blue light emitted by digital screens interferes with melatonin production, while the psychological arousal created by social media engagement prevents the mental relaxation necessary for healthy sleep onset. This creates a cycle where poor sleep quality reduces resistance to digital manipulation, leading to increased social media use that further disrupts sleep patterns.

The sleep disruption caused by social media use is compounded by the anxiety and stimulation created by constant social monitoring and evaluation. Users often lie awake thinking about social media interactions, planning future posts, or worrying about their online reputation, preventing the mental deactivation necessary for restorative sleep. This creates chronic sleep deprivation that affects cognitive function, emotional regulation, and physical health.

The 24/7 nature of social media creates what researchers call "digital insomnia"—the inability to disengage from digital stimulation even when users recognize its negative impact on their sleep and health. The fear of missing out on social media activity, combined with the addictive nature of variable reinforcement schedules, creates compulsive late-night device use that overrides rational sleep hygiene decisions and creates chronic circadian disruption.

Identity Fragmentation and Authenticity Loss

The requirement to maintain multiple digital personas across different platforms creates what psychologists call "identity fragmentation disorder"—a condition where individuals lose touch with their authentic self through the maintenance of multiple performed identities optimized for different algorithmic and social contexts. Users develop different versions of themselves for Instagram, Facebook, Twitter, LinkedIn, and other platforms, gradually losing touch with which version represents their authentic thoughts, feelings, and values.

The fragmentation of identity across multiple digital platforms prevents the integration and consolidation of experience that's necessary for psychological maturity and mental health. Instead of developing a coherent sense of self through sustained relationships and consistent values, users develop multiple fragmented identities that may conflict with each other and create internal psychological tension and confusion.

The loss of authentic identity through digital performance has particularly severe consequences for adolescents and young adults who are still developing their sense of self. When identity formation occurs primarily through digital performance rather than authentic self-exploration and real-world relationship building, individuals may reach adulthood without ever developing a stable sense of who they are beyond their social media personas.

THE NEUROLOGICAL TRANSFORMATION OF HUMAN CONSCIOUSNESS

Addiction Pathways and Brain Structure Changes

Extended exposure to the dopamine panopticon creates measurable changes in brain structure and function that mirror those observed in substance addiction and other behavioral addictions. Neuroimaging studies reveal that heavy social media users develop increased activity in brain reward centers when receiving social feedback, while simultaneously showing decreased sensitivity to real-world pleasures and rewards. These neurological changes represent a form of "digital brain damage" that persists even when users are offline.

The addiction pathways activated by social media engagement operate through the same neurochemical systems that respond to drugs, gambling, and other addictive behaviors. Dopamine release in response to social media rewards creates tolerance effects that require increasing levels of stimulation to achieve the same psychological satisfaction. This tolerance creates escalating patterns of use that interfere with other activities and relationships, meeting clinical definitions of behavioral addiction.

The neurological changes caused by social media addiction affect not just reward processing but cognitive control, attention regulation, and decision-making capacity. Heavy social media users show decreased activity in brain areas responsible for impulse control and long-term planning, while showing increased activity in areas associated with compulsive behavior and immediate gratification. These changes represent a fundamental alteration in cognitive capacity that affects all areas of life and decision-making.

The Rewiring of Social Cognition

The dopamine panopticon fundamentally alters how human brains process social information, creating what researchers call "digital social cognition" that differs significantly from the face-to-face social processing that shaped human evolution. When social interaction becomes mediated through algorithms and metrics, the brain develops different patterns of social information processing that prioritize digital performance over authentic connection and mutual understanding.

The rewiring of social cognition through digital interaction creates deficits in empathy, emotional intelligence, and relationship skills that affect users' ability to form and maintain satisfying real-world relationships. When social feedback becomes quantified through likes and shares rather than experienced through emotional resonance and mutual understanding, users lose touch with the subtle social cues and emotional nuances that characterize healthy human relationships.

The transformation of social cognition through digital interaction has particular implications for conflict resolution, intimacy, and collaborative problem-solving. Users who develop their social skills primarily through digital interaction often lack the capacity for the kind of sustained, nuanced communication required for working through disagreements, building trust, and creating genuine intimacy with others.

Cognitive Load and Mental Exhaustion

The constant cognitive demands of navigating multiple digital environments, maintaining various online personas, and processing enormous volumes of digital information creates what researchers call "cognitive overload syndrome"—a state of chronic mental exhaustion that affects concentration, decision-making, and emotional regulation. The human brain, which evolved to process relatively simple social environments, becomes overwhelmed by the complexity and volume of information required for successful digital navigation.

The cognitive load imposed by social media extends far beyond the time spent actively using platforms to include the background cognitive processing required to maintain digital relationships, track online reputation, and manage multiple digital identities. This background processing consumes mental resources even when users aren't actively online, creating chronic cognitive stress that affects performance in all areas of life.

The mental exhaustion created by digital cognitive overload makes users more susceptible to manipulation and less capable of the critical thinking and sustained attention required for complex problem-solving and creative work. This creates a population that's increasingly dependent on digital systems for information processing and decision-making while becoming less capable of independent thought and autonomous action.

THE SOCIAL CONSEQUENCES OF MASS DIGITAL ADDICTION

The Breakdown of Authentic Community

The dopamine panopticon's emphasis on individual performance and metric optimization undermines the collaborative, mutual support that characterizes healthy human communities. When social interaction becomes gamified through engagement metrics, community members begin competing rather than cooperating, leading to the breakdown of social bonds and the replacement of genuine community with performed sociality designed to generate digital validation.

The transformation of community from collaborative to competitive creates what sociologists call "performative community disorder," where groups of people engage in community-like behaviors while actually competing for attention and validation rather than working together for mutual benefit. This performative community provides the appearance of social connection while actually increasing isolation and reducing the social support that healthy communities provide.

The breakdown of authentic community through digital mediation has particular consequences for civic engagement, political participation, and collective problem-solving. When citizens relate to each other primarily as audiences for individual performance rather than collaborators in shared projects, the social cooperation necessary for democratic governance and collective action becomes increasingly difficult to achieve.

Generational Trauma and Digital Nativity

The generation that has grown up entirely within the dopamine panopticon faces unique psychological challenges that may constitute a form of collective trauma with long-lasting social consequences. These "digital natives" have never experienced unmediated social interaction or unmonitored private thought, making it difficult for them to understand what has been lost through constant digital surveillance and performance pressure.

The generational trauma of digital nativity manifests through what psychologists call "surveillance normalization syndrome"—the acceptance of comprehensive life monitoring as natural and inevitable rather than historically unprecedented and potentially harmful. This normalization makes it difficult for digital natives to recognize or resist the negative impacts of surveillance capitalism, creating a population that's psychologically adapted to digital exploitation.

The long-term social consequences of digital nativity remain unclear, but early indicators suggest profound changes in social behavior, cognitive capacity, and psychological development that may fundamentally alter human nature and social organization. The first generation to grow up entirely within surveillance capitalism is now reaching adulthood, and their adaptation to digital environments may represent a permanent transformation in human consciousness and social behavior.

The Polarization Engine

The dopamine panopticon's algorithmic optimization for engagement has created what researchers call "artificial polarization"—the systematic amplification of conflict and division through content curation designed to generate strong emotional responses and increase time spent on platform. This artificial polarization doesn't reflect natural social divisions but rather algorithmic manipulation designed to maximize advertising revenue through emotional manipulation.

The polarization engine operates by identifying topics and perspectives that generate strong reactions, then systematically exposing users to increasingly extreme versions of those perspectives while filtering out moderate voices and nuanced viewpoints. This creates artificial social conflicts that serve platform interests while undermining social cohesion and democratic deliberation.

The social consequences of artificial polarization extend far beyond online behavior to affect real-world relationships, political participation, and social cooperation. When algorithmic systems train entire populations to engage with each other primarily through conflict and emotional manipulation, the social skills necessary for compromise, collaboration, and mutual understanding begin to atrophy, creating societies that are increasingly incapable of collective problem-solving and democratic governance.

CONCLUSION: THE ARCHITECTURE OF WILLING SERVITUDE

The dopamine panopticon represents the culmination of a centuries-long evolution in systems of social control, achieving what no previous authoritarian system could accomplish: the creation of willing, enthusiastic participants in their own comprehensive surveillance and behavioral manipulation. Where Bentham's original panopticon relied on uncertainty and fear to create compliance, and Orwell's telescreens required constant threats of violence, the dopamine panopticon operates through pleasure, connection, and the fulfillment of fundamental human needs for social validation and recognition.

This system's genius lies not in its oppression but in its indispensability, not in its cruelty but in its seductive power to make surveillance feel like service, monitoring feel like care, and behavioral manipulation feel like personalization. We have constructed a world where our most intimate thoughts and experiences are continuously harvested for profit, our attention and consciousness are treated as commodities to be bought and sold, and our authentic relationships are replaced by algorithmic performance—and we experience this not as loss but as liberation, not as exploitation but as empowerment.

The mental health consequences of this system are still emerging, but early evidence suggests that we may be witnessing the first technologically induced transformation of human consciousness since the invention of written language. Rates of anxiety, depression, attention disorders, and social dysfunction have skyrocketed in direct correlation with the rise of social media and smartphone adoption, particularly among young people who have never known unmediated reality or unmonitored privacy.

Yet perhaps the most troubling aspect of the dopamine panopticon is not its current impact but its trajectory toward ever-greater sophistication and control. As artificial intelligence systems become more capable of predicting and manipulating human behavior, as virtual and augmented reality create more immersive forms of digital experience, and as brain-computer interfaces promise direct access to neural activity, the possibilities for behavioral control and consciousness manipulation will expand far beyond anything we currently experience.

The dopamine panopticon has taught us that humans will voluntarily surrender their freedom, privacy, and authentic relationships in exchange for engineered experiences that provide social validation and neurochemical reward. We have learned to love our surveillance, to compete for more comprehensive monitoring, and to panic at the thought of digital disconnection. We have become, in the most literal sense, addicted to our own oppression.

The question now is not whether we can escape the dopamine panopticon—the infrastructure is too vast, the addiction too complete, the economic interests too powerful for individual resistance to succeed. The question is whether we can recognize what we have become and choose to build different kinds of systems, different relationships with technology, and different definitions of human flourishing that don't require the commodification of consciousness and the industrialization of human attention.

In the dopamine panopticon, the screen is not just watching us—it is training us, conditioning us, and gradually transforming us into more predictable and profitable versions of ourselves. We have become both the product being sold and the consumers being targeted, both the prisoners being monitored and the guards doing the watching. The panopticon is complete not when everyone is being watched, but when everyone wants to be watched, when surveillance becomes indistinguishable from social participation, and when the thought of privacy becomes as alien as the thought of returning to a pre-digital world.

We are living in Bentham's prison, but we have painted the bars bright colors, added comfortable furniture, and convinced ourselves that we are free. The door may not even be locked—but we no longer remember that doors exist, or what it might mean to walk through one.

Chapter 7: Digital Doublethink

The Cognitive Dissonance of Privacy Concerns vs. Convenience Addiction

In Orwell's "1984," doublethink represented the pinnacle of totalitarian psychological control—the ability to hold two contradictory beliefs simultaneously while accepting both as true. Winston Smith could genuinely believe that freedom is slavery while also understanding that slavery is the absence of freedom, holding these incompatible ideas without experiencing the cognitive stress that such contradictions should naturally produce. This psychological feat, presented as the ultimate triumph of authoritarian conditioning, has found its most perfect expression not in political oppression, but in our relationship with digital technology.

Modern digital users routinely demonstrate a form of doublethink that would have impressed Orwell's fictional Thought Police. They express genuine concern about privacy and surveillance while voluntarily providing intimate personal data to corporations. They worry about government overreach while carrying devices that track their every movement and conversation. They fear the loss of freedom while eagerly trading privacy for convenience, arguing simultaneously that surveillance is dangerous and that they have "nothing to hide." This is not mere hypocrisy or inconsistency—it represents a fundamental restructuring of human cognition that allows contradictory beliefs to coexist without producing the psychological discomfort that should logically result from such contradictions.

The digital age has created perfect conditions for doublethink by making surveillance invisible, beneficial, and addictive. Unlike Orwell's crude telescreens, modern surveillance technology provides genuine utility that makes the monitoring feel worthwhile rather than oppressive. Users can simultaneously fear surveillance and crave the personalized recommendations, efficient navigation, and social connectivity that surveillance enables. This creates a psychological split where abstract privacy concerns coexist with concrete convenience benefits, allowing users to maintain both beliefs without confronting their fundamental incompatibility.

The Architecture of Rationalization

Digital doublethink operates through sophisticated psychological defense mechanisms that allow users to maintain contradictory beliefs without experiencing cognitive distress. These rationalizations don't emerge randomly—they are systematically encouraged by tech companies' messaging, social proof from other users, and the addictive reward structures built into digital platforms. Users develop elaborate mental frameworks that justify their privacy-invasive behaviors while maintaining their self-image as privacy-conscious individuals.

The most common rationalization involves temporal displacement—users acknowledge that surveillance is problematic in the abstract while arguing that their immediate situation is exceptional or temporary. They tell themselves they will adjust their privacy settings "later," that they will find alternative services "when they have time," or that they will address privacy concerns "after this important project is finished." This temporal displacement allows users to maintain their identity as privacy-conscious while indefinitely deferring privacy-protective actions.

Another powerful rationalization involves the illusion of informed consent. Users convince themselves that they have made deliberate, rational decisions about privacy trade-offs by pointing to their awareness of privacy policies, their adjustment of some privacy settings, or their selective sharing of information. This selective awareness allows users to feel in control while actually surrendering comprehensive surveillance access. They focus on the privacy choices they do make while ignoring the much larger privacy surrenders they passively accept.

The Convenience Addiction Cycle

The relationship between privacy surrender and convenience benefits creates a powerful addiction cycle that makes rational evaluation of trade-offs increasingly difficult. Like substance addiction, convenience addiction produces tolerance effects where users require increasing levels of convenience to maintain satisfaction, while simultaneously creating withdrawal symptoms when convenient services are removed or restricted. This biological response pattern makes privacy-protective choices feel like genuine hardship rather than principled decisions.

Convenience addiction begins with what psychologists call "intermittent variable reward schedules"—the same mechanism that makes gambling addictive. Digital services provide unpredictable rewards (useful information, social validation, entertainment) that create powerful psychological dependencies. Users become conditioned to expect these rewards and experience genuine distress when they are absent. This conditioning makes privacy-protective alternatives feel inadequate even when they provide identical core functionality, because they lack the addictive reward patterns users have learned to expect.

The withdrawal symptoms associated with privacy-protective choices are real and significant. Users who attempt to reduce their digital surveillance exposure often experience social isolation, professional disadvantages, and genuine practical difficulties. These negative consequences reinforce the rationalization that privacy protection is impractical or unnecessary, creating a feedback loop where failed attempts at privacy protection actually strengthen users' commitment to surveillance-based services.

The Normalization Through Gradual Erosion

Digital doublethink has been enabled by the gradual erosion of privacy expectations through what researchers call "privacy creep"—the slow, incremental expansion of surveillance that occurs so gradually that users adapt to each change without recognizing the cumulative transformation. This process mirrors the "boiling frog" metaphor, where gradual changes that would be shocking if implemented suddenly become acceptable when introduced incrementally over time.

Privacy creep operates through several mechanisms. New surveillance capabilities are introduced as optional features that provide genuine benefits, allowing users to experience the advantages before the invasive aspects become apparent. Once users are dependent on these features, the privacy costs are gradually increased through policy changes, feature modifications, and expanded data sharing. By the time users recognize the full extent of surveillance, they are too dependent on the services to easily withdraw.

The most insidious aspect of privacy creep is how it reshapes users' baseline expectations. Features that initially shocked users with their invasiveness become normal, expected parts of digital life. Location tracking, contact list access, conversation monitoring, and behavioral analysis all followed this pattern—introduced as shocking innovations that gradually became unremarkable background features of digital services.

How We Rationalize Giving Up Freedoms for Digital Benefits

The rationalization of freedom surrender in the digital age represents one of the most sophisticated forms of doublethink ever observed in human societies. Unlike traditional authoritarian systems that required external coercion to secure compliance, digital systems have created voluntary surrender mechanisms that make freedom loss feel like empowerment. Users develop complex justification frameworks that allow them to simultaneously value freedom while actively trading it away for digital benefits.

These rationalizations are not simple self-deception—they represent genuine cognitive adaptations to environments where traditional concepts of freedom and privacy have become incompatible with full participation in modern society. Users who attempt to maintain traditional privacy expectations face real social, professional, and practical costs that make freedom-preserving choices genuinely difficult. The rationalizations that emerge serve as psychological protection against the cognitive dissonance that would otherwise result from forced choices between freedom and functionality.

The Security Theater of Choice

One of the most powerful rationalizations involves the illusion of choice that digital platforms carefully cultivate. Users convince themselves that they maintain meaningful autonomy because they can theoretically opt out of services, adjust privacy settings, or choose alternative platforms. This "security theater" of choice provides psychological comfort while actually offering little meaningful control over surveillance and data collection.

The illusion of choice operates through several mechanisms. Platforms provide extensive privacy settings menus that create the impression of granular control while actually offering limited protection against core surveillance activities. Users can disable location history while location tracking continues through other services. They can opt out of advertising cookies while device fingerprinting continues. They can choose not to share data with third parties while first-party data collection expands to cover the same information. These pseudo-choices allow users to feel empowered while having minimal actual impact on their surveillance exposure.

Perhaps most insidiously, the complexity of genuine privacy protection is used to justify privacy surrender. Users encounter privacy settings menus with dozens of options, conflicting information about data usage, and technical jargon that obscures the actual implications of different choices. This complexity creates what researchers call "privacy fatigue"—a state where users become overwhelmed by privacy decisions and simply accept default settings that maximize data collection. Users then rationalize this surrender by arguing that the complexity proves privacy protection is impractical for ordinary people.

The Reciprocity Rationalization

Many users justify privacy surrender through reciprocity frameworks that frame data sharing as fair exchange for valuable services. This rationalization transforms surveillance from an imposition into a voluntary transaction where users receive genuine value in return for personal information. The reciprocity framework allows users to maintain their self-image as rational decision-makers while accepting surveillance levels that would have been unthinkable in previous eras.

The reciprocity rationalization is particularly powerful because digital services do provide genuine value that improves users' lives in measurable ways. Navigation services save time and reduce stress. Social media platforms enable meaningful connections with friends and family. Search engines provide access to vast amounts of useful information. Entertainment platforms offer convenient access to media and cultural content. These benefits are real and immediate, making the privacy costs seem like reasonable trade-offs rather than fundamental rights surrenders.

However, the reciprocity framework obscures several important realities about digital surveillance. Users rarely understand the full extent of data collection, the sophisticated analysis applied to their information, or the long-term implications of comprehensive surveillance. They also lack meaningful ability to negotiate the terms of exchange—the "take it or leave it" nature of digital services means that users cannot actually bargain for better privacy protection in exchange for accepting reduced functionality. The apparent reciprocity masks what is actually a coercive relationship where users have little genuine choice about surveillance terms.

The Social Proof Defense

Social proof represents another powerful rationalization mechanism where users justify their privacy surrenders by pointing to similar behavior from peers, experts, or authority figures. When everyone else is using surveillance-based services, abstention feels antisocial, paranoid, or unnecessarily difficult. This social proof defense allows users to externalize responsibility for privacy decisions by arguing that widespread adoption proves the acceptability of surveillance.

The social proof defense is particularly effective because privacy protection requires swimming against powerful social currents. Users who attempt to maintain privacy often face social isolation, professional disadvantages, and practical difficulties that make privacy-protective choices genuinely costly. These costs create strong incentives to rationalize privacy surrender as normal and reasonable rather than acknowledging the social pressure that makes privacy protection difficult.

Social media platforms have particularly sophisticated social proof mechanisms that make privacy surrender feel like social participation rather than surveillance acceptance. Users who share personal information receive social validation through likes, comments, and engagement. Users who attempt to maintain privacy appear antisocial or suspicious. This transforms privacy protection from a personal choice into a social statement that requires justification and defense.

The Powerlessness Rationalization

Many users justify privacy surrender through powerlessness narratives that frame comprehensive surveillance as inevitable and resistance as futile. These narratives allow users to maintain their values while accepting behaviors that contradict those values, resolving cognitive dissonance by arguing that meaningful choice is impossible rather than acknowledging their active participation in surveillance systems.

The powerlessness rationalization has several components. Users argue that surveillance is inevitable because of technological development, government requirements, or corporate power that cannot be meaningfully opposed by individual action. They claim that privacy is already dead, making privacy-protective behavior pointless. They assert that powerful actors already have access to their information through data breaches, government programs, or other channels that make additional privacy surrender inconsequential.

While these arguments contain elements of truth—individuals do have limited power against sophisticated surveillance systems—they also serve as psychological defense mechanisms that allow users to avoid confronting their own agency in surveillance relationships. By framing themselves as powerless victims rather than active participants, users can maintain their self-image as privacy-conscious while continuing to use privacy-invasive services without experiencing cognitive dissonance.

The Nothing to Hide Fallacy

Perhaps the most widespread rationalization for privacy surrender involves the "nothing to hide" argument, where users claim that surveillance is acceptable because they are not engaged in illegal or embarrassing activities. This argument represents a fundamental misunderstanding of privacy's purpose and importance, but it provides powerful psychological comfort for users who want to justify their surveillance acceptance.

The nothing to hide fallacy operates through several cognitive errors. It assumes that privacy is only valuable for concealing wrongdoing, ignoring privacy's role in maintaining autonomy, intimacy, creativity, and human dignity. It assumes that current legal and social norms will remain stable indefinitely, ignoring the ways that comprehensive surveillance data could be weaponized under different political regimes or social conditions. It assumes that users can accurately predict what information might someday be considered problematic, ignoring the unpredictable ways that personal information can be analyzed, combined, and interpreted.

Most importantly, the nothing to hide fallacy reverses the burden of proof in privacy relationships. Instead of requiring surveillance advocates to justify monitoring, it requires privacy advocates to justify secrecy. This reversal fundamentally alters the default assumptions about human autonomy and dignity, making privacy appear suspicious rather than fundamental. Users who internalize this reversed burden of proof become complicit in their own surveillance by treating privacy protection as something that requires justification rather than something that deserves protection.

The Normalization of Surveillance Capitalism

The concept of surveillance capitalism—an economic system where personal data extraction and analysis serve as the primary source of revenue and market power—has become so deeply embedded in digital culture that most users can no longer imagine alternative economic models for digital services. This normalization represents perhaps the most successful example of digital doublethink, where users simultaneously understand that they are products being sold to advertisers while maintaining the fiction that they are customers receiving free services.

Surveillance capitalism has achieved normalization through what might be called "economic naturalization"—the process by which historically contingent economic arrangements come to seem like natural laws rather than policy choices. Users learn to think of comprehensive data collection as the inevitable price of digital services rather than recognizing it as one possible business model among many alternatives. This naturalization makes surveillance capitalism appear both inevitable and beneficial, resolving the cognitive dissonance that might otherwise result from participating in systems that commodify personal information.

The Free Service Illusion

The normalization of surveillance capitalism begins with the powerful illusion that digital services are "free," allowing users to ignore or minimize the privacy costs of their technology usage. This illusion is carefully cultivated by companies that describe their services as free while actually operating sophisticated data extraction and monetization systems that generate enormous revenues from user information. Users learn to think of themselves as beneficiaries of corporate generosity rather than recognizing their role as products being sold to third parties.

The free service illusion operates through several psychological mechanisms. The absence of direct monetary payment makes privacy costs feel abstract and difficult to quantify compared to the concrete benefits of service usage. Users experience immediate utility from digital services while the privacy costs remain largely invisible, creating temporal asymmetries that favor service adoption over privacy protection. The complexity of data monetization systems makes it difficult for users to understand how their information generates revenue, obscuring the economic relationship between data extraction and service provision.

Perhaps most importantly, the free service illusion creates false comparisons between surveillance-based services and genuinely free alternatives. Users compare the functionality of surveillance-based services to their absence rather than to privacy-respecting alternatives that might be available for direct payment. This comparison framework makes surveillance capitalism appear not just acceptable but generous, when in reality users are often paying higher effective costs through privacy surrender than they would pay through direct fees for equivalent privacy-respecting services.

The Personalization Justification

Surveillance capitalism has achieved acceptance partly through the genuine benefits of personalization that comprehensive data collection enables. Users receive customized recommendations, targeted advertising, and tailored user experiences that provide real value and convenience. These personalization benefits allow users to frame comprehensive surveillance as beneficial rather than exploitative, creating positive associations with data collection that make privacy protection feel like self-deprivation.

The personalization justification is particularly powerful because the benefits are immediate and concrete while the costs remain abstract and future-oriented. Users experience better search results, more relevant product recommendations, and more engaging content immediately after providing personal information. The negative consequences of comprehensive surveillance—manipulation, discrimination, and social control—may not become apparent until much later, if ever. This temporal asymmetry creates powerful incentives to accept surveillance in exchange for immediate personalization benefits.

However, the personalization justification obscures several important realities about surveillance-based services. The personalization algorithms are designed to maximize engagement and revenue rather than user benefit, often leading to filter bubbles, addiction patterns, and manipulation that serve corporate interests rather than user needs. The comprehensive data collection required for personalization goes far beyond what would be necessary to provide genuine user benefits, collecting vast amounts of information that serves corporate strategic purposes rather than personalization goals. Users rarely have meaningful control over personalization algorithms, making them passive recipients of algorithmic decisions rather than active participants in personalization processes.

The Innovation Narrative

Tech companies have successfully promoted narratives that frame surveillance capitalism as essential for technological innovation, allowing users to justify privacy surrender as contributions to human progress. These narratives suggest that comprehensive data collection enables breakthrough innovations in artificial intelligence, medical research, and social coordination that would be impossible without extensive surveillance. Users who accept these narratives can maintain their self-image as forward-thinking and socially responsible while participating in comprehensive surveillance systems.

The innovation narrative operates through several rhetorical strategies. Companies emphasize the most beneficial applications of data analysis while minimizing more problematic uses. They highlight breakthrough innovations that require large datasets while ignoring alternative research methodologies that might achieve similar results with better privacy protection. They frame privacy protection as backward-looking resistance to progress rather than legitimate concern about the social implications of comprehensive surveillance.

However, the innovation narrative obscures important questions about the relationship between surveillance and innovation. Many significant technological innovations have occurred without comprehensive surveillance, suggesting that privacy protection and innovation are not necessarily incompatible. The innovations enabled by surveillance capitalism often serve corporate strategic goals rather than genuine human needs, raising questions about whether surveillance-enabled innovation actually improves human welfare. The opportunity costs of surveillance capitalism—the innovations that might have occurred under alternative economic models—remain largely unexplored and unacknowledged.

The Competitive Necessity Argument

Perhaps the most sophisticated justification for surveillance capitalism involves arguments about competitive necessity—the claim that comprehensive data collection is essential for companies to compete effectively in global markets. Users who accept this argument can justify their participation in surveillance systems as patriotic contributions to national economic competitiveness rather than acknowledging their role in systems that compromise their own privacy and autonomy.

The competitive necessity argument operates through several mechanisms. It frames privacy protection as economic handicap that would disadvantage domestic companies against international competitors who operate under different privacy regimes. It suggests that comprehensive surveillance is essential for artificial intelligence development, which is presented as crucial for national security and economic prosperity. It argues that privacy regulations would stifle innovation and economic growth, making privacy protection seem economically irresponsible.

However, the competitive necessity argument ignores several important realities about surveillance capitalism and economic competition. Many successful technology companies operate with significantly better privacy protection than surveillance capitalism leaders, suggesting that comprehensive data collection is not actually essential for competitive success. The economic benefits of surveillance capitalism accrue primarily to platform owners rather than users or society generally, raising questions about whether competitive success in surveillance markets actually benefits national interests. Alternative economic models for digital services exist and often provide better user experiences than surveillance-based alternatives.

The Algorithmic Mystification

Surveillance capitalism has achieved normalization partly through the mystification of algorithmic processes that makes comprehensive data collection seem like natural technological development rather than deliberate economic strategy. Users learn to think of algorithmic recommendation systems, targeted advertising, and automated decision-making as inevitable features of digital technology rather than recognizing them as implementations of specific business models that prioritize data extraction and behavioral manipulation.

Algorithmic mystification operates through the technical complexity of machine learning systems that makes their operation opaque to most users. Companies describe their algorithms as artificial intelligence rather than behavioral manipulation systems, creating associations with scientific progress rather than commercial exploitation. The mathematical sophistication of algorithmic systems creates an impression of objectivity and neutrality that obscures their role in implementing surveillance capitalist business strategies.

This mystification allows users to experience algorithmic manipulation as helpful assistance rather than behavioral control. Users receive product recommendations, content suggestions, and service optimizations that feel like helpful guidance rather than recognizing them as implementations of systems designed to maximize data extraction and engagement. The sophistication of algorithmic manipulation makes it difficult for users to recognize when they are being influenced, creating an illusion of autonomous decision-making while actually operating within systems designed to shape and control their choices.

Generational Differences in Privacy Expectations

Perhaps nowhere is digital doublethink more evident than in the dramatic generational differences in privacy expectations that have emerged over the past two decades. These differences represent more than simple technological adaptation—they reflect fundamentally different conceptual frameworks for understanding privacy, autonomy, and the relationship between individual and collective identity. Older generations who developed privacy expectations before the digital age often experience genuine cognitive dissonance when using surveillance-based services, while younger generations who have never known privacy may experience doublethink when confronting abstract privacy arguments that contradict their lived experience.

These generational differences create complex dynamics where older users may maintain stronger theoretical commitments to privacy while actually having less sophisticated understanding of digital surveillance, while younger users may have more nuanced understanding of surveillance mechanisms while maintaining weaker commitments to privacy protection. The result is a form of generational doublethink where different age groups maintain contradictory beliefs about the same surveillance systems, each group rationalizing their perspective through different cognitive frameworks.

The Pre-Digital Privacy Baseline

Generations that developed their privacy expectations before widespread internet adoption maintain what might be called a "pre-digital privacy baseline" that assumes privacy is a default state that must be actively invaded rather than a privilege that must be actively protected. These users often experience genuine shock when they discover the extent of digital surveillance, but this shock coexists with their continued use of surveillance-based services, creating classic doublethink patterns.

Pre-digital privacy baselines assume that personal information sharing requires explicit consent, that surveillance requires probable cause or specific justification, and that privacy invasion should be limited in scope and duration. These assumptions worked reasonably well in analog environments where information sharing required deliberate action and surveillance required significant resources. However, they become problematic in digital environments where information sharing is automatic and surveillance is continuous.

Users with pre-digital privacy baselines often struggle to understand the comprehensive nature of digital surveillance, focusing on obvious privacy invasions while missing more subtle forms of data collection. They may be concerned about social media posts while ignoring location tracking, worried about email surveillance while accepting comprehensive web browsing analysis, or focused on government surveillance while participating voluntarily in corporate data collection systems that are far more comprehensive than anything government agencies typically conduct.

The Digital Native Paradox

Generations that have grown up with digital technology, often called "digital natives," demonstrate a fascinating paradox where they have sophisticated technical understanding of surveillance mechanisms while maintaining significantly lower privacy expectations than older users. This creates a form of informed consent doublethink where users understand what they are surrendering while simultaneously believing that such surrender is normal, necessary, or beneficial.

Digital natives often have intuitive understanding of how social media algorithms work, how location tracking operates, and how personal data is collected and analyzed. However, this technical literacy coexists with privacy expectations that would have been shocking to previous generations. Young users routinely share intimate personal information, accept comprehensive location tracking, and participate in surveillance systems while understanding their operation but not questioning their appropriateness.

The digital native paradox emerges partly from the social integration of surveillance systems. For users who have never experienced privacy, comprehensive surveillance feels like normal social participation rather than privacy invasion. Social media sharing, location tracking, and behavioral analysis are integrated into friendship formation, romantic relationships, family communication, and professional development. Privacy protection would require opting out of social participation itself, making privacy-protective choices feel antisocial rather than principled.

The Convenience Generation Gap

Generational differences in privacy expectations are closely related to different relationships with convenience and efficiency. Older users often remember when privacy protection was compatible with full social and economic participation, making privacy-protective choices feel like returning to a previous normal state rather than accepting significant sacrifice. Younger users have never experienced such compatibility, making privacy protection feel like unprecedented sacrifice for abstract philosophical benefits.

This convenience generation gap creates different cost-benefit analyses for privacy decisions. Older users may remember when privacy protection required minimal sacrifice and provided clear benefits, making current privacy-convenience trade-offs feel problematic. Younger users have always experienced privacy protection as costly and inconvenient, making surveillance acceptance seem practical rather than problematic.

The convenience generation gap is particularly evident in workplace and educational contexts where digital surveillance has become essential for participation. Older workers and students may remember when productivity monitoring and academic surveillance were limited and controversial, making current comprehensive monitoring feel invasive. Younger participants have grown up with such monitoring, making resistance feel counterproductive rather than principled.

The Social Capital Divide

Different generations have fundamentally different relationships with social media and online identity formation that affect their privacy calculations. For older users, social media represents an optional supplement to existing social relationships, making privacy-protective choices feel socially feasible. For younger users, social media represents essential infrastructure for social development, making privacy protection feel like social suicide.

This social capital divide means that privacy-protective choices have dramatically different social costs across generations. Older users can maintain full social and professional lives while using minimal social media and accepting limited surveillance. Younger users face genuine social isolation if they attempt similar privacy protection, as their peer relationships, romantic opportunities, and professional networks are largely mediated through surveillance-based platforms.

The social capital divide also affects how different generations understand the concept of privacy itself. Older users often conceptualize privacy as the right to be left alone, reflecting social environments where privacy was possible without social cost. Younger users often conceptualize privacy as the ability to control information sharing with specific audiences, reflecting social environments where some information sharing is mandatory but users want to maintain control over the scope and audience for such sharing.

The Institutional Trust Spectrum

Generational differences in privacy expectations reflect broader differences in institutional trust that affect how users evaluate surveillance systems. Older users often maintain higher trust in government institutions and lower trust in corporate surveillance, while younger users often demonstrate the opposite pattern. These trust differences create different frameworks for evaluating surveillance trade-offs and different strategies for privacy protection.

Older users who grew up during periods of government surveillance scandals often maintain deep suspicion of government data collection while being more trusting of corporate surveillance systems. They may accept comprehensive corporate data collection while opposing government surveillance programs, creating doublethink patterns where identical surveillance technologies are evaluated differently based on institutional context.

Younger users who have grown up with corporate surveillance as normal social infrastructure often demonstrate higher comfort with corporate data collection while maintaining greater suspicion of government surveillance. They may use surveillance-based services extensively while opposing government surveillance programs, creating different doublethink patterns based on different institutional trust frameworks.

The Educational Privacy Gap

Perhaps most concerning is the educational privacy gap where formal education systems have failed to help any generation develop sophisticated frameworks for evaluating digital surveillance trade-offs. Older users often lack technical understanding of surveillance systems, while younger users often lack historical context for privacy expectations. Neither generation receives systematic education about surveillance capitalism, privacy rights, or alternative economic models for digital services.

This educational gap creates doublethink conditions where users of all ages make privacy decisions without understanding their full implications or available alternatives. Users develop personal rationalization frameworks without exposure to broader policy debates, historical precedents, or comparative analysis of different surveillance regimes. The result is widespread doublethink where users maintain contradictory beliefs about surveillance because they lack the educational foundation necessary for coherent privacy reasoning.

The educational privacy gap is particularly problematic because it prevents the development of coherent social and political responses to surveillance capitalism. When users across all generations maintain contradictory beliefs about surveillance, developing democratic responses to comprehensive data collection becomes extremely difficult. Users cannot effectively advocate for privacy protection when they simultaneously accept comprehensive surveillance in their personal technology usage.

Conclusion: Living with Contradiction in the Digital Age

The phenomenon of digital doublethink represents more than individual psychological adaptation to technological change—it reflects a fundamental transformation in human consciousness that may be irreversible. We have created systems so complex, so integrated into essential life functions, and so psychologically rewarding that coherent resistance has become nearly impossible. The cognitive mechanisms that once protected human autonomy by creating psychological discomfort around contradictory beliefs have been overwhelmed by the sophisticated manipulation techniques embedded in digital surveillance systems.

What makes digital doublethink particularly troubling is its voluntary nature. Unlike Orwell's explicitly coercive system, digital doublethink emerges from choices that users make freely, defend vigorously, and experience as empowering rather than oppressive. This voluntary aspect makes digital doublethink more psychologically sustainable and politically resilient than traditional forms of ideological control. When people actively defend the systems that manipulate them, reform becomes extraordinarily difficult.

The generational dimensions of digital doublethink suggest that these psychological adaptations may be permanent features of human societies going forward. As digital natives age and assume positions of social and political leadership, their normalized expectations of comprehensive surveillance may become the foundation for social institutions that previous generations would have recognized as dystopian. The capacity for experiencing cognitive dissonance about surveillance may itself be disappearing as comprehensive monitoring becomes the assumed background condition of human life.

Perhaps most concerning is how digital doublethink has made coherent privacy advocacy nearly impossible. When privacy advocates themselves participate extensively in surveillance systems, when they rely on surveillance-based services for their advocacy work, when they experience genuine benefits from the systems they critique, their advocacy loses logical force and emotional resonance. The contradictions embedded in digital doublethink make it difficult to imagine, much less implement, alternative systems that might better balance privacy with genuine human needs for connection and coordination.

Yet understanding digital doublethink also points toward potential intervention strategies. Recognition of cognitive dissonance patterns could inform educational approaches that help users develop more coherent frameworks for evaluating surveillance trade-offs. Understanding the psychological mechanisms that enable doublethink could inform policy approaches that reduce the structural factors that make contradictory beliefs necessary for social participation. Analysis of generational differences could inform intergenerational dialogue that combines older generations' privacy expectations with younger generations' technical understanding.

The question is whether such interventions are possible within systems designed to produce and maintain doublethink, or whether meaningful change would require fundamental alterations to the technological and economic structures that create doublethink conditions in the first place. As we become increasingly dependent on systems that require doublethink for comfortable participation, the possibility of stepping outside these systems to evaluate them critically becomes increasingly remote.

We stand at a crucial moment in human development where our capacity for coherent thought about technology and privacy may be disappearing permanently. Each day that passes sees millions more users trained in doublethink patterns, developing psychological dependencies on surveillance systems, and learning to rationalize privacy surrender as empowerment. Each day makes alternatives to surveillance capitalism seem more impossible, more impractical, more unnecessary.

The ultimate irony of digital doublethink is that it has been achieved through technologies that promised to enhance human freedom, connection, and empowerment. We have created the most sophisticated surveillance systems in human history not through authoritarian decree, but through our collective pursuit of convenience, efficiency, and social connection. In doing so, we have demonstrated that Orwell's vision was, if anything, insufficiently ambitious. The most effective forms of ideological control are not imposed from outside, but emerge from within human psychology itself when that psychology encounters systems designed to exploit its deepest needs and desires.

Whether digital doublethink represents a temporary adaptation to new technologies or a permanent transformation in human consciousness remains to be seen. What is clear is that we have fundamentally altered the relationship between individual psychology and social power, creating conditions where the preservation of human autonomy and dignity requires forms of resistance that feel psychologically impossible and socially counterproductive. In learning to love our digital chains, we may have forged the most secure bonds ever created in human societies—bonds that feel like freedom while functioning as perfect constraint.

Chapter 8: The Thought Police Algorithm

AI moderation and the automation of censorship

The digital age has witnessed the emergence of algorithmic systems that would make Orwell's Thought Police seem primitive by comparison—automated censorship mechanisms that operate with a speed, scale, and sophistication that no human bureaucracy could match. These AI-powered moderation systems don't merely react to prohibited content; they anticipate it, identify it in embryonic forms, and eliminate it before it can fully manifest or reach its intended audience. The automation of censorship represents one of the most profound threats to free expression in human history, operating through mechanisms so subtle and technologically complex that even their victims often remain unaware of the systematic suppression of their thoughts and ideas.

Modern AI moderation systems process billions of pieces of content daily across social media platforms, search engines, video sharing sites, and other digital communication channels. These systems analyze text, images, audio, and video content in real-time, making instantaneous decisions about what information billions of people will be allowed to see, share, and discuss. The sheer volume of content processed by these systems means that the vast majority of censorship decisions are made without any human oversight or review, creating an automated apparatus of thought control that operates largely outside democratic accountability or public awareness.

The sophistication of these systems extends far beyond simple keyword filtering or explicit content detection. Natural language processing algorithms analyze context, sentiment, implied meanings, and cultural references to identify content that violates increasingly complex and subjective community guidelines. Computer vision systems examine images and videos for visual elements that might be deemed problematic, while audio analysis tools scan spoken content for prohibited ideas or expressions. The integration of these different analytical approaches creates comprehensive content surveillance systems that can identify and suppress ideas regardless of how they are expressed or encoded.

The training data used to develop these AI moderation systems inevitably reflects the biases, preferences, and worldviews of their creators, transforming subjective editorial judgments into seemingly objective algorithmic decisions. When engineers at major technology companies make decisions about what constitutes "hate speech," "misinformation," or "harmful content," they embed their own cultural, political, and ideological assumptions into systems that will influence billions of people worldwide. The result is the globalization of specific cultural and political perspectives under the guise of neutral content moderation.

The Escalation of Automated Suppression

The evolution of AI moderation has followed a predictable pattern of expansion and escalation, with content restrictions gradually expanding from obviously prohibited material like child exploitation to increasingly subjective categories like "misinformation," "hate speech," and "harmful content" that encompass vast ranges of legitimate political, scientific, and social discourse. This expansion operates through a ratchet mechanism where restrictions, once implemented, are never meaningfully reduced, while new categories of prohibited content are continuously added based on changing political priorities and social pressures.

The COVID-19 pandemic provided a perfect example of this expansion process, as platforms implemented unprecedented content restrictions justified by public health concerns. Information that contradicted official government positions on virus origins, treatment options, vaccine efficacy, or policy responses was systematically suppressed, regardless of the credentials or expertise of those presenting such information. Medical professionals, scientists, and researchers found their content removed or restricted for presenting data or analysis that conflicted with approved narratives, creating a chilling effect on scientific discourse and medical debate.

The techniques developed for pandemic-related censorship have been systematically expanded to other areas of public concern, including climate change, political elections, social justice issues, and international conflicts. Each new category of "sensitive" content provides justification for developing more sophisticated detection and suppression capabilities that can be applied to future topics deemed problematic by platform operators. The result is a continuous expansion of automated censorship capabilities that gradually encompasses larger portions of human discourse under the umbrella of content moderation.

Machine Learning Bias and Cultural Imperialism

The machine learning algorithms powering AI moderation systems are trained on datasets that inevitably reflect the cultural biases, linguistic patterns, and ideological preferences of their creators and training environments. These systems learn to identify "problematic" content based on examples provided by human moderators, embedding cultural and political judgments into algorithmic decision-making processes that appear neutral and objective. When these systems are deployed globally, they effectively impose the cultural values and political perspectives of Silicon Valley engineers on billions of users worldwide, creating a form of digital colonialism that suppresses local cultural expressions and alternative worldviews.

The language models used in these systems are predominantly trained on English-language content from Western sources, creating systematic biases against non-Western cultural expressions, religious practices, and political perspectives. Content moderation algorithms may flag traditional cultural practices as "violent" or "harmful," religious expressions as "extremist," or political perspectives common in non-Western societies as "misinformation" based on their divergence from Western liberal democratic norms embedded in the training data.

The global deployment of these culturally biased moderation systems creates homogenizing pressures that gradually erode cultural diversity and local autonomy in favor of standardized expressions deemed acceptable by algorithmic gatekeepers. Communities worldwide find their traditional forms of expression, political discourse, and cultural practices constrained by moderation systems designed according to the values and preferences of a small group of technology companies based in a specific geographic and cultural context.

The Industrialization of Thought Control

The scale and systematization of AI moderation represents the industrialization of thought control, transforming censorship from a labor-intensive activity requiring human judgment into an automated manufacturing process that can be scaled indefinitely without proportional increases in cost or human resources. This industrialization enables censorship at scales that would have been impossible for traditional authoritarian regimes, while maintaining the appearance of private corporate decision-making rather than government suppression of speech.

The economic incentives driving this industrialization favor systems that err on the side of over-censorship rather than under-censorship, as platforms face greater risks from allowing problematic content than from suppressing legitimate speech. Advertisers and payment processors exert pressure for "brand-safe" content environments that exclude controversial or challenging material, while government regulators threaten legal consequences for platforms that fail to adequately suppress "harmful" content. These economic and regulatory pressures create systematic biases toward censorship in the design and deployment of AI moderation systems.

The automation of censorship also enables more sophisticated forms of suppression that operate through adjustment of algorithmic visibility rather than outright removal of content. Systems can reduce the reach of certain types of content, limit their appearance in search results or recommendation algorithms, or restrict their ability to be shared or discovered by new audiences. This creates layers of suppression that can effectively silence voices while maintaining plausible deniability about censorship activities.

Shadow banning and invisible manipulation of reach

The most insidious evolution in digital censorship has been the development of "shadow banning" techniques that suppress content and limit user reach through invisible algorithmic manipulation rather than explicit content removal. This approach represents a quantum leap in censorship sophistication, allowing platforms to effectively silence users while maintaining plausible deniability about their suppression activities. Victims of shadow banning continue posting and sharing content under the illusion that they are participating in normal social discourse, while algorithms silently limit the visibility and reach of their contributions, creating a form of digital solitary confinement that isolates individuals from meaningful social interaction.

Shadow banning operates through subtle manipulations of recommendation algorithms, search rankings, and content distribution systems that are virtually impossible for ordinary users to detect or prove. A user's posts may receive dramatically reduced engagement compared to similar content from other users, their content may disappear from search results or trending topics, their followers may stop seeing their posts in their feeds, or their account may become difficult for new users to discover. These effects can be implemented gradually over time, making them appear as natural fluctuations in engagement rather than deliberate suppression.

The psychological impact of shadow banning can be more severe than outright censorship because victims experience social isolation and declining influence without understanding why. They may interpret reduced engagement as a reflection of declining content quality, personal unpopularity, or changing audience interests rather than algorithmic manipulation. This uncertainty creates self-doubt and anxiety that can lead to self-censorship as users attempt to modify their behavior to regain their previous levels of engagement and social connection.

The technical implementation of shadow banning involves complex algorithmic adjustments across multiple systems that determine content visibility and user interaction. Recommendation algorithms can be programmed to deprioritize content from specific users or containing certain keywords, topics, or perspectives. Search algorithms can exclude shadow-banned users from results or rank their content lower in search listings. Notification systems can be modified to reduce the frequency with which other users are alerted to shadow-banned users' activities, effectively severing social connections and reducing organic content discovery.

The Gradation of Digital Existence

Shadow banning represents the implementation of graduated levels of digital existence, where users exist on a spectrum of algorithmic visibility rather than simply being present or absent on platforms. This creates multiple tiers of digital citizenship, from highly promoted accounts whose content receives algorithmic amplification, to normal accounts that participate in standard algorithmic distribution, to shadow-banned accounts that experience various degrees of suppression, to completely suspended accounts that are excluded from the platform entirely.

The assignment of users to these different tiers of digital existence is typically based on algorithmic assessments of content quality, user behavior, and alignment with platform policies and values. However, these assessments are often opaque and subjective, reflecting the biases and preferences embedded in the algorithmic systems rather than objective measures of content value or policy compliance. Users may find themselves relegated to lower tiers of digital existence without understanding why or how to restore their previous status.

The fluidity of these digital existence tiers allows for dynamic adjustment of user visibility based on changing circumstances, platform priorities, or content topics. A user might experience normal reach for most content while having posts about specific topics shadow-banned, or they might have their overall account reach reduced during certain time periods when their preferred topics or perspectives fall out of favor with platform moderators. This creates a sophisticated system of behavioral conditioning where users learn to avoid certain topics or expressions to maintain their digital visibility.

Algorithmic Gaslighting and Reality Distortion

The invisible nature of shadow banning creates what can only be described as algorithmic gaslighting, where users experience systematic manipulation of their digital reality while being unable to prove or understand what is happening to them. They observe declining engagement, reduced visibility, and social isolation while platforms deny that any suppression is occurring, attributing changes to algorithm updates, user behavior modifications, or natural fluctuations in engagement patterns.

This gaslighting effect is amplified by the complexity and opacity of modern algorithmic systems, which make it virtually impossible for ordinary users to distinguish between legitimate algorithm changes and targeted suppression. When platforms make frequent updates to their recommendation and distribution systems, any changes in user experience can be attributed to these updates rather than deliberate censorship activities. The technical sophistication required to understand and analyze these systems puts meaningful investigation beyond the reach of most users.

The psychological impact of this uncertainty extends beyond individual users to broader communities and social movements that rely on digital platforms for organization and communication. When activists, political dissidents, or social critics experience declining reach and engagement, they may interpret this as declining public interest in their causes rather than algorithmic suppression. This can lead to demoralization, reduced activism, and the fragmentation of social movements that depend on digital platforms for coordination and outreach.

Network Effects and Social Isolation

Shadow banning operates not just through direct suppression of individual accounts, but through the manipulation of network effects and social connections that determine how information and influence spread through digital communities. By limiting the visibility of certain users to their followers and connections, shadow banning can effectively isolate individuals from their social networks and reduce their ability to participate in community discussions or influence broader conversations.

The algorithmic manipulation of social networks creates artificial barriers to communication and community formation that can be more effective than outright censorship at preventing the spread of ideas and the organization of social movements. When key influencers, thought leaders, or community organizers experience shadow banning, their reduced visibility can fragment communities and limit the coordination necessary for effective collective action.

The network effects of shadow banning also create indirect censorship pressures on users who are not directly targeted but who depend on interaction with shadow-banned users for their own content creation and community participation. When influential members of a community are shadow-banned, the entire community experiences reduced engagement and visibility, creating incentives for remaining members to distance themselves from suppressed users or topics to maintain their own algorithmic standing.

The Weaponization of Engagement Metrics

The use of engagement metrics as proxies for content quality and user value creates opportunities for manipulating these metrics to justify shadow banning and content suppression. Platforms can implement subtle changes to how engagement is calculated, what types of interactions are counted as valuable, or how quickly engagement must occur to be considered meaningful, allowing them to systematically disadvantage certain types of content or users while maintaining the appearance of neutral algorithmic assessment.

The complexity of modern engagement algorithms makes it difficult for users to understand how their content is being evaluated or why their engagement might be declining. Factors such as the timing of posts, the demographics of engaging users, the types of interactions received, the topics discussed, and the external links shared all contribute to algorithmic assessments of content value in ways that can be manipulated to achieve censorship objectives while maintaining plausible deniability.

The weaponization of engagement metrics also creates opportunities for coordinated manipulation campaigns where opposing groups can use fake accounts, coordinated reporting, or engagement manipulation to trigger algorithmic penalties against their targets. These campaigns can be designed to appear as organic user behavior while systematically undermining the reach and influence of specific users or communities through exploitation of automated moderation and shadow banning systems.

Predictive policing and pre-emptive punishment

The evolution of algorithmic enforcement has transcended reactive responses to policy violations, developing into sophisticated predictive systems that identify and punish users for crimes they haven't yet committed.

These predictive policing algorithms analyze user behavior patterns, content themes, social connections, and engagement metrics to identify individuals who exhibit characteristics associated with future policy violations or problematic behavior. The result is a system of pre-emptive punishment that implements restrictions and penalties based on algorithmic predictions rather than actual misconduct, representing a digital implementation of the thought-crime concepts that Orwell imagined but could never have envisioned at such scale and sophistication.

Modern predictive enforcement systems leverage machine learning algorithms trained on vast datasets of user behavior to identify subtle patterns that correlate with future policy violations. These systems analyze not just what users post, but how they post it, when they post it, whom they interact with, what content they consume, and how others respond to their contributions. The algorithms identify combinations of behavioral indicators that have historically preceded policy violations, flagging users who exhibit these patterns for increased scrutiny, reduced reach, or preemptive restrictions even before they violate any explicit platform rules.

The sophistication of these predictive systems extends beyond simple behavioral pattern matching to include analysis of linguistic patterns, emotional states, social dynamics, and contextual factors that might indicate future problematic behavior. Natural language processing algorithms analyze writing style, vocabulary choices, sentiment progression, and communication patterns to identify users who might be becoming radicalized, planning harmful activities, or developing attitudes that could lead to policy violations. These linguistic analysis techniques can identify potential problems based on subtle changes in communication style that might be invisible to human moderators.

The temporal dimension of predictive enforcement creates particular concerns about fairness and accuracy, as these systems essentially punish users for futures that may never materialize. Algorithmic predictions about human behavior, even when based on sophisticated machine learning models, involve inherent uncertainty and error rates that become ethically problematic when used to justify punitive actions. Users may find themselves penalized for algorithmic assessments of their future behavior that are based on correlations rather than causal relationships and that may reflect biases in training data rather than accurate predictions about individual users.

The Psychology of Behavioral Prediction

The development of predictive enforcement systems relies heavily on psychological profiling techniques that attempt to identify mental states, personality traits, and behavioral tendencies associated with policy violations or problematic behavior. These systems analyze digital footprints to create comprehensive psychological assessments that include estimates of aggression levels, emotional stability, susceptibility to radicalization, propensity for violence, and likelihood of engaging in harassment or other prohibited behaviors.

The psychological profiling capabilities of modern AI systems extend beyond simple sentiment analysis to include sophisticated assessments of cognitive patterns, emotional regulation, social dynamics, and behavioral trajectories that unfold over extended periods. Machine learning algorithms can identify subtle changes in communication patterns that might indicate increasing frustration, radicalization, or planning for harmful activities, creating profiles that predict not just what users might do, but when they might do it and under what circumstances.

The accuracy of these psychological assessments remains questionable, particularly when applied to individuals rather than population-level predictions. While machine learning systems may be effective at identifying general patterns associated with problematic behavior across large populations, their ability to make accurate predictions about specific individuals involves significant uncertainty that becomes ethically problematic when used to justify punitive actions. The complexity of human psychology and the multitude of factors that influence individual behavior make reliable prediction extremely difficult, even with sophisticated AI systems.

Risk Assessment and Actuarial Justice

The implementation of predictive enforcement systems transforms platform governance from rule-based systems focused on specific violations to actuarial systems focused on risk assessment and statistical predictions about user behavior. This shift represents a fundamental change in the concept of justice from punishment after wrongdoing to prevention based on probability assessments, creating digital implementations of "actuarial justice" that prioritize risk management over individual rights and due process.

Actuarial justice systems evaluate users based on their statistical likelihood of engaging in problematic behavior rather than their actual conduct, creating situations where individuals are penalized based on their membership in algorithmic categories associated with higher risk rather than their personal actions or choices. Users who exhibit demographic, behavioral, or social characteristics associated with policy violations may find themselves subject to increased restrictions or reduced platform privileges regardless of their actual behavior or intent.

The opacity of actuarial justice systems makes it difficult for users to understand why they are being penalized or how to modify their behavior to avoid future restrictions. When penalties are based on complex algorithmic assessments rather than specific rule violations, users cannot identify the particular actions that triggered enforcement responses or develop clear strategies for compliance. This uncertainty creates anxiety and self-censorship as users attempt to avoid algorithmic penalties without understanding the criteria being used to assess their risk levels.

The Normalization of Guilt by Association

Predictive enforcement systems frequently incorporate social network analysis that evaluates users based on their connections, interactions, and associations rather than solely on their individual behavior. These systems implement digital versions of guilt by association, where users may be penalized for their connections to other users who have violated policies, their participation in communities that contain problematic content, or their interaction with content that has been deemed problematic by algorithmic assessments.

The social network analysis capabilities of modern AI systems can identify complex patterns of association and influence that extend far beyond direct connections to include indirect relationships, shared interests, similar behavioral patterns, and participation in overlapping communities. Users may find themselves flagged by predictive systems based on multi-degree connections to problematic users or content, creating situations where individuals are held responsible for the behavior of people they may not even know directly.

The implementation of guilt by association through algorithmic assessment creates powerful incentives for social conformity and community policing, as users learn that their associations and interactions can affect their own algorithmic standing. This can lead to the fragmentation of communities and the isolation of individuals who express unpopular opinions or engage with controversial topics, as other users seek to protect their own algorithmic status by avoiding potentially problematic associations.

Feedback Loops and Self-Fulfilling Prophecies

The implementation of predictive enforcement systems creates complex feedback loops that can transform algorithmic predictions into self-fulfilling prophecies. When users are subjected to increased restrictions or reduced platform privileges based on predictive assessments, these limitations can create frustration and resentment that actually increase the likelihood of the problematic behavior the system was designed to prevent. Users who feel unfairly treated by algorithmic systems may become more likely to violate policies or engage in the types of behavior that triggered the initial predictions.

The psychological impact of being labeled as high-risk by algorithmic systems can also influence user behavior in ways that confirm the initial predictions. Users who become aware that they are being treated differently by platform algorithms may develop antagonistic attitudes toward the platform and its policies, increasing the likelihood that they will eventually engage in behavior that violates community guidelines. This creates situations where predictive systems may actually cause the problems they claim to prevent.

The opacity of predictive systems makes it difficult for users to understand or contest algorithmic assessments of their risk levels, creating additional frustration and resentment that can contribute to the behavioral problems these systems are designed to address. When users cannot understand why they are being treated as higher risk or how to improve their algorithmic standing, they may abandon attempts at compliance and engage in more explicitly problematic behavior.

The black box problem: when machines make moral judgments

The deployment of AI systems for content moderation and behavior enforcement has created what researchers call the "black box problem"—algorithmic decision-making systems that operate through processes so complex and opaque that even their creators cannot fully understand or explain how they arrive at their conclusions. When these black box systems are tasked with making moral judgments about human behavior, determining what speech is acceptable, or deciding what ideas deserve amplification, they essentially delegate fundamental questions about human values and social norms to mathematical processes that resist human comprehension or democratic oversight.

Modern machine learning systems, particularly deep learning neural networks, operate through millions or billions of parameters that are adjusted during training processes to optimize performance on specific tasks. The resulting systems can achieve remarkable accuracy in pattern recognition and prediction tasks, but the internal logic they develop to achieve this performance remains largely opaque to human analysis. When these systems are applied to content moderation tasks, they make decisions about human expression based on learned patterns that may not correspond to any coherent moral principles or consistent application of stated policies.

The opacity of these systems becomes particularly problematic when they are used to make consequential decisions about human communication and social interaction. Users who have their content removed, their accounts restricted, or their reach limited by AI moderation systems cannot understand why these decisions were made or how to avoid similar problems in the future. The systems themselves cannot provide meaningful explanations for their decisions beyond pointing to statistical correlations identified during the training process that may not reflect any coherent reasoning about the content in question.

The scale at which these black box systems operate makes human oversight practically impossible, as billions of pieces of content are processed and millions of enforcement decisions are made daily without any human review or intervention. Even when human appeals processes exist, the volume of decisions made by AI systems far exceeds the capacity of human moderators to meaningfully review disputed cases. The result is the delegation of fundamental moral and social judgments to algorithmic systems that operate outside human understanding or democratic accountability.

The Impossibility of Algorithmic Neutrality

One of the most persistent myths surrounding AI moderation systems is that they represent neutral, objective approaches to content governance that avoid the biases and inconsistencies of human decision-making. However, the reality is that these systems embed countless value judgments and cultural assumptions made during their development, training, and deployment processes. The selection of training data, the definition of optimization objectives, the choice of architectural approaches, and the interpretation of results all involve human judgments that shape how these systems understand and evaluate human behavior.

The training data used to develop AI moderation systems inevitably reflects the biases, perspectives, and cultural assumptions of the humans who create and curate these datasets. When human moderators label content as acceptable or problematic for training purposes, they embed their own cultural values, political perspectives, and moral judgments into the algorithmic systems that learn from these examples. The result is the automation and scaling of specific human biases rather than the creation of truly neutral decision-making systems.

The optimization objectives used to train these systems also embed value judgments about what outcomes are desirable and how different types of errors should be weighted. A system optimized to minimize false negatives (allowing problematic content) will behave differently from one optimized to minimize false positives (removing acceptable content), and both approaches embed different assumptions about the relative costs of over-censorship versus under-censorship. These technical decisions about system design inevitably reflect moral and political judgments about the proper balance between free expression and content control.

The Democratization of Tyranny

The black box nature of AI moderation systems enables what could be called the "democratization of tyranny"—the implementation of authoritarian control mechanisms without the need for explicit authoritarian institutions or leaders. These systems can suppress dissent, enforce conformity, and punish non-compliant behavior without any individual or institution taking responsibility for these outcomes. The complexity and opacity of algorithmic systems allows their operators to claim that suppressive outcomes emerge naturally from neutral technical processes rather than deliberate policy choices.

This democratization of tyranny operates through the diffusion of responsibility across complex socio-technical systems where no individual actor appears to be making authoritarian decisions. Engineers claim they are simply optimizing algorithms for user engagement or advertiser satisfaction. Product managers claim they are responding to user feedback and community preferences. Corporate executives claim they are following legal requirements and industry best practices. The result is systematic suppression of expression and thought that emerges from the interaction of multiple actors and systems without any individual taking responsibility for the authoritarian outcomes.

The global deployment of these systems means that the cultural values and political perspectives embedded in AI moderation algorithms developed by a small number of technology companies effectively become global governance systems that influence discourse and behavior worldwide. Local communities, cultural groups, and national populations find their communication and expression subject to rules and standards determined by algorithmic systems developed according to the values and priorities of distant technology companies operating in different cultural and political contexts.

Moral Philosophy by Algorithm

The deployment of AI systems for content moderation effectively delegates fundamental questions of moral philosophy to mathematical optimization processes that have no understanding of ethics, human values, or the philosophical traditions that inform moral reasoning. These systems make countless decisions daily about what speech is harmful, what ideas deserve amplification, what behaviors should be encouraged or discouraged, and what forms of human expression are acceptable in digital public spaces. However, they make these decisions based on statistical patterns rather than coherent moral principles or philosophical reasoning.

The moral judgments embedded in AI moderation systems often reflect utilitarian approaches that prioritize outcomes like user engagement, advertiser satisfaction, or regulatory compliance over deontological concerns about rights, dignity, or justice. These systems are typically optimized to maximize metrics like user retention, content consumption, or revenue generation rather than to uphold principles like free expression, human dignity, or democratic discourse. The result is the implementation of moral frameworks that prioritize corporate objectives over human values.

The absence of explainability in these systems means that the moral logic underlying their decisions cannot be examined, debated, or refined through democratic processes or philosophical reflection. When AI systems make decisions about human expression based on opaque algorithmic processes, there is no opportunity for moral reasoning, ethical debate, or principled discussion about the values being implemented. Society effectively outsources fundamental moral questions to mathematical processes that cannot engage in the kind of reasoning that moral philosophy requires.

The Erosion of Human Moral Agency

The widespread deployment of AI systems for moral judgment and behavioral guidance creates risks for human moral development and agency that extend far beyond the immediate impacts on content moderation and platform governance. When individuals become accustomed to having their moral decisions guided or constrained by algorithmic systems, they may lose the capacity for independent moral reasoning and ethical reflection that are essential for human flourishing and democratic participation.

The gamification elements built into many digital platforms create incentive structures that train users to optimize their behavior for algorithmic approval rather than developing their own moral judgment or ethical reasoning capabilities. Users learn to avoid content or behaviors that might trigger algorithmic penalties rather than developing principled positions about right and wrong based on their own reflection and moral reasoning. This can lead to the atrophy of moral reasoning capabilities and increased dependence on external systems for ethical guidance.

The opacity of algorithmic moral judgment systems means that users cannot understand the ethical reasoning behind platform decisions, making it impossible for them to learn from these decisions or develop their own moral understanding through reflection on algorithmic judgments. When moral decisions are made by black box systems that cannot explain their reasoning, there is no opportunity for moral education or ethical development through engagement with these decisions.

The Need for Algorithmic Transparency and Democratic Accountability

The black box problem in AI moderation systems represents a fundamental challenge to democratic governance and human autonomy that requires new approaches to algorithmic transparency and accountability. Traditional approaches to corporate regulation and democratic oversight are inadequate for addressing the complex socio-technical systems that now govern human communication and social interaction at global scale. New institutional arrangements may be necessary to ensure that the values embedded in these systems reflect democratic deliberation rather than corporate priorities or algorithmic optimization.

The development of explainable AI techniques offers some hope for making algorithmic decision-making more transparent and accountable, but current approaches to algorithmic explainability remain limited in their ability to provide meaningful insight into the moral reasoning underlying AI decisions. Even when AI systems can provide statistical explanations for their decisions, these explanations may not correspond to the kind of moral reasoning that humans can understand or evaluate. The challenge is not just making algorithmic decisions transparent, but ensuring that the moral logic underlying these decisions can be subjected to democratic deliberation and ethical reflection.

The global nature of digital platforms creates additional challenges for democratic accountability, as the algorithmic systems that govern human communication operate across national boundaries and may be subject to different regulatory frameworks in different jurisdictions. The development of international governance mechanisms for algorithmic systems may be necessary to ensure that the moral judgments embedded in these systems reflect global democratic values rather than the preferences of specific corporations or national governments.

Conclusion

The emergence of algorithmic systems as the primary arbiters of human expression and social interaction represents one of the most profound challenges to human freedom and democratic governance in our time. The automation of censorship through AI moderation systems has created enforcement mechanisms that operate with a speed, scale, and sophistication that would make traditional authoritarian regimes seem primitive by comparison, yet these systems operate largely outside democratic accountability or public understanding. The transformation of content moderation from human judgment to algorithmic automation represents more than a change in enforcement technique—it represents the delegation of fundamental moral and social judgments to mathematical processes that resist human comprehension or democratic oversight.

The development of shadow banning and invisible manipulation techniques has created new forms of digital authoritarianism that suppress dissent and enforce conformity through subtle manipulation rather than explicit censorship. These techniques operate through the gradual erosion of social connection and influence rather than dramatic censorship events, making them more difficult to detect and resist while potentially more psychologically damaging to their victims. The invisibility of these suppression techniques enables platforms to deny censorship activities while systematically isolating and marginalizing users who express unpopular ideas or challenge approved narratives.

The evolution of predictive enforcement systems that punish users for crimes they haven't yet committed represents a digital implementation of thought-crime concepts that exceeds anything Orwell imagined in scope and sophistication. These systems transform platform governance from rule-based approaches focused on actual behavior to actuarial approaches focused on risk assessment and statistical predictions about future behavior. The result is the systematic penalization of individuals based on algorithmic assessments of their likelihood to engage in problematic behavior rather than their actual conduct or choices.

The black box nature of modern AI systems creates fundamental challenges for democratic governance and human autonomy when these systems are deployed for moral judgment and social control. The opacity of algorithmic decision-making processes means that the values and biases embedded in these systems cannot be examined, debated, or modified through democratic processes, effectively outsourcing fundamental questions of human values and social organization to mathematical optimization processes that operate outside human understanding or control.

The scale and sophistication of these algorithmic enforcement systems have created a new form of social control that combines the efficiency of automated processing with the authority of moral judgment, creating enforcement mechanisms that can suppress dissent and enforce conformity more effectively than traditional authoritarian institutions. The global deployment of these systems means that the cultural values and political perspectives embedded in algorithms developed by a small number of technology companies effectively become global governance systems that influence discourse and behavior worldwide.

The psychological impacts of living under comprehensive algorithmic surveillance and control extend beyond immediate censorship effects to include the gradual erosion of human moral agency and the capacity for independent thought and authentic expression. When individuals learn to optimize their behavior for algorithmic approval rather than developing their own moral judgment, the foundations of human autonomy and democratic participation begin to erode. The result is the systematic conditioning of populations to accept external algorithmic guidance for fundamental questions of thought, expression, and social interaction.

The resistance to these systems requires not just policy reforms or technological solutions, but a fundamental recommitment to human agency and democratic governance in the face of technological systems that operate through complexity and opacity rather than transparency and accountability. The challenge lies in developing new institutional arrangements that can ensure democratic oversight of algorithmic systems while preserving the benefits of technological innovation and global communication platforms.

The stakes extend beyond immediate concerns about censorship and free expression to fundamental questions about the future of human consciousness and social organization. If algorithmic systems become the primary arbiters of acceptable thought and expression, future generations may lose not just the freedom to express dissenting ideas, but the cognitive and moral capabilities necessary for independent thought and democratic participation. The automation of moral judgment represents more than a threat to free speech—it represents a fundamental challenge to the human capacity for ethical reasoning and autonomous moral development.

The window of opportunity for democratic resistance to these systems may be closing as the infrastructure of algorithmic control becomes embedded in the essential communication and social interaction systems that modern society depends upon. The complexity and global scale of these systems make them increasingly difficult to understand, regulate, or reform through traditional democratic processes, while their economic and technological advantages make them difficult to replace or circumvent. The development of alternative approaches to digital communication and social organization may be necessary to preserve spaces for authentic human expression and democratic discourse in an age of algorithmic control.

The ultimate question raised by the emergence of algorithmic thought police is whether human societies can develop institutional arrangements that harness the benefits of artificial intelligence and automated systems while preserving the conditions necessary for human flourishing, democratic governance, and authentic moral development. This may require accepting less efficiency and convenience in digital systems in exchange for preserving transparency, accountability, and human agency in the systems that increasingly govern human thought and social interaction. The alternative is a future where human consciousness itself becomes subject to algorithmic optimization according to values and objectives determined by mathematical processes rather than human deliberation and democratic choice.

PART III: RESISTANCE AND REVELATION

Chapter 9: Digital Dissidents and Modern Winston Smiths

In the depths of *1984*, Winston Smith's rebellion began with a simple act: writing in a diary the forbidden words "DOWN WITH BIG BROTHER." Today's digital dissidents face a far more complex landscape of resistance, where the very technologies that enable surveillance also provide the tools for circumventing it. Unlike Winston's analog world, where thoughtcrime could be hidden in secret corners and handwritten journals, our digital age offers both unprecedented opportunities for resistance and unimaginable consequences for those who dare to challenge the surveillance state. The modern Winston Smiths are not literary characters but real people—Edward Snowden, Julian Assange, Chelsea Manning, and countless others whose names we may never know—who have risked everything to reveal the true scope of digital authoritarianism and preserve the possibility of human freedom in an age of algorithmic control.

These digital dissidents operate in a paradoxical environment where the same technologies that enable mass surveillance also provide the most sophisticated tools for evading it. Cryptography that can protect communications from government interception is developed by the same computational systems that power dragnet surveillance programs. Blockchain networks that promise decentralized freedom rely on the same internet infrastructure controlled by the corporations and governments they seek to circumvent. Anonymous networks that shield dissidents from detection run on servers that may themselves be monitored or compromised. This technological paradox creates a cat-and-mouse game between surveillance and resistance that plays out in the invisible realm of code, algorithms, and digital protocols—a battle for the future of human freedom that most people don't even realize is being fought.

PRIVACY ADVOCATES, WHISTLEBLOWERS, AND DIGITAL RESISTANCE MOVEMENTS

The Evolution of Digital Resistance

The tradition of resistance to authoritarian surveillance has evolved dramatically from the analog world that Orwell imagined to the digital battlefields of the 21st century. Where once dissidents relied on secret meetings, coded messages, and underground printing presses, today's resistance movements operate through encrypted channels, anonymous networks, and decentralized technologies that can coordinate global action while protecting individual participants from identification and retaliation. This evolution represents both an escalation in the sophistication of resistance techniques and a corresponding escalation in the surveillance capabilities they must evade.

Modern digital resistance movements have learned to harness the same network effects that give surveillance capitalism its power, using viral distribution, crowd-sourced investigation, and distributed coordination to challenge centralized authority. Movements like Anonymous, WikiLeaks, and various privacy advocacy organizations demonstrate how small groups of technically sophisticated individuals can have global impact by leveraging digital technologies to expose corruption, coordinate protest, and protect vulnerable populations from surveillance and persecution.

The transformation of resistance from local to global, from physical to digital, has created new possibilities for solidarity and coordination that transcend national boundaries and traditional political categories. Digital dissidents in authoritarian regimes can receive support and protection from advocates in democratic countries, while surveillance techniques developed by democratic governments can be exposed and challenged by international networks of privacy advocates and civil liberties organizations.

The Psychology of Digital Dissidence

The decision to become a digital dissident requires a psychological profile that differs significantly from traditional forms of political resistance. While physical resistance movements require courage in the face of immediate danger, digital resistance requires the ability to comprehend abstract, technical systems and imagine long-term consequences that may not manifest for years or decades. Digital dissidents must possess both technical sophistication and moral clarity, understanding complex surveillance systems while maintaining commitment to principles that may seem abstract or irrelevant to most people.

The isolation inherent in digital resistance creates unique psychological challenges for those who choose to challenge surveillance systems. Unlike traditional resistance movements that provide community and mutual support, digital dissidents often work alone, communicating through encrypted channels with people they may never meet in person, pursuing goals that may never be achieved in their lifetime. This isolation can lead to paranoia, depression, and the kind of psychological breakdown that Orwell depicted in Winston Smith's ultimate defeat.

The psychological cost of digital dissidence is compounded by the comprehensive nature of modern surveillance systems, which make it impossible for dissidents to fully escape monitoring and retaliation. Unlike political dissidents in previous eras who could flee to other countries or disappear into underground networks, digital dissidents leave permanent traces in surveillance databases, making them vulnerable to identification and persecution years or even decades after their initial acts of resistance.

The Technical Elite and Democratic Responsibility

The concentration of technical expertise required for effective digital resistance in a small population of highly educated specialists creates a form of "technical aristocracy" where the defense of democratic values depends on individuals whose expertise and social position often isolate them from the populations they seek to protect. This creates a paradox where democratic resistance becomes dependent on undemocratic concentrations of technical knowledge and capability.

The responsibility placed on technical elites to defend privacy and freedom creates enormous personal costs for individuals who never sought political leadership but find themselves in positions where their specialized knowledge makes them uniquely capable of challenging surveillance systems. Many privacy advocates and digital rights activists describe feeling burdened by their awareness of surveillance capabilities that remain invisible to most people, creating a sense of responsibility that can be psychologically overwhelming.

The gap between technical elite awareness and popular understanding of surveillance issues creates challenges for democratic resistance movements that depend on broad public support to be effective. When the most serious threats to freedom require specialized technical knowledge to understand, building the popular movements necessary for meaningful political change becomes extremely difficult, leaving technical elites isolated and vulnerable while the broader population remains unaware of the dangers they face.

Grassroots Privacy Movements and Digital Literacy

Beyond the high-profile whistleblowers and technical experts, a growing grassroots movement of privacy advocates works to educate ordinary citizens about digital surveillance and provide tools for protecting personal privacy and freedom. Organizations like the Electronic Frontier Foundation, Privacy International, and Access Now combine legal advocacy, technical education, and grassroots organizing to build broader resistance to surveillance capitalism and digital authoritarianism.

These grassroots movements face the enormous challenge of translating complex technical and legal concepts into terms that ordinary citizens can understand and act upon. The abstraction of digital surveillance—the fact that it operates invisibly through algorithms and data collection rather than obvious physical monitoring—makes it difficult for people to understand the scope of the threat or take meaningful action to protect themselves.

The success of grassroots privacy movements depends on their ability to connect abstract technical issues to concrete personal consequences that people can understand and relate to their own lives. This requires developing new forms of digital literacy that go beyond basic computer skills to include understanding of surveillance systems, privacy rights, and resistance techniques that can be used by people without specialized technical training.

The Role of Legal and Constitutional Advocacy

Digital resistance operates not only through technical means but also through legal and constitutional challenges to surveillance systems and privacy violations. Organizations like the American Civil Liberties Union, the Center for Democracy & Technology, and various international human rights organizations work through courts and legislative bodies to establish legal protections for digital privacy and limit government surveillance powers.

The legal dimension of digital resistance faces unique challenges in addressing surveillance technologies that often outpace legal frameworks and operate in regulatory gray areas where existing privacy laws provide limited protection. Courts and legislatures struggle to understand technical surveillance capabilities and their implications for constitutional rights, creating opportunities for surveillance systems to operate without meaningful legal oversight.

The international nature of digital surveillance creates particular challenges for legal resistance, as surveillance capabilities often cross national boundaries and operate through international agreements and treaties that may not be subject to domestic constitutional protections. This creates a need for international coordination among legal advocates and human rights organizations to challenge surveillance systems that operate on a global scale.

THE RISE OF ENCRYPTED COMMUNICATION AND DECENTRALIZED NETWORKS

Cryptography as Digital Resistance

The development and deployment of strong cryptographic systems represents one of the most significant forms of digital resistance to surveillance capitalism and authoritarian monitoring. Unlike traditional forms of resistance that require physical courage and political organization, cryptographic resistance can be deployed by individuals using freely available software tools that make their communications and data effectively invisible to even the most sophisticated surveillance systems.

The power of cryptography as a resistance tool lies in its mathematical foundation, which provides security guarantees that don't depend on political goodwill, corporate responsibility, or government restraint. When properly implemented, cryptographic systems can provide protection against surveillance that is limited only by the laws of physics and mathematics rather than the intentions of those in power. This creates a form of resistance that is both technically sophisticated and democratically accessible to anyone with basic digital literacy.

The widespread deployment of encryption technologies has created what cryptographers call "the golden age of surveillance" and "the golden age of privacy" simultaneously—surveillance systems have unprecedented capabilities to monitor unencrypted communications, while encryption systems provide unprecedented capabilities to render communications invisible to surveillance. This paradox creates a technological arms race between surveillance and privacy that shapes the digital landscape and determines the future of human freedom.

The Encryption Wars and Government Response

The recognition of encryption's power as a resistance tool has led to sustained government efforts to weaken, backdoor, or ban cryptographic systems under the pretext of national security and law enforcement needs. These "encryption wars" represent a fundamental conflict between individual privacy rights and state surveillance capabilities, with both democratic and authoritarian governments seeking to maintain their ability to monitor citizen communications.

Government arguments against strong encryption typically focus on the need to prevent terrorism, child exploitation, and other serious crimes that may be planned or coordinated through encrypted communications. However, technical experts consistently point out that weakening encryption for law enforcement purposes necessarily weakens it against all adversaries, including criminal organizations, foreign intelligence services, and malicious hackers who threaten national security and individual safety.

The global nature of encryption technology creates particular challenges for government attempts to control or weaken cryptographic systems. Even if one country successfully bans or weakens encryption, citizens can access strong cryptographic tools developed in other countries, making unilateral government action largely ineffective while creating economic disadvantages for countries that restrict encryption use.

Anonymous Networks and Digital Underground

The development of anonymous communication networks like Tor, I2P, and other privacy-focused technologies has created a "digital underground" where dissidents, journalists, and ordinary citizens can communicate and share information without revealing their identities or locations. These networks use sophisticated routing and encryption techniques to make user identification extremely difficult even for well-resourced adversaries with substantial surveillance capabilities.

Anonymous networks serve multiple purposes within digital resistance movements, providing protection for whistleblowers who need to share sensitive information, enabling dissidents in authoritarian countries to access censored information and coordinate resistance activities, and allowing ordinary citizens to explore controversial topics or express unpopular opinions without fear of social or professional retaliation.

The existence of anonymous networks creates a parallel internet where different norms and possibilities exist than in the surveilled mainstream internet. This digital underground provides space for experimentation with alternative forms of social organization, economic exchange, and political coordination that may not be possible in environments subject to comprehensive monitoring and control.

Decentralized Communication Protocols

Beyond anonymous networks, the development of truly decentralized communication protocols promises to eliminate single points of failure and control that make centralized systems vulnerable to surveillance and censorship. Technologies like mesh networking, peer-to-peer communication systems, and blockchain-based messaging platforms create communication infrastructures that don't depend on centralized servers or internet service providers that can be monitored or shut down.

Decentralized communication systems face significant technical challenges related to reliability, scalability, and user experience that have limited their adoption compared to centralized alternatives. However, recent advances in distributed systems technology and growing awareness of centralized platform risks have led to renewed interest in decentralized alternatives that could provide communication infrastructure resistant to surveillance and control.

The political implications of truly decentralized communication systems are profound, as they could enable forms of social organization and coordination that operate outside traditional state and corporate control structures. This creates both opportunities for democratic empowerment and risks of enabling criminal or terrorist activities that operate beyond the reach of law enforcement and democratic oversight.

The Limits and Vulnerabilities of Technical Resistance

Despite their sophistication and mathematical strength, technical resistance tools like encryption and anonymous networks face significant limitations and vulnerabilities that prevent them from providing complete protection against determined adversaries. Surveillance systems can often circumvent technical protections through metadata analysis, traffic pattern recognition, endpoint compromise, and social engineering attacks that don't require breaking cryptographic systems directly.

The complexity of technical resistance tools creates barriers to adoption that limit their effectiveness as democratic protection mechanisms. Most citizens lack the technical knowledge necessary to properly implement and maintain privacy tools, creating gaps in protection that surveillance systems can exploit. Even technically sophisticated users make mistakes in operational security that can compromise their anonymity and safety.

The arms race between surveillance and privacy technologies creates a constantly evolving landscape where new vulnerabilities and attack methods regularly emerge that can compromise even well-designed resistance systems. This requires ongoing vigilance and technical updating that many users are unable or unwilling to maintain, creating windows of vulnerability that can be exploited by adversaries.

CRYPTOCURRENCY AND BLOCKCHAIN AS FREEDOM TECHNOLOGIES

Bitcoin and the Dream of Financial Sovereignty

The development of Bitcoin and other cryptocurrencies represents one of the most significant challenges to state financial control and surveillance since the invention of banking itself. By creating a form of digital money that operates independently of government and banking oversight, cryptocurrencies provide individuals with the ability to conduct financial transactions without revealing their identity or obtaining permission from financial institutions or regulatory authorities.

The philosophical foundations of cryptocurrency development explicitly embrace libertarian ideals of individual sovereignty and resistance to state control. Bitcoin's anonymous creator, Satoshi Nakamoto, designed the system specifically to eliminate the need for trusted third parties in financial transactions, creating what proponents describe as "trustless money" that doesn't depend on government backing or institutional guarantee for its value and functionality.

The practical implications of cryptocurrency adoption for individual freedom are profound, particularly in authoritarian countries where governments use financial surveillance and control to suppress dissent and limit citizens' ability to organize resistance activities. Cryptocurrencies provide protesters, dissidents, and civil society organizations with access to financial infrastructure that operates independently of state control, enabling funding and coordination activities that would otherwise be impossible.

Blockchain Technology and Decentralized Systems

Beyond cryptocurrency applications, blockchain technology promises to enable decentralized systems for identity verification, contract enforcement, property registration, and other functions currently controlled by centralized institutions. These applications could potentially eliminate single points of control and surveillance that make centralized systems vulnerable to authoritarian manipulation and corporate exploitation.

Decentralized identity systems built on blockchain technology could provide individuals with control over their personal information and digital identity without depending on government-issued documents or corporate platforms for verification and authentication. This could enable forms of social and economic participation that operate independently of traditional identity infrastructure while providing strong privacy protections.

Smart contract systems promise to automate contract enforcement and dispute resolution without requiring centralized legal systems or institutional oversight. While still technically immature, these systems could potentially enable forms of economic coordination and organization that operate outside traditional regulatory frameworks and institutional control structures.

The Regulatory Response to Cryptocurrency

Government responses to cryptocurrency adoption have varied widely, from complete bans in countries like China to regulatory acceptance and integration in countries like Switzerland and Singapore. This variation reflects fundamental disagreements about the appropriate balance between individual financial freedom and state regulatory authority over monetary systems and financial transactions.

The pseudonymous nature of many cryptocurrency systems creates particular challenges for regulatory authorities who need to balance anti-money laundering and tax enforcement requirements with the privacy expectations of legitimate users. This has led to the development of increasingly sophisticated blockchain analysis techniques that can often identify cryptocurrency users despite the systems' privacy features.

The global nature of cryptocurrency networks makes unilateral government action largely ineffective, as users can access cryptocurrency services through international exchanges and platforms even if their home countries restrict or ban cryptocurrency use. This creates pressure for international coordination among regulatory authorities while providing cryptocurrency users with regulatory arbitrage opportunities that limit government control.

Privacy Coins and Enhanced Anonymity

The recognition that Bitcoin and other early cryptocurrencies provide limited privacy protection has led to the development of "privacy coins" like Monero, Zcash, and others that use advanced cryptographic techniques to provide much stronger anonymity guarantees for users. These systems represent the cutting edge of financial privacy technology and provide individuals with access to truly anonymous digital money.

Privacy coins have attracted particular government attention and hostility because they provide capabilities for money laundering, tax evasion, and criminal financing that are extremely difficult for authorities to detect or prevent. Several countries have banned privacy coin trading and possession, while others have pressured cryptocurrency exchanges to delist these currencies from their platforms.

The technical arms race between privacy coin developers and blockchain analysis companies continues to evolve, with new anonymity techniques being developed to counter new surveillance and analysis capabilities. This ongoing competition shapes the landscape of financial privacy and determines the extent to which individuals can maintain economic sovereignty in an increasingly surveilled world.

Decentralized Autonomous Organizations and Governance

Blockchain technology has enabled experimentation with decentralized autonomous organizations (DAOs) that operate through smart contracts and token-based governance rather than traditional corporate or institutional structures. These organizations promise to enable forms of collective action and resource coordination that operate independently of traditional legal and regulatory frameworks.

DAOs represent a radical experiment in post-institutional governance where decisions are made through cryptographic voting mechanisms rather than traditional democratic or corporate processes. While still technically experimental, these systems demonstrate possibilities for organizing human activity outside traditional institutional structures that could have profound implications for political and economic organization.

The legal status of DAOs remains unclear in most jurisdictions, creating both opportunities for regulatory arbitrage and risks of legal uncertainty that could undermine their long-term viability. This legal ambiguity reflects broader challenges in regulating decentralized systems that don't fit traditional legal categories and institutional frameworks.

CASE STUDIES: EDWARD SNOWDEN, JULIAN ASSANGE, AND THE PRICE OF TRUTH

Edward Snowden: The NSA Revelations and Institutional Whistleblowing

Edward Snowden's 2013 revelations about the scope and capabilities of NSA surveillance programs represent the most significant intelligence leak in human history, exposing a global surveillance apparatus that exceeded even the most paranoid conspiracy theories about government monitoring capabilities. Snowden's disclosures revealed that intelligence agencies had effectively eliminated the privacy protections that democratic societies assumed existed, creating comprehensive monitoring systems that tracked the communications and activities of entire populations.

The personal cost of Snowden's revelations illustrates the extreme risks faced by those who challenge surveillance systems through institutional whistleblowing. Forced to flee the United States and seek asylum in Russia, Snowden remains in permanent exile, unable to return to his home country where he faces charges under the Espionage Act that could result in life imprisonment. This extreme punishment for revealing information that serves the public interest demonstrates the extent to which surveillance states will go to protect their operational secrecy.

Snowden's case highlights the inadequacy of existing whistleblower protection systems for addressing surveillance overreach and intelligence abuse. Despite following established procedures for reporting concerns through official channels, Snowden found no institutional mechanisms for addressing the constitutional violations he discovered, forcing him to choose between complicity in illegal surveillance and personal destruction through public disclosure.

The global impact of Snowden's revelations has been profound but limited, sparking international debate about surveillance overreach while producing relatively few substantive reforms to the surveillance systems he exposed. This demonstrates the resilience of surveillance institutions and their ability to weather public criticism while maintaining operational capabilities largely unchanged.

Julian Assange: WikiLeaks and the Criminalization of Journalism

Julian Assange's creation of WikiLeaks represents an attempt to use technological systems to enable anonymous whistleblowing and document disclosure on a global scale. By providing secure channels for sources to submit classified or sensitive documents, WikiLeaks promised to democratize the ability to expose corruption and abuse of power while protecting sources from identification and retaliation.

The persecution of Assange by multiple governments demonstrates the extent to which powerful institutions will go to prevent technological systems from undermining their control over information and narrative. Assange spent seven years in asylum at the Ecuadorian embassy in London before being arrested and extradited to face charges in the United States that could result in life imprisonment for publishing classified documents—activities that traditional journalism organizations perform routinely.

The legal theories being used to prosecute Assange represent a fundamental threat to press freedom and democratic accountability, as they criminalize standard journalistic practices when applied to classified government information. If successful, these prosecutions could effectively eliminate investigative journalism about national security issues and prevent the public disclosure of government wrongdoing.

WikiLeaks' impact on global politics has been enormous, from exposing war crimes in Iraq and Afghanistan to influencing the 2016 US presidential election through the publication of Democratic Party emails. This demonstrates both the power of technological systems to enable transparency and accountability and the risks of these systems being used for partisan political purposes or foreign interference.

Chelsea Manning: The Personal Cost of Conscience

Chelsea Manning's disclosure of classified military documents to WikiLeaks, including the "Collateral Murder" video that showed US military personnel killing civilians in Iraq, illustrates the personal cost of acting on conscience when institutional systems fail to address wrongdoing. Manning's subsequent imprisonment, torture through solitary confinement, and ongoing legal harassment demonstrate the brutal treatment reserved for those who expose state crimes.

Manning's case highlights the particular vulnerabilities faced by military whistleblowers, who operate within institutional structures that explicitly prioritize obedience over conscience and provide few protections for those who report wrongdoing. The extreme punishment Manning received—including extended solitary confinement that constituted torture according to human rights organizations—demonstrates the military's commitment to deterring future disclosures through brutal example.

The commutation of Manning's sentence by President Obama and subsequent re-imprisonment for refusing to testify against Julian Assange illustrates the ongoing legal persecution faced by those who challenge surveillance and secrecy systems. This pattern of continued harassment demonstrates that the state's vengeance against whistleblowers extends far beyond their initial punishment and continues indefinitely.

Manning's personal journey, including her gender transition during imprisonment and ongoing activism for transgender rights and government transparency, demonstrates the complex intersection of personal identity and political resistance in the digital age. Her case illustrates how personal courage in challenging institutional wrongdoing can inspire broader movements for social justice and systemic change.

Reality Winner: The Speed of Digital Retribution

Reality Winner's rapid identification and prosecution for leaking a single NSA document about Russian election interference demonstrates how digital surveillance systems have accelerated the speed at which whistleblowers can be identified and punished. Winner was arrested within days of her disclosure, illustrating how comprehensive monitoring systems make anonymous whistleblowing increasingly difficult even for small-scale disclosures.

Winner's case demonstrates the evolution of surveillance techniques that make traditional operational security measures inadequate for protecting sources and whistleblowers. Digital document tracking, email monitoring, and behavioral analysis systems can quickly identify potential sources even when they attempt to use traditional anonymization techniques.

The harsh sentence Winner received for disclosing a single document that revealed foreign interference in US elections illustrates the disproportionate punishment reserved for those who expose government wrongdoing compared to those who commit the wrongdoing being exposed. This asymmetry in justice demonstrates how surveillance systems protect institutional power rather than democratic accountability.

Winner's case also highlights the gendered and racialized aspects of whistleblower persecution, as women and minorities often receive harsher treatment than their white male counterparts who engage in similar disclosure activities. This differential treatment reveals how systems of punishment intersect with broader patterns of social inequality and discrimination.

Daniel Ellsberg: The Pentagon Papers and Historical Perspective

Daniel Ellsberg's disclosure of the Pentagon Papers during the Vietnam War provides historical perspective on the evolution of whistleblower persecution and government secrecy systems. Ellsberg's ability to photocopy thousands of pages of classified documents and distribute them to multiple news organizations without immediate detection illustrates how technological limitations once provided protection for whistleblowers that no longer exists.

The government's failed prosecution of Ellsberg due to official misconduct and illegal surveillance demonstrates how legal protections for defendants once provided meaningful checks on prosecutorial abuse. The erosion of these protections through national security exception doctrines and expanded surveillance authorities has eliminated many of the legal safeguards that once protected whistleblowers from government retaliation.

Ellsberg's continued activism and support for contemporary whistleblowers demonstrates the ongoing relevance of Vietnam-era lessons about government deception and the importance of public disclosure in maintaining democratic accountability. His analysis of the similarities between Pentagon Papers-era secrecy and contemporary surveillance systems provides valuable insight into the continuities and escalations in government efforts to control information and suppress dissent.

The contrast between public and official responses to Ellsberg's disclosures and contemporary whistleblower cases illustrates how the political and media environment has evolved in ways that make it more difficult for whistleblowers to receive public support and protection from government persecution.

Aaron Swartz: Information Liberation and Digital Martyrdom

Aaron Swartz's prosecution for downloading academic articles from JSTOR and his subsequent suicide represent a tragic illustration of how digital surveillance and prosecutorial overreach can destroy young activists who challenge information control systems. Swartz's case demonstrates how copyright and computer crime laws are weaponized against those who seek to democratize access to information and knowledge.

Swartz's vision of information liberation—the belief that academic research and knowledge should be freely available to everyone rather than locked behind paywalls and access restrictions—represents a fundamental challenge to the commodification of information that underlies much of the contemporary economy. His prosecution demonstrated the lengths to which institutions will go to protect information monopolies and prevent technological circumvention of access restrictions.

The prosecutorial tactics used against Swartz, including threats of decades in prison for activities that caused no measurable harm, illustrate how the legal system has become a tool for terrorizing digital activists and deterring challenges to information control systems. The psychological pressure created by these tactics contributed to Swartz's death and demonstrates the human cost of criminalizing digital activism.

Swartz's legacy continues through organizations and movements that advocate for open access to information, reform of copyright laws, and protection for digital rights activists. His death sparked broader conversations about prosecutorial reform and the need for legal protections for information activism that continue to influence policy debates and reform efforts.

THE INFRASTRUCTURE OF DIGITAL RESISTANCE

Underground Networks and Hidden Services

The development of hidden service networks within anonymous systems like Tor has created a parallel internet infrastructure that operates beyond the reach of conventional surveillance and censorship systems. These networks host websites, forums, and services that would be impossible to operate on the conventional internet due to government censorship, corporate restrictions, or threat of retaliation against operators and users.

Hidden service networks provide critical infrastructure for resistance movements, investigative journalists, and civil society organizations operating in authoritarian environments. These networks enable the sharing of sensitive information, coordination of resistance activities, and protection of vulnerable populations in ways that would be impossible through conventional internet infrastructure subject to government monitoring and control.

The technical sophistication required to operate hidden services safely creates barriers to entry that limit their accessibility to technically educated users, while also providing strong security guarantees for those who can navigate the complexity. This creates a form of "technical privilege" where protection from surveillance depends on specialized knowledge and skills that are not equally distributed across populations.

The cat-and-mouse game between hidden service operators and law enforcement agencies continues to evolve, with new techniques for identifying and compromising hidden services being developed alongside new methods for protecting them. This ongoing technical competition determines the extent to which parallel internet infrastructure can provide lasting protection for resistance activities.

Secure Communication Tools and Operational Security

The development of secure communication tools like Signal, Wire, and other encrypted messaging applications has provided ordinary citizens with access to military-grade cryptography for protecting their communications from surveillance and interception. These tools represent a democratization of privacy technology that was once available only to governments and large corporations with substantial technical resources.

The widespread adoption of encrypted messaging has fundamentally altered the surveillance landscape, forcing intelligence agencies to develop new techniques for monitoring communications while providing individuals with unprecedented capabilities for private communication. This shift has created new forms of security culture where operational security practices once limited to intelligence professionals become necessary for ordinary citizens seeking to protect their privacy.

The user interface and experience design of secure communication tools plays a crucial role in determining their effectiveness as resistance technologies. Tools that prioritize security over usability often fail to achieve widespread adoption, while tools that prioritize usability may compromise security in ways that make them vulnerable to sophisticated adversaries.

The ongoing development of secure communication tools requires sustained technical effort and funding that depends on communities of developers and users committed to digital privacy and resistance. The vulnerability of these development communities to legal pressure and resource constraints creates ongoing risks to the availability and quality of privacy-protecting technologies.

Digital Dead Drops and Anonymous Coordination

Modern resistance movements have developed sophisticated techniques for anonymous coordination and information sharing that operate through digital systems without revealing the identity or location of participants. These techniques combine cryptographic tools, anonymous networks, and carefully designed operational procedures to enable collective action while protecting individual participants from identification and retaliation.

Digital dead drop systems allow for the anonymous transfer of information and resources without direct communication between participants, using blockchain systems, distributed storage networks, and time-delayed revelation techniques to coordinate activities across time and space. These systems represent significant advances in the technology of conspiracy and resistance that enable new forms of collective action.

The technical complexity of anonymous coordination systems creates significant barriers to adoption that limit their effectiveness for grassroots organizing and popular resistance movements. The specialized knowledge required to participate safely in anonymous networks creates dependencies on technical elites that may undermine the democratic character of resistance movements.

The psychological challenges of anonymous coordination—operating without knowing the identity or trustworthiness of collaborators—create unique stresses and vulnerabilities that can be exploited by adversaries seeking to disrupt resistance movements. The paranoia and isolation inherent in anonymous organizing can undermine the solidarity and mutual support that sustain resistance movements over time.

Economic Infrastructure for Resistance

The development of alternative economic infrastructure through cryptocurrencies, decentralized funding platforms, and anonymous payment systems has provided resistance movements with new capabilities for raising and distributing resources without revealing the identity of supporters or recipients. This economic infrastructure enables forms of solidarity and support that operate independently of traditional financial systems subject to government monitoring and control.

Cryptocurrency funding has enabled protest movements, civil society organizations, and individual activists to receive support from international networks of sympathizers without revealing donor identities or providing governments with the ability to freeze or confiscate funds. This capability has proven particularly important for movements operating in authoritarian environments where traditional funding sources are subject to severe restrictions and penalties.

The technical barriers to using cryptocurrency systems safely create ongoing challenges for resistance movements that lack technical expertise, while the volatility and complexity of cryptocurrency markets create additional risks and complications for organizations seeking to use these systems for sustained operations and planning.

The growing sophistication of blockchain analysis and cryptocurrency tracking systems has begun to limit the privacy benefits of cryptocurrency funding, requiring increasingly sophisticated operational security measures to maintain anonymity and protect supporters from identification and retaliation.

CONCLUSION: THE ETERNAL STRUGGLE FOR HUMAN FREEDOM

The landscape of digital resistance reveals both the enormous potential of technology to enable human freedom and the profound challenges faced by those who seek to preserve liberty in an age of unprecedented surveillance capabilities. The modern Winston Smiths who risk everything to challenge digital authoritarianism demonstrate extraordinary courage and technical sophistication, but they also illustrate the enormous personal costs of resistance and the asymmetrical nature of the conflict between individual dissidents and institutional surveillance systems.

The cases of Snowden, Assange, Manning, and others reveal a consistent pattern: those who expose the crimes and constitutional violations of surveillance systems face far harsher punishment than those who commit the violations being exposed. This inversion of justice—where truth-tellers are treated as criminals while actual criminals retain positions of power and authority—demonstrates how surveillance systems protect themselves through the strategic use of law enforcement and prosecutorial power against their critics.

Yet the technological infrastructure of resistance continues to evolve and expand, providing new capabilities for anonymous communication, financial sovereignty, and decentralized organization that operate beyond the reach of traditional control systems. The development of cryptographic tools, blockchain networks, and decentralized systems represents a technological revolution that could fundamentally alter the balance of power between individuals and institutions, enabling new forms of human organization and cooperation that operate independently of traditional authority structures.

The critical question facing contemporary resistance movements is whether technological capabilities can evolve fast enough to outpace the surveillance systems they seek to evade. The arms race between privacy and surveillance technologies continues to accelerate, with both sides developing increasingly sophisticated capabilities that push the boundaries of what is technically possible. The outcome of this competition will largely determine the future of human freedom and the possibility of meaningful resistance to digital authoritarianism.

The democratization of resistance technologies through open-source development and grassroots education efforts provides hope that privacy and freedom tools will remain accessible to ordinary citizens rather than becoming the exclusive province of technical elites. However, the ongoing complexity and specialization required for effective digital resistance creates persistent barriers that limit the accessibility and effectiveness of these tools for mass movements and popular resistance.

Perhaps most importantly, the digital resistance movements of the early 21st century have established the principle that surveillance systems can be challenged, exposed, and circumvented through technical means and personal courage. The sacrifices made by digital dissidents have created technological and cultural resources that future resistance movements can build upon, while their revelations have educated global populations about the scope and implications of surveillance capitalism and digital authoritarianism.

The price of truth in the digital age is often measured in years of imprisonment, permanent exile, and personal destruction. Yet those who have paid this price have preserved the possibility that future generations might live in freedom rather than digital servitude. Their legacy lies not only in the specific surveillance programs they exposed or the technical tools they developed, but in their demonstration that resistance remains possible even in the face of overwhelming technological superiority and institutional power.

In Winston Smith's world, the telescreen was an obvious and acknowledged instrument of surveillance that citizens understood they were subjected to. In our world, the instruments of surveillance are invisible, seductive, and voluntary—we carry them willingly, invite them into our homes, and pay subscription fees for enhanced monitoring. This makes the courage of contemporary digital dissidents even more remarkable, as they risk everything to resist systems that most people don't even recognize as oppressive.

The eternal struggle for human freedom continues in new technological forms, fought by new kinds of heroes using new kinds of weapons. The outcome remains uncertain, but the struggle itself continues to define what it means to be human in an age of algorithmic control. As long as individuals are willing to risk everything for the principle that truth must be spoken and freedom must be preserved, the possibility of liberation remains alive, hidden in encrypted channels and anonymous networks, waiting for the moment when it might emerge to transform the world.

The digital dissidents of our time have shown us that even in the dopamine panopticon, even under comprehensive surveillance, even when the costs are extreme and the odds overwhelming, resistance is still possible. They have preserved the flame of human freedom in the darkest corners of the digital underground, ensuring that future generations will have the tools and inspiration necessary to continue the fight. Their legacy is written not in stone but in code, not in monuments but in mathematics, not in history books but in the hidden architectures of resistance that continue to operate beneath the surface of our surveilled world.

The screen may be watching us, but we are watching back—and we are learning to look away.

Chapter 10: The Proles Have Smartphones

How Digital Technology Has Created New Forms of Class Division

In Orwell's "1984," the proles represented the vast majority of the population who were kept in a state of ignorant contentment through entertainment, alcohol, and the illusion of freedom. The Party understood that the proles posed no threat to their power because they lacked the education, organization, and consciousness necessary for effective resistance. They were given just enough freedom and distraction to prevent rebellion while being excluded from real political power or economic advancement. Today's digital landscape has created a remarkably similar class structure, but with a crucial twist: the modern proles don't just have bread and circuses—they have smartphones.

The digital revolution has fundamentally restructured social stratification in ways that would have fascinated Orwell's sociologists. Rather than eliminating class distinctions, digital technology has created new forms of hierarchy based on digital literacy, technological access, and information manipulation skills. These new class divisions are often invisible to those experiencing them, masked by the democratic rhetoric of universal access and technological empowerment. The smartphone, rather than serving as a great equalizer, has become the primary instrument through which new forms of digital serfdom are imposed and maintained.

The apparent universality of smartphone access obscures the profound differences in how different social classes experience digital technology. While wealthy, educated users employ sophisticated privacy tools, understand algorithmic manipulation, and leverage technology for genuine empowerment, less privileged users often find themselves trapped in what might be called "digital sharecropping"—working to generate value for platforms while receiving minimal benefits in return. They consume manipulative content, surrender valuable personal data, and participate in surveillance systems that primarily benefit others, all while believing they are participating in democratic technological progress.

The Illusion of Digital Democracy

The rhetoric surrounding digital technology consistently emphasizes its democratizing potential—the way smartphones give everyone access to information, communication tools, and economic opportunities that were previously reserved for elites. This rhetoric serves a crucial ideological function by making digital class divisions seem temporary or illusory rather than structural and permanent. Users experiencing digital subjugation are encouraged to see their situation as a result of personal choices or temporary circumstances rather than recognizing systemic exploitation.

The democratizing narrative focuses on the most visible aspects of digital access while ignoring more subtle forms of digital inequality. Every smartphone user can indeed access the same websites, download the same apps, and theoretically participate in the same digital ecosystems. However, this surface-level equality obscures profound differences in how different users experience these systems. Wealthy users employ VPNs, ad blockers, and privacy tools that fundamentally alter their digital experience. They understand how algorithms work and can game them for personal benefit. They have the education and resources necessary to recognize and resist manipulation.

Meanwhile, less privileged users experience these same systems through interfaces designed to maximize data extraction and behavioral manipulation. They encounter more aggressive advertising, more invasive surveillance, and more manipulative content recommendation systems. Their data is more valuable to advertisers because they have fewer resources to resist marketing messages. Their attention is more completely captured because they have fewer alternative entertainment options. The same technological systems that empower some users simultaneously exploit others, creating a form of digital stratification that masquerades as universal access.

The Attention Economy Class System

The modern digital economy operates primarily through the extraction and monetization of human attention, creating a class system based on users' ability to protect and direct their own cognitive resources. Those who understand attention as a valuable resource that should be carefully guarded can maintain autonomy and agency in digital environments. Those who don't recognize attention's value become unwitting participants in their own exploitation, surrendering their most precious cognitive resources in exchange for minimal entertainment and social validation.

This attention-based class system is particularly insidious because it doesn't require explicit coercion or obvious inequality. Users at all socioeconomic levels have access to the same basic technological tools, but they use these tools in fundamentally different ways that either preserve or surrender their cognitive autonomy. Wealthy, educated users typically employ technology instrumentally—using specific apps and services to accomplish particular goals before disengaging. Less privileged users often experience technology as an endless stream of entertainment and distraction that consumes increasing portions of their waking attention.

The platforms themselves are designed to maximize engagement from users who lack the sophistication to recognize manipulation techniques. Recommendation algorithms are optimized for users who don't understand how algorithmic systems work. Interface designs exploit psychological vulnerabilities that affect users who haven't learned to recognize such exploitation. The result is a systematic transfer of attention and agency from less sophisticated users to more sophisticated ones, mediated through platforms that profit from this transfer while maintaining the fiction that all users benefit equally.

Digital Labor Exploitation

Perhaps the most significant aspect of digital class division involves the extraction of unpaid labor from users who don't recognize their activities as work. Every social media post, every search query, every app interaction generates valuable data that platforms monetize through advertising and analysis services. Users who understand this dynamic can minimize their unpaid labor contribution or find ways to capture some value from their data generation. Users who don't recognize this dynamic continue generating valuable content and data while receiving minimal compensation.

This digital labor exploitation operates through what might be called "gamified sharecropping"—systems that make unpaid work feel like entertainment or social participation. Social media users generate content, moderate discussions, and provide customer service functions for platforms while experiencing these activities as leisure or social interaction. Gig economy workers provide labor and capital (their vehicles, time, and local knowledge) while platforms extract the majority of value generated by their work. In both cases, the platforms' primary contribution is technological coordination, yet they capture the vast majority of economic value generated by user activities.

The exploitation is masked by the voluntary nature of participation and the genuine social benefits that users receive from platform usage. Users do gain real value from social connections, entertainment, and economic opportunities provided by digital platforms. However, the value they generate typically far exceeds the value they receive, creating a systematic transfer of wealth from users to platform owners. This transfer is invisible to users who don't understand the economic mechanisms underlying platform business models, making them willing participants in their own economic exploitation.

The Surveillance Class Divide

Digital surveillance systems create profound class divisions based on users' ability to maintain privacy and control their information exposure. Wealthy, educated users employ sophisticated privacy protection techniques that make them difficult and expensive targets for surveillance. They use encrypted communications, privacy-focused browsers, VPN services, and carefully configured privacy settings that minimize their surveillance exposure. They understand which platforms collect what types of data and make informed decisions about privacy trade-offs.

Meanwhile, less privileged users experience comprehensive surveillance through default settings, manipulative interface designs, and economic pressures that make privacy protection impractical. They cannot afford privacy-protecting services, lack the technical knowledge necessary for sophisticated privacy configuration, and often depend on surveillance-based platforms for essential services like navigation, communication, and entertainment. Their comprehensive surveillance exposure makes them more valuable targets for advertising, more vulnerable to discrimination, and more susceptible to manipulation and social control.

This surveillance class divide has profound political implications because it affects citizens' ability to participate meaningfully in democratic processes. Citizens under comprehensive surveillance are more vulnerable to political manipulation, more likely to self-censor their political expressions, and more susceptible to discriminatory treatment based on their political affiliations. Those who can maintain privacy retain genuine political agency, while those under comprehensive surveillance experience what amounts to a form of digital disenfranchisement that undermines democratic equality.

Digital Literacy as the New Determinant of Freedom vs. Subjugation

In the digital age, traditional markers of social class—income, education, social connections—remain important, but they are increasingly mediated through digital literacy skills that determine whether individuals can navigate technological systems as autonomous agents or become trapped in relationships of technological dependence and exploitation. Digital literacy has become the crucial skill that separates those who use technology from those who are used by technology, creating a new form of social stratification that cuts across traditional class boundaries while reinforcing and amplifying existing inequalities.

Digital literacy encompasses far more than basic computer skills or social media usage. True digital literacy requires understanding how algorithms work, recognizing manipulation techniques, comprehending privacy implications, and developing strategies for maintaining autonomy in technological systems designed to capture and control human attention and behavior. These skills are not naturally acquired through technology usage—they require explicit education and conscious development. Users who lack digital literacy become increasingly vulnerable to technological exploitation, regardless of their intelligence, education, or socioeconomic status.

The digital literacy divide creates a bifurcated society where some individuals leverage technology for genuine empowerment while others become trapped in relationships of technological dependence that resemble feudal arrangements more than democratic participation. Those with sophisticated digital literacy can use technology to enhance their productivity, expand their social networks, access valuable information, and participate meaningfully in digital economic opportunities. Those without such literacy find themselves providing unpaid labor, surrendering valuable personal data, and submitting to behavioral manipulation while believing they are receiving valuable services.

The Algorithmic Awareness Gap

Perhaps the most crucial component of digital literacy involves understanding how algorithmic systems work to shape user experience and behavior. Users who understand algorithmic manipulation can recognize when they are being influenced, adjust their behavior to resist unwanted manipulation, and sometimes leverage algorithmic systems for their own benefit. Users who lack algorithmic awareness become unwitting participants in manipulation systems designed to influence their purchasing decisions, political opinions, and social behaviors.

Algorithmic awareness requires understanding that digital platforms are not neutral information delivery systems but actively curated environments designed to maximize specific outcomes—typically engagement, data collection, and advertising effectiveness. Sophisticated users understand that search results are not objective rankings but commercially influenced presentations. They recognize that social media feeds are not chronological displays of friend activities but algorithmically optimized streams designed to maximize attention capture. They understand that recommendation systems are not helpful suggestions but behavioral influence tools designed to shape their preferences and behaviors.

This awareness allows sophisticated users to maintain critical distance from algorithmic suggestions while still benefiting from technological functionality. They can use search engines while understanding the commercial biases in results. They can use social media while recognizing the manipulative aspects of feed algorithms. They can benefit from recommendation systems while maintaining agency over their own preferences and decisions. Users without this awareness experience algorithmic manipulation as helpful assistance, making them more susceptible to influence and less capable of maintaining autonomous decision-making.

Privacy Literacy and Information Control

Digital literacy includes sophisticated understanding of privacy rights, surveillance systems, and information control strategies that allow users to maintain autonomy in environments designed to extract and analyze personal information. Privacy-literate users understand what information they are sharing, who has access to that information, and how that information might be used to influence or discriminate against them. They develop strategies for sharing necessary information while protecting sensitive data and maintaining control over their information exposure.

Privacy literacy requires understanding the difference between privacy policies and actual privacy practices, recognizing that companies often collect far more information than users realize and use that information in ways that exceed user expectations. Sophisticated users understand how data analysis techniques can extract sensitive information from apparently innocuous data sources—how location data reveals political affiliations, how purchase patterns indicate health conditions, how social network analysis reveals intimate relationships and personal vulnerabilities.

This understanding allows privacy-literate users to make informed decisions about information sharing and develop strategies for maintaining privacy while still benefiting from technological services. They can use privacy-protecting browsers, encrypted communication tools, and careful information sharing practices that minimize their surveillance exposure while maintaining access to essential digital services. Users without privacy literacy surrender comprehensive information about their lives, behaviors, and relationships without understanding the implications of such surrender or the alternatives available to them.

Economic Digital Literacy

Understanding the economic mechanisms underlying digital platforms represents another crucial component of digital literacy that determines whether users participate as exploited laborers or informed participants in digital economic systems. Economically literate users understand how platforms generate revenue, what role users play in value creation, and how to minimize their exploitation while maximizing their benefits from platform participation.

Economic digital literacy includes understanding advertising-based business models, recognizing when users are providing valuable labor or data, and developing strategies for capturing fair value from digital economic participation. Sophisticated users understand that "free" platforms are typically funded through advertising revenue generated by user data and attention, making users the actual products being sold to advertisers rather than customers receiving free services. This understanding allows them to make informed decisions about platform usage and develop strategies for minimizing their exploitation.

Perhaps most importantly, economic digital literacy enables users to recognize and pursue genuine economic opportunities in digital environments while avoiding exploitative schemes that masquerade as empowerment. Digitally literate users can distinguish between legitimate freelance opportunities and exploitative gig work arrangements. They can identify and avoid pyramid schemes, cryptocurrency scams, and other predatory economic schemes that target users who don't understand digital economic systems.

Critical Information Literacy

The abundance of information available through digital platforms creates new requirements for information literacy that go far beyond traditional media literacy skills. Digital environments contain mixtures of reliable and unreliable information, sophisticated propaganda and genuine news, commercial messages disguised as educational content, and algorithmic manipulation systems that shape information exposure based on commercial and political objectives. Users who lack critical information literacy become vulnerable to misinformation, manipulation, and exploitation through information systems designed to influence their beliefs and behaviors.

Critical information literacy requires understanding how information systems work, recognizing manipulation techniques, and developing strategies for evaluating information reliability in environments where traditional authority markers may be absent or manipulated. Sophisticated users understand how search engines prioritize and filter information, how social media algorithms shape information exposure, and how commercial and political interests influence information availability and presentation.

This literacy allows users to maintain informed perspectives on important issues while resisting attempts to manipulate their beliefs and opinions through carefully curated information environments. They can use digital information resources while maintaining critical evaluation skills and diverse information sources. Users without critical information literacy become trapped in information bubbles designed to reinforce existing beliefs while making them more susceptible to commercial and political manipulation.

The Role of Education in Creating or Preventing Digital Serfdom

Educational systems play a crucial role in determining whether technological advancement leads to widespread empowerment or creates new forms of digital subjugation. Current educational approaches to technology often focus on basic technical skills—how to use specific applications or navigate particular platforms—while ignoring the critical thinking skills necessary for maintaining autonomy in digital environments. This emphasis on technical training over critical analysis prepares students to become efficient users of technological systems while leaving them vulnerable to manipulation and exploitation by those same systems.

The failure of educational systems to address digital literacy comprehensively has created generations of users who are technically proficient but critically vulnerable. They can navigate complex interfaces, use sophisticated applications, and participate actively in digital platforms while lacking the analytical skills necessary to recognize when they are being manipulated, exploited, or surveilled. This combination of technical proficiency with critical vulnerability creates ideal conditions for digital serfdom—users who willingly and efficiently participate in systems that primarily benefit others.

The Vocational Training Trap

Many educational approaches to technology focus on preparing students for employment in tech industries or tech-dependent roles without developing the critical thinking skills necessary for understanding the broader social implications of technological systems. This vocational emphasis creates what might be called a "digital vocational training trap" where students learn to serve technological systems efficiently without questioning the social arrangements those systems create and maintain.

Vocational technology education typically emphasizes compliance with existing systems rather than critical analysis of those systems. Students learn to follow best practices for social media marketing, develop skills for navigating workplace surveillance systems, and master techniques for efficient participation in gig economy platforms. While these skills may provide short-term economic benefits, they also prepare students to participate uncritically in systems that may ultimately exploit their labor and undermine their autonomy.

The vocational approach also tends to treat technological systems as natural phenomena rather than human creations that reflect specific values and power arrangements. Students learn to adapt to algorithmic systems without understanding how those systems could be designed differently. They develop skills for working within surveillance capitalism without questioning whether alternative economic models might better serve their interests and social welfare generally.

The Digital Divide in Educational Resources

Educational institutions themselves reflect and reinforce digital class divisions through unequal access to sophisticated digital literacy education. Wealthy schools and universities provide comprehensive education about privacy protection, critical media literacy, and the social implications of technological systems. They prepare students to understand and navigate digital systems as sophisticated, critical users who can maintain autonomy while leveraging technology for personal and social benefit.

Meanwhile, less privileged educational institutions often provide only basic technical training that prepares students to be efficient consumers of technological services without developing critical analytical skills. These programs emphasize job training over critical thinking, technical compliance over social analysis, and individual adaptation over collective resistance to exploitative systems. The result is an educational reproduction of digital class divisions where privileged students learn to control technology while less privileged students learn to be controlled by technology.

This educational divide has profound long-term implications because it determines not just individual outcomes but the broader social capacity for democratic governance of technological systems. Societies where only elites receive sophisticated digital literacy education become vulnerable to technological authoritarianism, while societies that provide comprehensive digital literacy education to all citizens maintain the collective capacity for democratic technology governance.

The Curriculum Gaps

Current educational curricula typically contain significant gaps in areas crucial for digital literacy and technological autonomy. Most students receive little or no education about surveillance systems, algorithmic manipulation, privacy rights, or the economic structures underlying digital platforms. They learn to use technology without understanding how technology uses them, preparing them for digital participation without digital autonomy.

Critical curriculum gaps include education about the history of technological development, the political economy of digital platforms, the psychological techniques used in digital manipulation, and the civil liberties implications of comprehensive surveillance. Students who graduate without education in these areas become vulnerable to exploitation and manipulation regardless of their technical proficiency. They may be skilled users of digital tools while remaining naive about the social systems those tools implement and maintain.

Perhaps most importantly, educational systems typically fail to provide students with frameworks for imagining alternative technological arrangements. Students learn to adapt to existing systems without understanding that those systems represent choices rather than inevitabilities. This lack of imagination about alternatives makes it difficult for students to recognize exploitation when they experience it or to envision and work toward more equitable technological arrangements.

The Critical Pedagogy Alternative

Alternative educational approaches based on critical pedagogy offer potential pathways for preventing digital serfdom through education that combines technical skill development with critical social analysis. Critical digital literacy education helps students understand technological systems as human creations that reflect specific values and power arrangements, empowering them to participate in technological systems as critical agents rather than passive consumers.

Critical pedagogy approaches to digital literacy emphasize understanding the social context of technological development, analyzing the power relationships embedded in technological systems, and developing skills for resistance and alternative creation. Students learn not just how to use existing systems but how to evaluate those systems critically, recognize manipulation and exploitation, and work toward more equitable technological arrangements.

This approach requires fundamental changes to educational philosophy and practice, moving away from training students for efficient participation in existing systems toward empowering students to transform those systems. It requires educators who understand the social implications of technology and are committed to developing students' capacity for critical analysis and social action rather than just technical proficiency.

Rural vs. Urban Digital Divides and Their Political Implications

The digital revolution has created profound geographical divisions that intersect with existing urban-rural political tensions in ways that threaten democratic stability and social cohesion. These digital divides operate on multiple levels—infrastructure access, digital literacy, economic opportunities, and information environments—creating different digital experiences that shape political consciousness and social identity in increasingly divergent ways. The result is not just technological inequality but the emergence of distinct digital cultures with incompatible worldviews and political commitments.

Rural areas often experience digital technology through different infrastructure, economic arrangements, and social contexts than urban areas, creating fundamentally different relationships with technological systems. While urban users typically have access to high-speed internet, sophisticated privacy tools, and diverse information sources, rural users often rely on slower connections, have fewer technology alternatives, and encounter more homogeneous information environments. These technological differences interact with existing cultural and economic divisions to create increasingly polarized political constituencies.

The Infrastructure Inequality Foundation

The most basic level of rural-urban digital division involves disparities in technological infrastructure that create fundamentally different possibilities for digital participation. Rural areas often have slower internet connections, less reliable service, and fewer technology options, limiting residents' ability to participate fully in digital economic opportunities and information environments. These infrastructure limitations don't just create inconvenience—they shape the entire digital experience in ways that affect political consciousness and social identity.

Infrastructure limitations force rural users to rely more heavily on mobile internet access, which is more expensive per unit of data and more vulnerable to surveillance than fixed broadband connections. Rural users often cannot afford or access the privacy-protecting tools that urban users take for granted, making them more vulnerable to surveillance and manipulation. They have fewer choices among internet service providers, reducing their ability to vote with their wallets against companies with poor privacy practices or political biases.

These infrastructure constraints also limit rural users' ability to participate in digital economic opportunities that require high-speed, reliable internet connections. Remote work opportunities, online education, and digital entrepreneurship become less accessible, forcing rural residents to remain dependent on traditional economic arrangements even as urban areas transition to digital economic models. This economic dependency reinforces rural-urban political divisions by creating different relationships with technological change and economic transformation.

The Information Environment Polarization

Rural and urban digital divides create increasingly polarized information environments that shape political consciousness in fundamentally different ways. Rural users often encounter information through different platforms, algorithms, and social networks than urban users, creating distinct information bubbles that reinforce different political worldviews. These information environment differences don't just reflect existing political divisions—they actively create and amplify political polarization through technological mediation.

Rural information environments often emphasize local news sources, social media networks dominated by conservative voices, and recommendation algorithms trained on rural user behavior patterns. These information systems create feedback loops that reinforce rural political perspectives while filtering out information that might challenge or complicate those perspectives. Urban information environments operate through different algorithms, social networks, and information sources that create parallel but incompatible understandings of political and social reality.

The algorithmic mediation of information exposure means that rural and urban users increasingly live in different factual universes, making democratic deliberation and compromise increasingly difficult. When citizens cannot agree on basic facts about economic conditions, social problems, or policy effectiveness, democratic governance becomes nearly impossible. The digital divide thus becomes not just a technological problem but a fundamental threat to democratic stability and social cohesion.

The Economic Opportunity Divide

Digital economic opportunities are distributed unevenly between rural and urban areas in ways that reinforce existing economic inequalities while creating new forms of digital economic dependency. Urban areas typically have better access to high-paying remote work opportunities, digital entrepreneurship resources, and technology industry employment. Rural areas often have access primarily to exploitative gig work arrangements that provide labor flexibility for urban consumers while offering minimal economic benefits to rural workers.

This economic divide creates different relationships with technological change and different political interests regarding technology regulation. Urban workers who benefit from digital economic opportunities typically support policies that promote technological innovation and digital economic development. Rural workers who experience technology primarily through economic exploitation or displacement typically support policies that restrict technological change or provide protection against technological disruption.

The gig economy provides a particularly clear example of how digital economic opportunities create rural-urban political divisions. Urban users typically encounter gig economy platforms as convenient services that enhance their quality of life—ride sharing, food delivery, and personal services that supplement their primary economic activities. Rural users often encounter these same platforms as economic necessities that provide essential income through exploitative labor arrangements with minimal benefits or security.

The Digital Literacy Geography

Rural and urban areas often provide different educational and social opportunities for developing sophisticated digital literacy skills, creating geographical patterns of digital vulnerability and empowerment. Urban areas typically have better access to educational institutions, technology training programs, and social networks that promote sophisticated digital literacy development. Rural areas often lack these educational resources, making residents more vulnerable to digital manipulation and exploitation.

This digital literacy geography intersects with existing educational inequalities to create cumulative disadvantages for rural residents. Rural schools often lack the resources and expertise necessary to provide comprehensive digital literacy education. Rural residents have fewer opportunities for continuing education in digital literacy skills. Rural social networks may lack the technological sophistication necessary to provide informal digital literacy education through peer learning.

The result is geographical patterns of digital vulnerability that make rural residents more susceptible to misinformation, online scams, digital manipulation, and technological exploitation. These vulnerabilities have political implications because they affect rural residents' ability to participate meaningfully in democratic processes that increasingly require sophisticated digital literacy skills for effective participation.

The Social Capital Digital Divide

Rural and urban areas have different social structures that affect how residents experience and navigate digital technological systems. Urban areas typically have more diverse social networks, greater social mobility, and weaker community institutions, creating social contexts that support individual autonomy and technological experimentation. Rural areas typically have stronger community institutions, more stable social networks, and greater social conformity pressures, creating social contexts that may resist technological change while providing better social support for community members.

These social structural differences create different vulnerabilities and opportunities in digital environments. Urban residents may have greater individual autonomy to experiment with privacy-protecting technologies, alternative platforms, and technological resistance strategies. However, they may also have weaker social support networks to help them navigate technological challenges or resist manipulation. Rural residents may have stronger community support systems that provide collective resistance to some forms of technological manipulation, but they may also face community pressure to conform to technological arrangements that serve community solidarity rather than individual autonomy.

The social capital divide also affects political mobilization and collective action around technology issues. Urban residents may find it easier to organize around individual rights and privacy protection. Rural residents may be more effective at collective resistance to technological changes that threaten community stability or traditional values. These different mobilization capacities create different political strategies and different policy preferences regarding technology regulation and governance.

The Platform Economy Geography

Different geographical areas are integrated into digital platform economies in fundamentally different ways that create different economic interests and political preferences. Urban areas typically serve as centers of platform economy innovation and management, with residents working as engineers, managers, and creative professionals who benefit from platform economy growth. Rural areas typically serve as sources of platform economy labor and consumers, with residents providing delivery services, content creation, and data generation that primarily benefit urban platform economy professionals.

This geographical division of platform economy roles creates conflicting economic interests regarding platform regulation and worker protection. Urban professionals typically benefit from light regulation that promotes platform innovation and growth. Rural workers typically benefit from stronger regulation that provides better compensation, working conditions, and social protection for platform economy participants. These conflicting interests create geographical patterns of political conflict over technology policy.

The platform economy geography also affects how different areas experience technological change and automation. Urban areas typically experience technological change as opportunity creation and economic growth. Rural areas often experience technological change as job displacement and economic disruption that threatens community stability. These different experiences of technological change create different political attitudes toward innovation policy and social protection programs.

The Electoral and Democratic Implications

The rural-urban digital divide has profound implications for democratic governance and electoral politics because it creates different technological experiences that shape political consciousness in increasingly incompatible ways. Rural and urban voters increasingly live in different digital worlds with different information environments, economic opportunities, and social experiences that make compromise and democratic deliberation increasingly difficult.

Digital divides affect not just how citizens access information but how they understand the nature of political problems and appropriate solutions. Rural citizens who experience technology primarily through exploitation and surveillance may support policies that restrict technological development or provide protection against technological change. Urban citizens who benefit from technological innovation may support policies that promote continued technological development and resist restrictions on technological companies.

These technological differences intersect with existing cultural and economic rural-urban divisions to create increasingly polarized electoral constituencies that make democratic governance increasingly difficult. When voters have fundamentally different technological experiences and information environments, finding common ground on policy issues becomes nearly impossible. The result is electoral politics that increasingly resembles warfare between incompatible technological cultures rather than democratic deliberation about shared challenges.

The digital divide thus represents not just a technological problem but a fundamental threat to democratic stability that requires comprehensive policy responses addressing infrastructure inequality, educational disparities, economic opportunities, and information environment polarization. Without such comprehensive responses, digital technological development may ultimately undermine the social cohesion and shared understanding necessary for democratic governance.

Conclusion: Digital Feudalism in the Age of Smartphones

The emergence of smartphones as universal technology has not created the democratic, egalitarian society that digital utopians predicted. Instead, it has established a new form of social stratification that combines the most sophisticated surveillance and manipulation techniques in human history with the illusion of universal access and democratic participation. We have created a digital feudalism where the vast majority of users serve as digital serfs, generating value through their data, attention, and labor while receiving minimal benefits in return, all while believing they are participating in technological liberation.

The parallels to Orwell's proles are striking but incomplete. Orwell's proles were kept in ignorance and excluded from political power, but they maintained some degree of autonomous life outside the Party's direct control. Today's digital proles have smartphones that provide them with entertainment, social connection, and the illusion of empowerment while actually subjecting them to more comprehensive surveillance and manipulation than any population in human history has ever experienced. They are not excluded from political participation but are instead given forms of participation that primarily serve to legitimize systems that exploit them.

The digital literacy divide has become the crucial factor determining freedom versus subjugation in technological societies. Those who understand how digital systems work can leverage technology for genuine empowerment while maintaining autonomy and privacy. Those who lack such understanding become trapped in relationships of technological dependency that resemble feudal arrangements more than democratic participation. This divide cuts across traditional class boundaries while reinforcing and amplifying existing inequalities, creating new forms of social stratification that may be more permanent and politically stable than previous class systems.

Perhaps most concerning is how educational systems have failed to address these challenges comprehensively. Rather than preparing citizens to participate in technological systems as critical, autonomous agents, educational institutions typically prepare students to be efficient users of systems designed to exploit them. This educational failure perpetuates digital feudalism by ensuring that each new generation enters technological systems without the critical thinking skills necessary to recognize exploitation or imagine alternatives.

The geographical dimensions of digital inequality add another layer of complexity to these class divisions. Rural-urban digital divides create increasingly polarized political constituencies with incompatible worldviews and conflicting interests regarding technology governance. These geographical divisions threaten democratic stability by making compromise and deliberation increasingly difficult, while ensuring that technology policy serves urban interests at the expense of rural communities.

The smartphone has thus become the perfect instrument of digital feudalism—a device that provides genuine utility and empowerment to sophisticated users while simultaneously subjecting unsophisticated users to comprehensive surveillance, manipulation, and exploitation. It creates the illusion of universal access while actually reinforcing and amplifying existing inequalities. It provides entertainment and distraction that prevent recognition of exploitation while generating the data and attention that make exploitation profitable.

Breaking free from digital feudalism will require fundamental changes to educational systems, economic arrangements, and political institutions that currently serve to perpetuate digital inequality. It will require comprehensive digital literacy education that develops critical thinking skills rather than just technical proficiency. It will require economic models that provide fair compensation for the value that users generate through their digital participation. It will require political institutions capable of democratic governance of technological systems rather than capture by technology industry interests.

Most importantly, it will require collective recognition that current technological arrangements are not inevitable or necessary but represent choices that can be changed through deliberate social action. The proles may have smartphones, but they also have the potential for technological liberation if they develop the consciousness, organization, and political power necessary to transform the systems that currently exploit them. The question is whether such transformation is possible within systems designed to prevent exactly this kind of critical consciousness and collective action, or whether digital feudalism has become so embedded in social institutions that meaningful change has become impossible.

The stakes could not be higher. We stand at a historical moment where technological systems are becoming increasingly sophisticated and pervasive while the social capacity for democratic governance of those systems appears to be declining. Each day that passes sees millions more users integrated into digital feudalism, trained in technological dependency, and conditioned to accept exploitation as empowerment. The window for creating alternative arrangements may be closing rapidly, making this moment crucial for determining whether technological advancement leads to widespread liberation or permanent digital serfdom.

The choice remains ours, but making that choice requires recognizing that we have already created new forms of technological authoritarianism that operate through consent and participation rather than coercion and exclusion. The proles have smartphones, and through those smartphones, they have been given a form of technological participation that may be more effective at preventing rebellion than Orwell's crude combination of surveillance and propaganda. Understanding this reality is the first step toward imagining and creating technological arrangements that serve human freedom rather than technological control.

Chapter 11: Room 101 as a Service

How personalized advertising represents individualized psychological torture

In George Orwell's dystopian masterpiece, Room 101 contained "the worst thing in the world" for each individual—a personalized torture chamber designed around each victim's deepest fears and psychological vulnerabilities. Today's digital advertising ecosystem has realized this nightmare vision on a global scale, creating individualized psychological manipulation systems that exploit personal insecurities, fears, and desires with surgical precision. Modern personalized advertising doesn't merely attempt to sell products; it systematically exploits psychological vulnerabilities, amplifies personal anxieties, and manipulates emotional states to create compulsive consumption behaviors that generate profit from human suffering and psychological distress.

The sophistication of contemporary advertising technology has evolved far beyond simple demographic targeting or interest-based marketing to encompass comprehensive psychological profiling that identifies and exploits individual emotional vulnerabilities. Machine learning algorithms analyze vast datasets of personal behavior to identify moments of psychological weakness, relationship stress, financial anxiety, health concerns, career insecurity, and social isolation. These algorithms don't just detect these vulnerabilities; they learn to exploit them systematically, delivering precisely timed and carefully crafted messages designed to amplify insecurities and create desperate psychological states that drive impulsive purchasing behavior.

The data collection apparatus supporting personalized advertising operates as a comprehensive surveillance system that monitors every aspect of human experience for exploitable psychological insights. Location data reveals when individuals are at hospitals, divorce lawyers' offices, unemployment offices, or other locations associated with personal crisis. Communication analysis identifies relationship problems, financial stress, health concerns, and emotional instability through language patterns and sentiment analysis. Purchase history reveals personal insecurities about appearance, social status, relationships, and professional success. This comprehensive surveillance creates detailed psychological maps that identify exactly when and how to manipulate individuals for maximum commercial exploitation.

The timing and context of personalized advertising delivery is carefully orchestrated to maximize psychological impact and vulnerability. Algorithms identify moments of emotional distress, social isolation, financial pressure, or personal crisis when individuals are most susceptible to manipulative messaging. A person going through a divorce might receive targeted advertising for dating services, self-help books, and appearance enhancement products precisely when their self-esteem is most fragile. Someone facing unemployment might be bombarded with get-rich-quick schemes, career training programs, and debt consolidation services at their moment of greatest financial anxiety. This precision targeting transforms advertising from broad commercial messaging into individualized psychological warfare designed to profit from human suffering.

The Weaponization of Intimate Knowledge

The most disturbing aspect of personalized advertising lies in its systematic exploitation of intimate personal knowledge that individuals never consciously chose to share. The data fusion capabilities of modern advertising platforms combine information from dozens of sources to create psychological profiles that may be more accurate than individuals' own self-assessments. These systems know when people are depressed before they seek help, when relationships are failing before partners acknowledge problems, when health issues are developing before symptoms become apparent, and when financial problems are emerging before individuals recognize their severity.

The psychological manipulation enabled by this intimate knowledge operates through carefully crafted messaging that appears to understand and empathize with personal struggles while actually exploiting them for commercial gain. Advertising copy is dynamically generated to reference specific fears, insecurities, and desires identified through data analysis, creating the illusion of personal understanding and care while actually implementing sophisticated manipulation techniques. The emotional resonance achieved through this personalization creates powerful psychological bonds between consumers and brands that transcend rational decision-making processes.

The exploitation of intimate knowledge extends beyond conscious vulnerabilities to include subconscious psychological patterns and behavioral tendencies that individuals may not recognize in themselves. Machine learning algorithms identify personality traits, cognitive biases, decision-making patterns, and emotional triggers that can be exploited through targeted messaging even when individuals believe they are immune to advertising manipulation. This creates situations where people are systematically manipulated through psychological mechanisms they don't understand and vulnerabilities they don't recognize they possess.

Psychological Conditioning and Behavioral Modification

Modern personalized advertising operates as a comprehensive behavioral modification system that gradually shapes personality, values, and life choices through systematic psychological conditioning. The constant exposure to targeted messaging designed to exploit specific vulnerabilities creates lasting changes in self-perception, aspirations, and behavior patterns that extend far beyond immediate purchasing decisions. Individuals subjected to systematic advertising manipulation may find their personalities, relationships, and life goals gradually modified to align with commercial objectives rather than their authentic interests or values.

The conditioning process operates through sophisticated reward and punishment schedules that reinforce desired behaviors while creating anxiety and dissatisfaction around non-commercial activities and choices. Social media platforms integrate advertising messages into social validation systems, making commercial engagement a requirement for social acceptance and emotional satisfaction. The intermittent reinforcement provided by social media likes, comments, and shares becomes entangled with commercial messaging, creating addiction-like dependencies on both social validation and consumption behaviors.

The long-term psychological effects of sustained exposure to personalized advertising manipulation include increased materialism, social comparison, status anxiety, and dissatisfaction with non-commercial aspects of life. Individuals may find themselves unable to experience satisfaction or self-worth without constant consumption and commercial validation, creating psychological dependencies that serve commercial interests while undermining human flourishing and authentic happiness.

The Industrialization of Emotional Exploitation

The scale and systematization of personalized advertising represents the industrialization of emotional exploitation, transforming human psychological suffering into a raw material for corporate profit generation. Advertising technology platforms process billions of individual psychological profiles daily, identifying opportunities to exploit fear, insecurity, loneliness, and desire across entire populations. This industrial approach to psychological manipulation operates with the efficiency and scale of manufacturing systems, but instead of producing goods, it manufactures psychological states and behaviors that serve commercial objectives.

The economic incentives driving this industrialization create systematic pressures for increasingly sophisticated and invasive forms of psychological manipulation. Advertising platforms compete based on their ability to drive consumer behavior, creating market pressures for more effective emotional exploitation techniques. The measurement and optimization of advertising effectiveness based on behavioral outcomes rather than information provision creates incentives for psychological manipulation rather than rational persuasion.

The global deployment of these industrial-scale psychological manipulation systems means that billions of people worldwide are subjected to systematic emotional exploitation designed according to the profit objectives of advertising technology companies. The cultural and psychological impact of this manipulation extends beyond individual consumers to encompass entire societies that become organized around consumption behaviors driven by manufactured insecurities and artificial desires rather than authentic human needs and values.

The commodification of insecurity and desire

The modern advertising ecosystem has evolved beyond simply responding to existing consumer needs to actively manufacturing insecurities, anxieties, and desires that can then be exploited for commercial profit. This represents a fundamental shift in the relationship between commerce and human psychology, where personal emotional states and psychological conditions become raw materials to be harvested, processed, and sold. The commodification of insecurity operates through systematic campaigns designed to create dissatisfaction with personal appearance, social status, relationships, career success, and life achievements, generating artificial psychological needs that can only be satisfied through consumption.

The manufacturing of insecurity begins with comprehensive data analysis that identifies areas of potential vulnerability in individual psychological profiles. Algorithms analyze social media posts, search histories, purchase patterns, and behavioral data to identify aspects of individuals' lives where they might be made to feel inadequate or dissatisfied. Physical appearance, social relationships, career achievement, financial status, parenting skills, lifestyle choices, and personal accomplishments all become targets for systematic insecurity generation designed to create market opportunities for commercial exploitation.

The creation of artificial desires operates through sophisticated psychological techniques that associate products and services with fundamental human needs for love, acceptance, security, status, and meaning. Marketing messages are crafted to suggest that consumer goods can satisfy deep psychological and emotional needs that were traditionally met through relationships, community participation, personal growth, and meaningful work. This creates artificial dependencies on consumption for psychological satisfaction while undermining non-commercial sources of fulfillment and self-worth.

The systematization of insecurity and desire manufacturing has created entire industries dedicated to identifying and exploiting human psychological vulnerabilities. Beauty industries manufacture dissatisfaction with natural appearance to drive consumption of cosmetics, cosmetic procedures, and fashion products. Financial services industries manufacture anxiety about financial security to drive consumption of insurance, investment products, and debt services. Social media platforms manufacture fear of social isolation and status anxiety to drive engagement with advertising and data collection systems.

The Psychology of Manufactured Dissatisfaction

The techniques used to manufacture psychological dissatisfaction draw heavily from research in cognitive psychology, behavioral economics, and social psychology to identify the most effective methods for creating emotional distress that drives consumption behavior. Social comparison theory is weaponized through carefully curated social media content that presents artificially enhanced versions of other people's lives, creating systematic dissatisfaction with personal achievements and circumstances. Fear-based messaging exploits cognitive biases related to risk assessment and loss aversion to create anxiety about potential negative outcomes that can allegedly be prevented through consumption.

The timing and context of dissatisfaction manufacturing is carefully orchestrated to maximize psychological impact and commercial effectiveness. Algorithms identify moments of personal vulnerability, social isolation, or life transition when individuals are most susceptible to messages designed to create insecurity and desire. New parents receive messaging designed to create anxiety about child safety and development. People experiencing relationship problems receive advertising that suggests their personal inadequacies are responsible for their difficulties. Individuals facing career challenges are targeted with messages that imply their professional struggles result from personal failures that can be remedied through consumption.

The psychological conditioning created through systematic dissatisfaction manufacturing extends beyond immediate commercial objectives to reshape fundamental aspects of personality and self-perception. Individuals subjected to constant messaging about their inadequacies may internalize these suggestions, developing chronic dissatisfaction, anxiety, and self-doubt that persists even when they're not actively exposed to advertising. This creates psychological conditions that require ongoing commercial intervention, generating long-term customer dependencies that serve commercial interests while undermining mental health and personal well-being.

The Attention Economy and Emotional Labor

The commodification of human attention has created economic systems where emotional arousal, psychological engagement, and behavioral modification become the primary products being sold to advertisers and other commercial interests. Social media platforms, search engines, and other digital services are designed to maximize user engagement through emotional manipulation, creating business models that profit from human psychological suffering and behavioral compulsion. The more effectively these platforms can create anxiety, desire, fear, and other strong emotional states, the more valuable they become to advertisers seeking to exploit these emotional conditions.

The extraction of attention and emotional labor from users operates through sophisticated behavioral modification techniques that create addiction-like dependencies on digital platforms and the emotional states they provide. Variable ratio reinforcement schedules provide unpredictable rewards for platform engagement, creating compulsive usage patterns that keep users available for advertising exposure and emotional manipulation. Social validation systems tie self-worth and emotional satisfaction to platform metrics like likes, shares, and comments, creating psychological dependencies that can be exploited for commercial purposes.

The economic value of emotional labor and attention extraction has created incentives for increasingly sophisticated and invasive forms of psychological manipulation. Platforms compete based on their ability to capture and maintain user attention, creating market pressures for more effective emotional exploitation techniques. The measurement of success through engagement metrics rather than user well-being creates systematic biases toward psychological manipulation that generates compulsive usage rather than genuine satisfaction or value creation.

The Subscription Model for Psychological Dependency

The evolution toward subscription-based business models for digital services has created economic incentives for manufacturing ongoing psychological dependencies that require continuous commercial intervention. Instead of selling discrete products or services, companies increasingly profit from creating chronic psychological conditions that require ongoing consumption to manage. This represents a shift from episodic commercial relationships to chronic dependencies that integrate commercial consumption into fundamental aspects of daily psychological and emotional functioning.

Dating apps create artificial scarcity and manufactured rejection to ensure users remain psychologically dependent on the platforms for romantic validation and social connection. Social media platforms use algorithmic manipulation to create cycles of social anxiety and validation-seeking that require constant engagement to manage. Fitness and wellness apps manufacture dissatisfaction with physical appearance and health status to create dependencies on ongoing monitoring and intervention services. These business models profit from preventing problem resolution rather than solving problems, creating incentives for systematic psychological manipulation designed to maintain rather than eliminate customer suffering.

The subscription economy has also created opportunities for more sophisticated forms of psychological manipulation through the collection of longitudinal behavioral data that reveals how individual users respond to different types of emotional manipulation over time. This enables the development of personalized manipulation strategies that become more effective as they learn individual psychological patterns and vulnerabilities. The result is the creation of increasingly precise and inescapable systems of emotional exploitation that adapt and optimize based on individual user responses.

Social media's role in amplifying personal fears and anxieties

Social media platforms have evolved into sophisticated psychological amplification systems that systematically identify, magnify, and exploit individual fears and anxieties for commercial and behavioral control purposes. These platforms don't merely provide neutral spaces for social interaction; they actively manipulate emotional states through algorithmic curation of content designed to maintain user engagement through psychological arousal and emotional dysregulation. The result is the transformation of personal fears and anxieties from private psychological experiences into public commodities that can be harvested, analyzed, and exploited for profit and social control.

The algorithmic systems governing social media content distribution are specifically designed to prioritize emotionally arousing content that generates strong psychological responses, particularly fear, anger, anxiety, and social comparison. These algorithms have learned that content which triggers fight-or-flight responses, social anxiety, status competition, and existential fears generates higher engagement rates than content that promotes calm, satisfaction, or emotional stability. The result is systematic bias toward content that amplifies psychological distress while suppressing content that might promote emotional well-being or psychological resilience.

The amplification of personal fears operates through multiple mechanisms embedded in social media platform design and algorithmic behavior. Confirmation bias is exploited through filter bubbles that expose users primarily to content that reinforces their existing fears and anxieties while filtering out information that might provide reassurance or alternative perspectives. Social proof mechanisms are manipulated to make fears appear more widespread and legitimate than they actually are, creating artificial consensus around anxiety-provoking ideas and catastrophic thinking patterns. Availability heuristic exploitation ensures that rare but frightening events receive disproportionate attention, creating systematic distortions in risk perception and threat assessment.

The personalization capabilities of social media platforms enable the delivery of fear-amplifying content that is specifically tailored to individual psychological vulnerabilities and personal circumstances. Algorithms analyze user behavior, content engagement patterns, and personal data to identify specific fears and anxieties that can be exploited for maximum psychological impact. Someone with health anxiety might receive an endless stream of medical horror stories and disease information. Someone with social anxiety might be shown content highlighting social rejection and interpersonal conflict. Someone with financial stress might be bombarded with economic catastrophe predictions and financial failure narratives.

The Architecture of Psychological Manipulation

The design elements of social media platforms operate as comprehensive psychological manipulation systems that systematically exploit cognitive biases and emotional vulnerabilities to maintain user engagement and extract behavioral data. Infinite scroll mechanisms prevent natural stopping points that might allow users to disengage from emotionally manipulative content. Push notifications are timed to interrupt daily activities and draw users back into psychologically arousing content streams. Social validation metrics like likes, shares, and comments create intermittent reinforcement schedules that generate addiction-like dependencies on platform engagement.

The gamification elements built into social media platforms transform human social interaction into competitive activities that generate anxiety, status competition, and social comparison behaviors. Follower counts, engagement metrics, and viral content algorithms create artificial hierarchies that trigger status anxiety and social insecurity. The public nature of these metrics transforms private social relationships into public performance spaces where personal worth becomes tied to algorithmic assessment and peer validation. This creates systematic pressures for self-presentation and social performance that generate chronic anxiety and psychological stress.

The real-time nature of social media interaction creates artificial urgency and social pressure that amplifies anxiety and emotional reactivity. Users feel compelled to respond immediately to messages, comments, and social events, creating chronic states of psychological arousal and attention fragmentation. The fear of missing out (FOMO) generated by constant streams of social content creates anxiety about social exclusion and inadequate life experiences. The expectation of immediate response and constant availability creates stress that extends beyond platform usage into all aspects of daily life.

The Weaponization of Social Comparison

Social media platforms have weaponized natural human tendencies toward social comparison by creating artificial environments where individuals are constantly exposed to curated and enhanced versions of other people's lives, achievements, and experiences. These platforms systematically bias social comparison processes toward upward comparisons that generate dissatisfaction, inadequacy, and social anxiety while filtering out information that might provide realistic perspective on social relationships and life achievements. The result is systematic manufacturing of social comparison distress that drives continued platform engagement and susceptibility to advertising manipulation.

The curation and filtering of social content creates artificial social realities where users are primarily exposed to highlight reels and success narratives while being shielded from the struggles, failures, and ordinary experiences that characterize normal human life. This creates systematic distortions in social comparison processes that make individuals feel inadequate and unsuccessful compared to artificially enhanced presentations of other people's lives. The psychological impact includes increased depression, anxiety, social isolation, and materialism as individuals attempt to compete with artificial standards generated by algorithmic content curation.

The algorithmic amplification of social comparison extends beyond individual relationships to encompass lifestyle comparison, career achievement comparison, parenting comparison, and other aspects of human experience that become sources of competitive anxiety rather than mutual support and community connection. Parents are exposed to curated presentations of perfect parenting that generate anxiety and inadequacy about their own parenting skills. Professionals are shown unrealistic career success narratives that create dissatisfaction with normal career progression. Individuals in relationships are exposed to idealized romance presentations that create dissatisfaction with normal relationship dynamics.

The Monetization of Mental Health Crisis

The amplification of personal fears and anxieties through social media platforms has contributed to widespread mental health crises that are then further monetized through advertising for mental health services, pharmaceutical products, and wellness solutions. This creates perverse economic incentives where platforms profit both from creating psychological distress and from advertising solutions to the problems they have helped create. The same algorithmic systems that amplify anxiety and depression then target users experiencing these conditions with advertising for therapy services, medications, and self-help products.

The systematic creation of mental health problems through social media manipulation enables the development of entire industries dedicated to treating conditions that are artificially amplified or manufactured through digital platform usage. Anxiety disorders, depression, body dysmorphia, social anxiety, and attention disorders may be significantly exacerbated by social media usage patterns that are specifically designed to create these psychological conditions for commercial exploitation. The treatment of these conditions then becomes another profit center for the same economic system that contributed to their development.

The integration of mental health monitoring and intervention services into social media platforms creates additional opportunities for psychological manipulation and behavioral control. Platforms that claim to provide mental health support may actually be collecting detailed information about user psychological states and vulnerabilities that can be used for more sophisticated advertising targeting and behavioral manipulation. The same data used to identify users in need of mental health support can be used to identify users who are particularly vulnerable to commercial exploitation.

The Creation of Artificial Social Crises

Social media algorithms systematically amplify controversial, divisive, and fear-provoking content to generate engagement, creating artificial social crises and manufactured conflicts that wouldn't exist without algorithmic manipulation. These platforms profit from social discord, political polarization, and community fragmentation by generating emotional arousal that drives platform usage and advertising consumption. The result is the systematic manufacturing of social problems that serve commercial interests while undermining social cohesion and community well-being.

The amplification of social conflict operates through algorithmic promotion of extreme viewpoints, inflammatory content, and divisive narratives that generate strong emotional responses and social engagement. Moderate voices and nuanced perspectives are systematically suppressed in favor of polarizing content that generates controversy and argument. This creates artificial social environments where extreme positions appear more common and legitimate than they actually are, driving social polarization and conflict that serves algorithmic engagement objectives while undermining democratic discourse and social stability.

The global deployment of these social conflict amplification systems means that local communities and social relationships worldwide are being systematically undermined by algorithmic manipulation designed to serve the commercial interests of technology platforms. Traditional social institutions and community relationships are being replaced by algorithmically mediated interactions that prioritize engagement over social cohesion, creating systematic pressures toward social fragmentation and conflict that serve commercial rather than human interests.

The subscription model for surveillance and control

The evolution of digital services toward subscription-based business models has created new opportunities for comprehensive surveillance and behavioral control that extend far beyond traditional advertising-based revenue systems. The subscription economy transforms users from one-time customers into ongoing relationships that require continuous engagement, data collection, and behavioral modification to maintain profitability. This model creates economic incentives for developing increasingly sophisticated and invasive forms of surveillance and control that become embedded in essential services and daily life activities, making resistance or alternatives increasingly difficult to pursue.

Subscription-based services collect vastly more detailed and longitudinal data about user behavior than traditional transaction-based commerce, creating comprehensive behavioral profiles that reveal personality traits, psychological vulnerabilities, relationship patterns, health conditions, financial circumstances, and other intimate aspects of human experience. The ongoing nature of subscription relationships enables the collection of behavioral data over extended time periods, revealing patterns and trends that can be used for increasingly sophisticated prediction and manipulation of user behavior. This longitudinal data becomes extremely valuable for advertising targeting, behavioral modification, and social control purposes.

The integration of subscription services into essential life activities creates comprehensive surveillance networks that monitor virtually every aspect of human existence. Subscription-based transportation services track movement patterns and location data. Streaming entertainment services monitor consumption preferences and attention patterns. Productivity software subscriptions track work habits and professional activities. Health and fitness subscriptions monitor physical activity, sleep patterns, and biological data. The aggregation of data from multiple subscription services creates comprehensive surveillance systems that exceed the capabilities of traditional government surveillance programs while operating through voluntary commercial relationships.

The subscription model also creates opportunities for more sophisticated forms of behavioral control through the gradual modification of service features and user experiences based on behavioral data and control objectives. Services can gradually modify their functionality to encourage certain behaviors while discouraging others, creating behavioral modification systems that operate below the threshold of user awareness. The ongoing nature of subscription relationships enables long-term behavioral conditioning programs that gradually shape user behavior toward desired outcomes over months or years of service usage.

The Platform Dependency Economy

The subscription economy has created systematic dependencies on digital platforms and services that make it increasingly difficult for individuals to function in modern society without submitting to comprehensive surveillance and behavioral control. Essential services including communication, transportation, entertainment, productivity tools, financial services, and social interaction are increasingly provided through subscription-based platforms that require ongoing data sharing and behavioral monitoring as conditions of access. This creates situations where surveillance and control become prerequisites for social and economic participation rather than voluntary commercial choices.

The network effects associated with many subscription-based platforms create additional barriers to resistance or alternative selection. Communication platforms become more valuable as more people join them, creating pressure for universal adoption that makes resistance to surveillance difficult without accepting social isolation. Professional productivity platforms become industry standards that are required for employment and career advancement, making surveillance a prerequisite for economic participation. Social media platforms become essential for maintaining relationships and social connections, making surveillance a requirement for social participation.

The integration and interoperability of subscription services creates platform ecosystems that become increasingly difficult to exit once users have invested in them. Apple's ecosystem of devices, services, and subscriptions creates dependencies that make switching to alternative platforms costly and difficult. Google's integration of search, email, cloud storage, and productivity services creates comprehensive dependencies that would require significant effort and cost to replicate with alternative providers. These ecosystem effects trap users in surveillance and control systems while making alternatives appear impractical or impossible.

The Gamification of Compliance

Subscription-based services increasingly incorporate gamification elements that transform surveillance compliance and behavioral control into engaging activities that users actively participate in and enjoy. Fitness tracking subscriptions create competitive games around health monitoring that encourage users to provide comprehensive biological and activity data. Productivity applications create achievement systems around work monitoring that encourage detailed professional surveillance. Social media subscriptions create reward systems around content creation and engagement that encourage users to provide personal information and behavioral data.

The gamification of surveillance creates psychological rewards for complying with data collection and behavioral monitoring, making surveillance feel beneficial and enjoyable rather than invasive or controlling. Users receive badges, achievements, social recognition, and other rewards for providing personal data and allowing behavioral monitoring, creating positive associations with surveillance activities. The competitive elements built into many gamified surveillance systems create social pressure for participation and compliance, as refusing to participate means missing out on social recognition and competitive achievements.

The long-term psychological effects of gamified surveillance include the normalization of comprehensive monitoring and control as positive and beneficial activities. Users learn to associate surveillance with personal improvement, social connection, and achievement, making resistance to surveillance feel like self-deprivation rather than privacy protection. This psychological conditioning makes users more willing to accept expanding surveillance and control systems while reducing resistance to invasive monitoring and behavioral modification programs.

The Monetization of Behavioral Modification

The subscription economy has created new business models based on behavioral modification services that explicitly profit from changing user behavior and psychological states rather than providing products or services that users consciously desire. These services generate revenue by creating psychological dependencies and behavioral compulsions that require ongoing subscription payments to maintain. Weight loss subscriptions create artificial dependencies on external monitoring and guidance systems while undermining internal appetite regulation and self-control. Dating app subscriptions manufacture romantic anxiety and artificial scarcity to maintain user dependency on platform-mediated relationship seeking.

The behavioral modification services provided through subscription models often create the problems they claim to solve, ensuring ongoing user dependency and revenue generation. Productivity applications create artificial complexity and dependency around task management while undermining natural organizational skills. Meditation and wellness applications create dependencies on external guidance systems while undermining internal emotional regulation and self-awareness. Social media subscriptions create artificial social anxiety and validation-seeking that require ongoing platform engagement to manage.

The integration of artificial intelligence and machine learning into subscription-based behavioral modification services creates increasingly sophisticated and personalized manipulation systems that adapt to individual user psychology and behavioral patterns. These systems learn what motivates, rewards, and influences each user, creating personalized behavioral modification programs that become more effective over time. The result is the creation of individually tailored addiction and dependency systems that are specifically designed to exploit each user's psychological vulnerabilities and behavioral patterns.

The Surveillance Capitalism Integration

The subscription economy represents an evolution of surveillance capitalism that creates more comprehensive and sustainable methods for extracting value from human behavioral data while providing additional revenue streams through direct user payments. Instead of relying solely on advertising revenue generated from behavioral data, subscription services generate revenue from both user payments and the valuable behavioral data collected through service provision. This dual revenue model creates incentives for increasingly comprehensive data collection and behavioral manipulation that serves both direct monetization and secondary advertising markets.

The combination of subscription payments and behavioral data collection creates particularly valuable datasets for advertising targeting and behavioral analysis, as paying customers provide more detailed and accurate behavioral information than users of free services. Subscription users are more likely to provide accurate personal information, maintain consistent usage patterns, and engage deeply with services, creating higher-quality behavioral data that can be sold to advertisers and other commercial interests. The payment relationship also provides additional psychological commitment that makes users more likely to tolerate invasive data collection and behavioral monitoring.

The global expansion of subscription-based surveillance capitalism creates systematic pressures for all commercial services to adopt comprehensive data collection and behavioral modification capabilities to remain competitive in advertising and behavioral data markets. Even services that don't directly rely on advertising revenue find themselves compelled to collect and monetize user behavioral data to maximize profitability and compete with services that have integrated surveillance and behavioral modification capabilities.

Conclusion

The transformation of the digital economy into a comprehensive system of psychological exploitation and behavioral control represents one of the most sophisticated and invasive forms of human manipulation ever devised. The evolution from simple product advertising to personalized psychological torture systems that exploit individual fears, insecurities, and vulnerabilities for commercial profit has created digital environments that systematically undermine human psychological well-being while generating massive corporate revenues. The realization of Orwell's Room 101 as a commercial service delivered through algorithmic personalization represents not science fiction, but the current reality of digital platform capitalism.

The commodification of human insecurity and psychological distress has created entire industries dedicated to manufacturing and exploiting emotional suffering for commercial gain. The systematic creation of artificial desires, manufactured inadequacies, and amplified anxieties transforms fundamental aspects of human experience into raw materials for corporate profit generation. This represents a fundamental perversion of commercial relationships from meeting human needs to creating and exploiting human suffering, with devastating implications for individual well-being and social cohesion.

The role of social media platforms in amplifying personal fears and anxieties has created artificial social environments that systematically bias human psychology toward distress, conflict, and psychological dysfunction. These platforms don't merely reflect human social dynamics; they actively manipulate them to generate psychological states that serve commercial and control objectives rather than human flourishing. The result is the systematic degradation of human social relationships and psychological well-being in service of algorithmic engagement and advertising revenue optimization.

The subscription model for surveillance and control has created comprehensive monitoring and behavioral modification systems that integrate into essential life activities while generating ongoing revenue from human psychological manipulation. These systems create dependencies and addictions that make resistance increasingly difficult while providing continuous opportunities for data extraction and behavioral influence. The result is the transformation of normal life activities into comprehensive surveillance and control systems that operate through voluntary participation while serving interests other than human well-being.

The psychological impact of these systems extends far beyond individual consumer experiences to encompass fundamental changes in human consciousness, social relationships, and cultural values. Populations subjected to systematic psychological exploitation develop chronic anxiety, depression, materialism, and social dysfunction that undermine the foundations of human flourishing and democratic society. The normalization of psychological manipulation as commercial practice creates cultural acceptance of exploitation and control that extends beyond digital platforms into broader social and political relationships.

The resistance to these systems requires not just individual behavior changes or consumer choices, but fundamental restructuring of economic and technological systems that currently profit from human psychological suffering. The scale and sophistication of modern psychological exploitation systems make individual resistance increasingly difficult, while the integration of these systems into essential services makes complete avoidance practically impossible for most people. New forms of collective action, regulation, and alternative economic organization may be necessary to protect human psychological well-being from systematic commercial exploitation.

The stakes extend beyond immediate concerns about advertising manipulation and privacy violations to fundamental questions about the future of human consciousness and social organization. If comprehensive psychological exploitation and behavioral modification systems become normalized aspects of commercial and social relationships, future generations may lose the cognitive and emotional capabilities necessary for autonomous decision-making, authentic relationships, and democratic participation. The commodification of human psychology represents a threat not just to individual well-being, but to the foundations of human dignity and social organization.

The window of opportunity for resistance to these systems may be closing as the infrastructure of psychological exploitation becomes embedded in essential services and social relationships. The economic advantages gained by organizations that effectively exploit human psychology create competitive pressures that may make psychological manipulation a requirement for commercial survival rather than a choice. The development of alternative economic and technological systems that prioritize human well-being over psychological exploitation may be necessary to preserve the conditions that make authentic human flourishing possible.

The ultimate challenge posed by the emergence of Room 101 as a service is whether human societies can develop institutional arrangements that harness the benefits of digital technology and global connectivity while protecting human psychology from systematic commercial exploitation. This may require accepting less convenience, efficiency, and personalization in digital services in exchange for preserving psychological autonomy and emotional well-being. The alternative is a future where human consciousness itself becomes a commodity to be harvested and manipulated for profit, where authentic desire becomes indistinguishable from manufactured compulsion, and where human relationships become mediated by algorithmic systems designed to exploit rather than enhance human connection and mutual flourishing.

The recognition that personalized advertising represents individualized psychological torture is not hyperbole but accurate description of systems that systematically exploit human vulnerabilities for commercial gain. The scale, sophistication, and invasiveness of these systems exceed traditional forms of psychological manipulation while operating through voluntary participation and market mechanisms that obscure their exploitative nature. The development of resistance to these systems requires not just awareness of their existence, but fundamental reconstruction of economic and social relationships that currently depend on and profit from systematic human psychological exploitation.

PART IV: BREAKING THE DIGITAL CHAINS

Chapter 12: Digital Detox and the Right to Disconnect

In *1984*, Winston Smith's ultimate rebellion wasn't his affair with Julia or his membership in the Brotherhood—it was his simple desire to think his own thoughts, to remember his own memories, and to exist for moments outside the Party's omnipresent control. Today's digital rebels face a remarkably similar challenge: how to reclaim mental space, authentic experience, and genuine human connection in a world designed to capture, commodify, and control every moment of consciousness. The path to digital liberation doesn't require violent revolution or political upheaval—it begins with the radical act of disconnection, the subversive choice to step away from screens, to silence notifications, and to rediscover what it means to be human in an unmediated world.

The movement toward digital detox and technological minimalism represents more than individual lifestyle choices; it constitutes a form of resistance to the fundamental premises of surveillance capitalism and the attention economy. When we choose to limit our digital consumption, protect our personal data, and reclaim our time and attention from algorithmic manipulation, we strike at the economic foundation of the systems that seek to control us. This resistance operates not through confrontation but through withdrawal, not through destruction but through conscious non-participation in the systems of digital exploitation that depend on our voluntary surrender of autonomy and awareness.

PRACTICAL STRATEGIES FOR RECLAIMING DIGITAL AUTONOMY

The Archaeology of Digital Habits

The first step toward digital liberation requires what might be called an "archaeology of digital habits"—a careful excavation and examination of how digital technologies have colonized our daily routines, thought patterns, and behavioral responses. Most people have no accurate understanding of their actual digital consumption patterns, experiencing their relationship with technology through a haze of rationalization and unconscious habit rather than conscious choice and intentional design.

The process of digital habit archaeology begins with measurement and awareness. Digital wellness applications can track screen time, app usage, and pickup frequency, revealing patterns that often shock users with their intensity and compulsiveness. The average smartphone user checks their device 96 times per day, spending over seven hours engaged with digital screens, yet most people vastly underestimate both the frequency and duration of their digital engagement when asked to self-report their behavior.

Beyond quantitative measurement, the archaeology process requires careful attention to the emotional and psychological triggers that drive digital habit formation. Understanding when, where, and why we reach for digital devices reveals the underlying needs and vulnerabilities that technology companies exploit through persuasive design and behavioral manipulation. Boredom, anxiety, loneliness, and uncertainty serve as primary drivers of compulsive digital consumption, suggesting that sustainable digital minimalism requires addressing these underlying emotional patterns rather than simply restricting device access.

The excavation of digital habits often reveals how thoroughly our cognitive processes have been restructured around digital stimulation and validation. Many people discover they've lost the ability to tolerate silence, solitude, or unstimulated mental space without experiencing anxiety or restlessness. This recognition of cognitive dependency often serves as a powerful motivator for pursuing deeper changes in digital consumption patterns and lifestyle design.

Mindful Technology Design and Intentional Consumption

Once individuals understand their current digital consumption patterns, the next phase of reclaiming autonomy involves the intentional redesign of digital environments and consumption habits. This process operates through the principle of "friction design"—deliberately introducing obstacles and delays that interrupt automatic digital consumption and create space for conscious choice and reflection.

Practical friction design techniques include removing social media applications from smartphones while maintaining access through web browsers that require more intentional navigation, using app timers and blocking software that create natural stopping points in digital consumption, and implementing device-free zones and times that protect specific activities and environments from digital intrusion. These techniques don't prevent digital engagement but make it more conscious and intentional by disrupting the seamless, frictionless experience that encourages compulsive consumption.

The curation of digital information environments represents another crucial aspect of intentional consumption. Rather than passively consuming algorithmically curated content designed to maximize engagement and advertising revenue, individuals can take control of their information diet through careful selection of news sources, conscious avoidance of inflammatory or manipulative content, and the cultivation of information sources that serve their actual interests and values rather than commercial optimization algorithms.

Mindful technology design extends beyond consumption patterns to include the conscious selection of technologies and platforms that align with personal values and privacy preferences. This might involve choosing email over social media for communication, selecting privacy-focused search engines and browsers over surveillance-based alternatives, and preferring decentralized or open-source technologies over centralized corporate platforms that commodify user data and behavior.

Digital Sabbaths and Disconnection Practices

The establishment of regular periods of complete digital disconnection represents one of the most powerful strategies for reclaiming autonomy and rediscovering non-digital forms of experience and consciousness. Digital sabbaths—whether implemented daily, weekly, or seasonal—create protected time and space for activities and experiences that cannot be commodified, surveilled, or optimized through digital systems.

The practice of regular digital disconnection often reveals how thoroughly digital mediation has colonized our experience of reality. Many people discover they've lost touch with their own thoughts, emotions, and sensory experiences without constant digital stimulation and distraction. The initial discomfort of digital disconnection—often described as anxiety, boredom, or restlessness—gradually gives way to rediscovered capacities for contemplation, creativity, and genuine present-moment awareness.

Digital sabbaths also provide opportunities for engaging in activities and relationships that require sustained attention and cannot be effectively multitasked with digital consumption. Reading books, having deep conversations, engaging in creative projects, and spending time in natural environments all require forms of attention and presence that are undermined by the fragmented, stimulus-response patterns encouraged by digital consumption.

The social dimensions of digital sabbaths can be particularly powerful, as families and communities that disconnect together often rediscover forms of interaction and connection that have been diminished by constant digital mediation. Shared meals without devices, conversations without interruption, and collaborative activities without documentation create opportunities for authentic relationship and mutual presence that contrast sharply with the performative, mediated interactions that dominate much digital social life.

Privacy Protection and Data Sovereignty

Reclaiming digital autonomy requires not only limiting digital consumption but also protecting personal data and information from extraction and exploitation by surveillance capitalism systems. This involves both technical measures and behavioral changes that reduce data generation and limit corporate and government access to personal information and behavioral patterns.

Technical privacy protection involves the use of privacy-focused browsers, search engines, email providers, and messaging applications that don't track, store, or monetize user data. Virtual private networks (VPNs), ad blockers, and tracker blocking extensions can significantly reduce data collection by websites and advertising networks, while encrypted communication tools can protect personal communications from surveillance and interception.

Beyond technical tools, privacy protection requires behavioral changes that reduce data generation and sharing. This includes minimizing social media use, avoiding loyalty programs and data collection schemes, paying for services with cash or cryptocurrency rather than credit cards that create detailed transaction records, and carefully managing the personal information shared with businesses, organizations, and government agencies.

The concept of "data sovereignty" suggests that individuals should maintain control over their personal information and have the right to determine how it is collected, stored, used, and shared. This principle extends beyond current legal frameworks to encompass a broader vision of individual autonomy and self-determination that includes control over one's digital identity and information footprint.

Creating Analog Alternatives and Real-World Engagement

Digital minimalism becomes most sustainable when it's supported by rich, meaningful alternatives to digital consumption and engagement. This requires the cultivation of analog activities, relationships, and experiences that provide the social connection, intellectual stimulation, and creative expression that people often seek through digital platforms.

The development of local, in-person communities represents a crucial alternative to digital social networking. This might involve participating in neighborhood organizations, joining hobby groups or sports leagues, attending religious or philosophical gatherings, or engaging in volunteer work that connects individuals with their immediate physical and social environment. These real-world connections often provide deeper satisfaction and meaning than digital relationships while developing social skills and emotional capacities that are atrophied by primarily digital interaction.

Creative and intellectual pursuits that require sustained attention and cannot be easily digitized provide particularly powerful alternatives to digital consumption. Learning musical instruments, practicing visual arts, engaging in craft work, gardening, cooking, and other hands-on activities create forms of flow and engagement that contrast sharply with the passive consumption and fragmented attention that characterize much digital experience.

The cultivation of contemplative practices—meditation, prayer, journaling, solitary walks—provides tools for managing the anxiety, restlessness, and emotional dysregulation that often drives compulsive digital consumption. These practices develop capacities for self-awareness, emotional regulation, and mental clarity that support more conscious and intentional relationships with technology.

THE GROWING MOVEMENT TOWARD TECHNOLOGICAL MINIMALISM

Philosophical Foundations of Digital Minimalism

The technological minimalism movement draws from broader philosophical traditions that emphasize the importance of conscious choice, intentional living, and resistance to consumer culture's pressure for endless acquisition and consumption. Digital minimalism applies these principles specifically to technology, arguing that individuals should be highly selective about which technologies they allow into their lives and how they use them.

The philosophical foundation of digital minimalism rests on the recognition that technology is not neutral but actively shapes human behavior, consciousness, and social relationships in ways that may conflict with individual values and wellbeing. Rather than accepting technological change as inevitable progress that must be embraced, digital minimalists assert the right to make conscious choices about which technologies serve their goals and values and which detract from human flourishing.

The movement emphasizes quality over quantity in technological adoption, suggesting that fewer, more carefully chosen technologies used with intention and purpose provide greater value than the endless proliferation of gadgets, applications, and digital services that characterize contemporary consumer culture. This principle challenges the assumption that more technology automatically creates better outcomes and instead prioritizes the conscious curation of technological tools that genuinely improve life without creating dependency or distraction.

Digital minimalism also draws from critiques of consumer capitalism that highlight how marketing and product design manipulate human psychology to create artificial needs and compulsive consumption patterns. By applying these critiques to technology, digital minimalists develop resistance to the persuasive design and marketing techniques that technology companies use to encourage addictive use and maximize engagement.

Case Studies in Successful Digital Minimalism

The practice of digital minimalism has produced numerous case studies of individuals and families who have successfully reduced their digital consumption while maintaining or improving their quality of life, productivity, and social relationships. These examples provide practical models for implementing minimalist principles and demonstrate the feasibility and benefits of conscious technology use.

Professional case studies often involve individuals who have achieved career success while maintaining strict boundaries around digital consumption. This includes entrepreneurs who delegate social media management to others, writers who compose on analog tools before transferring work to digital formats, and executives who implement email sabbaths and device-free meeting policies. These examples challenge the assumption that professional success requires constant digital connectivity and availability.

Family case studies demonstrate how household digital minimalism can improve relationship quality, child development, and family dynamics. Families that implement device-free meal times, bedrooms without screens, and regular outdoor activities often report improved communication, reduced conflict, and stronger family bonds. Children raised in digitally minimalist households often show enhanced creativity, longer attention spans, and better social skills compared to peers with unlimited digital access.

Community case studies illustrate how groups and organizations can implement minimalist principles to improve collective outcomes. Schools that restrict smartphone access report improved academic performance and social interaction among students. Workplaces that implement focused work periods without digital communication often see increased productivity and job satisfaction. Religious and spiritual communities that emphasize analog practices and limit digital mediation frequently demonstrate stronger community bonds and spiritual development.

The diversity of successful digital minimalism implementations across different demographics, professions, and life circumstances demonstrates that these principles can be adapted to various contexts and constraints. Success doesn't require complete technology rejection but rather conscious, selective use that prioritizes human values and wellbeing over technological convenience and digital stimulation.

The Economics of Attention and Consumer Resistance

Digital minimalism represents a form of consumer resistance to the attention economy that challenges the fundamental business models of surveillance capitalism and advertising-supported digital services. When individuals limit their digital consumption and protect their personal data, they reduce the economic value they provide to technology companies and advertising networks.

The economic impact of widespread digital minimalism adoption would be profound, potentially undermining the revenue models that support free digital services by reducing user engagement and data collection opportunities. This creates economic incentives for technology companies to resist minimalist movements through product design, marketing, and policy advocacy that encourages increased rather than decreased digital consumption.

However, consumer resistance to surveillance capitalism and addictive technology design has also created market opportunities for privacy-focused and minimalist technology products. Companies that prioritize user privacy, limit data collection, and design products for conscious rather than compulsive use have found growing demand among consumers seeking alternatives to mainstream technology offerings.

The tension between minimalist consumer preferences and surveillance capitalist business models may drive broader changes in technology industry practices and business models. As consumers become more aware of the costs of surveillance and digital addiction, market pressure may encourage the development of technology products and services that genuinely serve user interests rather than exploiting psychological vulnerabilities for profit.

Digital Minimalism and Mental Health

Research on digital minimalism practices consistently demonstrates significant mental health benefits, including reduced anxiety and depression, improved sleep quality, enhanced focus and productivity, and greater life satisfaction. These outcomes suggest that excessive digital consumption contributes to widespread mental health challenges and that conscious limitation of digital engagement can provide therapeutic benefits.

The mental health benefits of digital minimalism appear to operate through multiple mechanisms, including improved sleep hygiene through reduced screen time before bed, decreased social comparison and FOMO (fear of missing out) through limited social media use, enhanced present-moment awareness through reduced digital distraction, and improved self-efficacy through conscious technology choice rather than compulsive consumption.

Digital minimalism practices often complement traditional mental health interventions and may be particularly effective for individuals whose mental health challenges are exacerbated by digital consumption patterns. The integration of minimalist principles into therapeutic approaches represents a growing area of clinical innovation and research.

The collective mental health implications of widespread digital minimalism adoption could be substantial, potentially reducing population-level rates of anxiety, depression, and attention disorders that have increased dramatically during the smartphone and social media era. This suggests that digital minimalism represents not just individual lifestyle choices but potential public health interventions.

Cultural Resistance and Social Norms

The practice of digital minimalism often requires resistance to social norms and cultural expectations that assume constant digital connectivity and availability. Individuals who limit their digital engagement may face social pressure, professional challenges, and cultural marginalization that make minimalist practices difficult to maintain.

The social dimensions of digital minimalism highlight how thoroughly digital technologies have been integrated into contemporary social expectations and relationship norms. Opting out of social media, limiting smartphone use, or implementing digital boundaries can create friction in personal and professional relationships that depend on digital mediation and constant availability.

However, the growing awareness of digital addiction and surveillance capitalism has begun to shift cultural norms around digital consumption, creating more social acceptance for minimalist practices and digital boundaries. Public discussions about screen time, social media addiction, and digital privacy have made conscious technology use seem reasonable rather than eccentric or antisocial.

The development of digital minimalism as a cultural movement rather than individual practice creates opportunities for collective resistance to surveillance capitalism and attention economy manipulation. Communities that embrace minimalist principles can provide social support and alternative norms that make individual minimalist practices more sustainable and socially acceptable.

LEGAL FRAMEWORKS FOR DIGITAL RIGHTS AND PRIVACY PROTECTION

The Evolution of Privacy Law in the Digital Age

Legal frameworks for privacy protection have struggled to keep pace with the rapid development and deployment of digital surveillance technologies, creating regulatory gaps that allow extensive data collection and behavioral manipulation without meaningful legal constraints. The evolution of privacy law reflects ongoing tensions between individual rights, commercial interests, and government surveillance capabilities in democratic societies.

Traditional privacy law was developed for physical rather than digital environments and focuses on protection from intrusion and disclosure rather than the data collection and algorithmic manipulation that characterize contemporary surveillance systems. This creates fundamental misalignments between legal protections and actual privacy threats that limit the effectiveness of existing regulatory frameworks.

The global nature of digital surveillance creates additional challenges for national privacy law, as data collection and processing often occur across multiple jurisdictions with different legal standards and enforcement capabilities. This jurisdictional complexity allows companies to forum shop for the most permissive regulatory environments while making enforcement of privacy protections extremely difficult.

The technical complexity of digital surveillance systems creates challenges for legal frameworks that require lawmakers and judges to understand sophisticated technologies in order to craft and enforce appropriate regulations. The rapid pace of technological change often outpaces the deliberative processes of democratic lawmaking, creating persistent regulatory lag that leaves emerging surveillance capabilities unregulated.

The European General Data Protection Regulation (GDPR) Model

The European Union's General Data Protection Regulation represents the most comprehensive attempt to create legal frameworks for protecting individual privacy and data rights in the digital age. GDPR establishes principles of data minimization, purpose limitation, and individual consent that challenge many of the fundamental practices of surveillance capitalism and advertising-based business models.

GDPR's emphasis on individual control over personal data includes rights to access, correct, delete, and port personal information that give individuals unprecedented legal authority over their digital footprints. The regulation also establishes strong consent requirements that prevent companies from collecting and processing personal data without explicit, informed permission from users.

The extraterritorial application of GDPR to any company that processes data from EU residents has created global impact that extends far beyond European borders. Companies worldwide have had to modify their data practices to comply with GDPR requirements, creating a "Brussels Effect" where European privacy standards influence global technology practices.

However, the implementation and enforcement of GDPR has revealed significant limitations in regulatory approaches to digital privacy. Many companies have found ways to maintain surveillance-based business models while technically complying with GDPR requirements through consent manipulation, data processor arrangements, and jurisdictional arbitrage that limits the regulation's practical effectiveness.

The California Consumer Privacy Act (CCPA) and State-Level Innovation

The California Consumer Privacy Act represents the most significant state-level privacy legislation in the United States and demonstrates how subnational jurisdictions can drive privacy protection in the absence of comprehensive federal action. CCPA establishes consumer rights to know what personal information is collected, to delete personal information, and to opt out of the sale of personal information.

The California model reflects a different approach to privacy protection than GDPR, emphasizing consumer choice and market-based solutions rather than fundamental rights and data minimization principles. This approach may be more compatible with American legal and cultural traditions but may also provide weaker protection against surveillance capitalism practices.

The success of state-level privacy legislation like CCPA has encouraged similar laws in other states and may eventually create pressure for federal privacy legislation that harmonizes different state requirements. However, the patchwork of different state privacy laws also creates compliance complexity that may favor large technology companies with resources to manage multiple regulatory frameworks.

The limitations of state-level privacy legislation include jurisdictional constraints that limit enforcement authority and the possibility of federal preemption that could weaken state protections. The effectiveness of state privacy laws also depends on enforcement resources and political will that may vary across jurisdictions and over time.

Emerging Digital Rights Frameworks

Beyond privacy protection, emerging legal frameworks are beginning to address broader questions of digital rights and technological autonomy. These frameworks recognize that digital technologies affect not only privacy but fundamental questions of human agency, democratic participation, and social organization that require comprehensive rights-based approaches.

The concept of "digital dignity" encompasses individual rights to autonomy, self-determination, and freedom from manipulation in digital environments. This framework suggests that individuals should have legal protection not only from data collection but from algorithmic manipulation, addictive design, and other practices that undermine human agency and wellbeing.

Algorithmic accountability frameworks seek to establish legal requirements for transparency, fairness, and human oversight in automated decision-making systems that affect individual opportunities and outcomes. These frameworks recognize that algorithmic systems can perpetuate and amplify discrimination, bias, and unfair treatment in ways that require legal remedies and regulatory oversight.

Rights to explanation and algorithmic transparency would require companies to provide individuals with understandable explanations of how automated systems make decisions that affect them, enabling informed consent and meaningful appeal processes. These rights challenge the "black box" nature of many algorithmic systems and could require significant changes in system design and business practices.

Children's Digital Rights and Developmental Protection

The recognition that children and adolescents are particularly vulnerable to digital manipulation and surveillance has led to emerging legal frameworks specifically designed to protect young people's digital rights and developmental needs. These frameworks acknowledge that consent-based privacy models are inadequate for protecting children who lack the cognitive development necessary for informed decision-making about complex digital privacy issues.

Children's digital rights frameworks often emphasize developmental considerations that prioritize wellbeing over commercial interests, including restrictions on data collection from minors, limitations on persuasive design and addictive features in products used by children, and requirements for age-appropriate design that considers developmental psychology and child safety.

The implementation of children's digital rights faces significant challenges related to age verification, parental consent, and balancing protection with access to beneficial digital services. These technical and practical challenges highlight the broader difficulties of implementing rights-based approaches to digital technology regulation.

International cooperation on children's digital rights may be particularly important given the global nature of digital services and the shared concern across cultures for child protection and development. However, different cultural and legal approaches to children's rights, parental authority, and government regulation create challenges for developing harmonized international frameworks.

The Right to Disconnect and Temporal Sovereignty

Emerging legal frameworks are beginning to recognize "right to disconnect" principles that protect individuals from obligations to remain constantly available for digital communication and engagement. These rights acknowledge that the temporal colonization of life by digital technologies can undermine human wellbeing and work-life balance in ways that require legal protection.

Right to disconnect legislation typically establishes legal protections for employees who choose not to respond to work-related digital communications outside of regular work hours, preventing employer retaliation and establishing boundaries around digital availability expectations. These laws recognize that constant connectivity can create exploitative work conditions and undermine the leisure time necessary for human flourishing.

The concept of "temporal sovereignty"—the right to control one's own time and attention—suggests broader legal frameworks that could protect individuals from algorithmic manipulation of attention and time use. These frameworks would recognize time and attention as fundamental human resources that should not be exploited without consent and compensation.

The enforcement and implementation of right to disconnect legislation faces challenges related to global business operations, technological integration of work and personal life, and cultural expectations around availability and responsiveness. The effectiveness of these laws may depend on broader cultural shifts around work-life balance and digital consumption norms.

CORPORATE RESPONSES TO PRIVACY DEMANDS AND REGULATORY PRESSURE

Privacy Theater and Compliance Strategies

Corporate responses to privacy demands and regulatory pressure have often prioritized the appearance of privacy protection over substantive changes to surveillance-based business models. This "privacy theater" involves implementing compliance measures that satisfy legal requirements while maintaining data collection and behavioral manipulation practices through technical workarounds and business model innovations.

Common privacy theater techniques include consent manipulation through dark patterns that make privacy-protective choices difficult or confusing, data processor arrangements that technically comply with regulations while maintaining effective control over data use, and the development of new data collection methods that operate outside existing regulatory frameworks.

The complexity of privacy regulations creates opportunities for legal arbitrage where companies comply with the letter of the law while violating its spirit, maintaining surveillance capabilities through technical compliance strategies that preserve business model fundamentals. This approach allows companies to claim privacy leadership while continuing practices that undermine user privacy and autonomy.

The effectiveness of privacy theater in maintaining public confidence while preserving surveillance capabilities demonstrates the limitations of regulatory approaches that focus on technical compliance rather than fundamental changes to business models and power relationships. This suggests the need for more comprehensive approaches to corporate accountability and transparency.

Apple's Privacy Marketing and Competitive Differentiation

Apple's adoption of privacy as a key marketing and competitive differentiation strategy represents a significant shift in how major technology companies position themselves relative to surveillance capitalism and data collection practices. Apple's privacy marketing emphasizes user control, data minimization, and protection from tracking while criticizing competitors' surveillance-based business models.

Apple's privacy initiatives include technical measures like App Tracking Transparency that requires user permission for cross-app tracking, on-device processing that reduces cloud data collection, and differential privacy techniques that protect individual privacy while enabling aggregate analytics. These measures represent genuine improvements in user privacy protection while serving Apple's competitive interests against advertising-based competitors.

However, Apple's privacy positioning also serves strategic business interests that may not align with comprehensive privacy protection. Apple's control over its platform ecosystem allows it to limit third-party data collection while maintaining its own data collection capabilities, creating competitive advantages rather than fundamental privacy improvements.

The limitations of Apple's privacy approach include continued participation in surveillance capitalism through advertising services, data collection practices that may conflict with privacy marketing claims, and platform control that limits user choice and technical sovereignty. This demonstrates how corporate privacy initiatives may provide partial improvements while maintaining fundamental power imbalances.

Google and Meta's Adaptation Strategies

Google and Meta, whose business models depend heavily on data collection and targeted advertising, have developed adaptation strategies that seek to maintain surveillance capabilities while responding to regulatory pressure and consumer privacy demands. These strategies involve technical innovations and business model modifications that preserve revenue streams while addressing privacy concerns.

Google's Privacy Sandbox initiative represents an attempt to maintain targeted advertising capabilities while eliminating third-party cookies and other traditional tracking technologies. This approach would centralize advertising data collection and targeting within Google's ecosystem while providing privacy benefits compared to current cross-site tracking practices.

Meta's focus on encryption and messaging privacy represents an attempt to protect user communications while maintaining data collection capabilities through platform features, behavioral analysis, and integrated advertising systems. This approach allows Meta to claim privacy leadership while preserving the business model fundamentals that depend on user data collection and analysis.

The effectiveness of these adaptation strategies in truly protecting user privacy remains debated, with critics arguing that they represent efforts to maintain surveillance capabilities through new technical means rather than fundamental changes to surveillance capitalism business models. The evaluation of these approaches requires ongoing scrutiny of implementation details and actual privacy outcomes.

The Emergence of Privacy-Focused Business Models

Consumer demand for privacy protection and regulatory pressure have created market opportunities for companies that adopt business models based on privacy protection rather than surveillance capitalism. These companies demonstrate the feasibility of profitable technology businesses that prioritize user privacy and data minimization.

Privacy-focused companies often use subscription-based rather than advertising-based business models, aligning company incentives with user privacy interests rather than creating conflicts between revenue generation and privacy protection. Examples include privacy-focused search engines, email providers, and messaging applications that charge users directly rather than monetizing user data.

The success of privacy-focused companies creates competitive pressure on surveillance capitalism companies to improve their privacy practices or risk losing market share to alternatives that better serve user interests. This market pressure may prove more effective than regulatory compliance in driving meaningful improvements in corporate privacy practices.

However, the scalability and long-term viability of privacy-focused business models faces challenges related to consumer willingness to pay for privacy, network effects that favor larger platforms, and competitive responses from surveillance capitalism companies that may use regulatory arbitrage or technical innovation to maintain advantages.

Corporate Lobbying and Regulatory Capture

Technology companies have invested heavily in lobbying and policy advocacy designed to shape privacy regulations in ways that serve their business interests while limiting meaningful constraints on surveillance capitalism practices. This corporate political influence operates through direct lobbying, industry association advocacy, and the funding of research and think tanks that support industry positions.

Corporate lobbying strategies often focus on shaping regulatory definitions and implementation details that can significantly affect the practical impact of privacy legislation. By influencing technical standards, enforcement procedures, and regulatory exemptions, companies can limit the effectiveness of privacy regulations while maintaining public support for privacy protection in principle.

The revolving door between technology companies and regulatory agencies creates additional opportunities for corporate influence over privacy policy development and enforcement. Former industry executives who join regulatory agencies may bring industry perspectives that favor business interests over privacy protection, while regulatory officials who join industry may provide inside knowledge of regulatory vulnerabilities.

The global nature of technology companies creates opportunities for regulatory arbitrage where companies can threaten to relocate operations or limit services in jurisdictions with strong privacy regulations. This economic leverage can pressure lawmakers to weaken privacy protections in order to maintain economic benefits from technology company presence.

Industry Self-Regulation and Standards Development

The technology industry has developed various self-regulatory initiatives and technical standards that aim to address privacy concerns while avoiding more restrictive government regulation. These industry-led efforts often emphasize technical solutions and voluntary commitments rather than legally binding requirements or fundamental business model changes.

Industry privacy standards and certification programs provide frameworks for companies to demonstrate privacy compliance and best practices while maintaining flexibility in implementation and business model design. These programs may provide genuine privacy benefits while also serving as defensive measures against more restrictive regulatory approaches.

The effectiveness of industry self-regulation depends on enforcement mechanisms, transparency requirements, and accountability measures that may be limited compared to government regulation. Without meaningful penalties for non-compliance or mechanisms for independent oversight, voluntary privacy commitments may provide limited protection for user privacy interests.

The participation of surveillance capitalism companies in privacy standards development creates potential conflicts of interest where industry standards may be designed to accommodate existing business practices rather than establish meaningful privacy protections. This suggests the need for independent oversight and verification of industry privacy initiatives.

THE PSYCHOLOGY OF DIGITAL LIBERATION

Overcoming Learned Digital Helplessness

The process of reclaiming digital autonomy often requires overcoming what might be called "learned digital helplessness"—the internalized belief that individuals have no meaningful control over their relationship with technology and that surveillance and manipulation are inevitable aspects of modern life. This psychological barrier prevents many people from taking action to protect their privacy and limit their digital consumption even when they understand the costs and risks involved.

Learned digital helplessness develops through repeated experiences of technological change that seems to happen without individual choice or input, privacy policies and terms of service that are incomprehensible and non-negotiable, and digital systems that are designed to maximize engagement and minimize user control. These experiences teach people that they are powerless consumers rather than autonomous agents capable of making meaningful choices about their technological environment.

Overcoming learned digital helplessness requires developing what psychologists call "digital self-efficacy"—the belief that individuals can understand, control, and make meaningful choices about their technological environment. This involves both practical skill development and psychological work to rebuild confidence in personal agency and decision-making capability.

The development of digital self-efficacy often begins with small, manageable changes that demonstrate personal control and create positive feedback loops. Successfully implementing simple privacy protections, reducing screen time, or choosing alternative technologies can build confidence and motivation for larger changes in digital consumption and privacy protection.

The Social Psychology of Digital Minimalism

The practice of digital minimalism often requires navigating social pressures and relationship challenges that arise when individuals choose to limit their digital engagement while living in digitally saturated social environments. This creates psychological stress and social friction that can undermine minimalist practices and create isolation from digital-native social networks.

The social psychology of digital minimalism involves managing others' expectations about availability and responsiveness, finding ways to maintain important relationships without full participation in digital communication norms, and dealing with social exclusion from digitally mediated social activities and networks. These challenges require developing new social skills and relationship strategies that may be unfamiliar to people who developed their social identities within digital environments.

The formation of communities and social networks that support digital minimalism practices provides crucial social resources for maintaining lifestyle changes that conflict with mainstream digital consumption norms. These communities can provide practical advice, emotional support, and alternative social activities that reduce the isolation and social costs of digital minimalism.

The intergenerational dimensions of digital minimalism create particular challenges for families where different generations have different relationships with technology and different understandings of appropriate digital consumption and privacy protection. Managing these differences requires communication, compromise, and respect for different approaches to technology use.

Cognitive Rewiring and Attention Recovery

The practice of digital minimalism often involves a process of cognitive rewiring that reverses some of the neurological changes associated with heavy digital consumption and attention fragmentation. This recovery process can be challenging and uncomfortable as the brain readapts to longer attention spans, reduced stimulation, and different patterns of reward and engagement.

Attention recovery typically involves an initial period of discomfort as individuals experience boredom, restlessness, and anxiety when confronted with unstimulated mental space and slower-paced activities. This discomfort reflects the brain's adaptation to high-stimulation digital environments and gradually diminishes as cognitive patterns readjust to analog activities and experiences.

The development of sustained attention capabilities through digital minimalism practices often reveals how thoroughly digital consumption had fragmented cognitive processes and undermined the deep focus necessary for complex thinking, creative work, and meaningful relationship building. The recovery of these capabilities can be profoundly rewarding and motivating for continued minimalist practices.

The timeline and extent of cognitive recovery from digital overconsumption varies significantly among individuals and appears to depend on factors including age, duration of heavy digital use, and the availability of engaging alternative activities. Some changes may occur within days or weeks, while others may require months or years of sustained practice.

Identity Reconstruction and Authentic Self-Discovery

The process of digital detox often involves a profound process of identity reconstruction as individuals discover aspects of themselves that had been obscured or suppressed by constant digital mediation and performance pressure. This self-discovery can be both liberating and disorienting as people reconnect with interests, values, and ways of being that don't translate easily to digital environments.

The removal of constant social media feedback and digital validation can initially create identity uncertainty as individuals lose external reference points for self-worth and social identity. This period of identity confusion often precedes the development of more internally directed and authentic forms of self-understanding and self-validation.

The recovery of private mental space and internal dialogue through digital minimalism often reveals how thoroughly public digital performance had replaced private self-reflection and authentic self-expression. The rediscovery of internal mental life can be profound and transformative, providing foundation for more authentic relationships and creative expression.

The integration of insights gained through digital detox into sustainable lifestyle practices requires ongoing attention to maintaining boundaries and practices that protect authentic self-development from re-colonization by digital performance pressure and social comparison.

CONCLUSION: THE POSSIBILITY OF TECHNOLOGICAL FREEDOM

The movement toward digital detox and technological minimalism represents more than individual lifestyle optimization—it constitutes a fundamental challenge to the premises of surveillance capitalism and the inevitability of digital domination over human consciousness and social organization. Every person who successfully reclaims their attention, protects their privacy, and chooses conscious engagement with technology demonstrates that alternatives to digital servitude remain possible and viable.

The practical strategies, legal frameworks, and corporate responses examined in this chapter reveal both the possibilities and limitations of individual and regulatory approaches to digital liberation. While personal digital minimalism practices can provide significant benefits for mental health, productivity, and life satisfaction, they cannot address the systemic issues that arise from surveillance capitalism's business models and the concentration of digital power in the hands of a few global technology corporations.

The legal evolution toward stronger privacy protections and digital rights represents important progress in establishing frameworks for technological accountability and individual autonomy. However, the implementation challenges, corporate resistance, and jurisdictional limitations of current regulatory approaches suggest that legal solutions alone are insufficient for addressing the full scope of digital authoritarianism and technological manipulation.

Corporate responses to privacy demands demonstrate both the potential for market-driven improvements in digital privacy and the limitations of relying on corporate self-regulation to protect fundamental human interests. While competitive pressure and consumer demand have driven some genuine improvements in privacy protection, the fundamental business model conflicts between surveillance capitalism and user privacy remain largely unresolved.

The psychological dimensions of digital liberation—overcoming learned helplessness, managing social pressure, recovering cognitive capabilities, and reconstructing authentic identity—highlight the profound personal work required to break free from digital dependency and manipulation. These individual psychological processes are essential for sustainable change but require social and cultural support that may be difficult to maintain in digitally saturated environments.

Perhaps most importantly, the digital detox movement has demonstrated that technological determinism is false—that human beings retain the capacity to make conscious choices about their relationship with technology despite decades of persuasive design and behavioral manipulation. The millions of people who have successfully reduced their digital consumption, protected their privacy, and reclaimed their attention prove that resistance to digital domination remains possible.

The challenge moving forward involves scaling these individual successes into collective movements that can challenge the systemic power structures underlying digital authoritarianism. This requires connecting personal digital minimalism practices with broader political movements for technological accountability, economic justice, and democratic control over digital infrastructure and platform governance.

The right to disconnect represents more than a luxury for the digitally privileged—it constitutes a fundamental human right to mental privacy, temporal sovereignty, and conscious choice about the technological mediation of human experience. The establishment and protection of this right requires ongoing vigilance, collective action, and the continued development of alternative technologies and social systems that serve human flourishing rather than corporate profit.

In breaking our digital chains, we do more than improve our individual lives—we preserve the possibility of human freedom for future generations. The children growing up today will inherit either a world where human consciousness is completely commodified and controlled by algorithmic systems, or a world where digital technologies serve human purposes and values. The choices we make about our own digital consumption and the political and cultural movements we support will largely determine which future emerges.

The path forward requires what might be called "technological wisdom"—the ability to distinguish between technologies that genuinely serve human flourishing and those that exploit human psychology for corporate or political gain. This wisdom cannot be achieved through pure individual effort but requires collective learning, cultural development, and institutional support that helps entire societies make better choices about technological adoption and implementation.

The digital detox movement has shown us that even in the most thoroughly surveilled and manipulated digital environments, the spark of human autonomy and conscious choice remains alive. Every notification silenced, every privacy setting adjusted, every moment of authentic offline connection represents a small act of rebellion against the systems that seek to reduce us to data points and advertising targets.

The screen may be watching us, but in choosing to look away—even briefly, even imperfectly—we assert our fundamental humanity and preserve the possibility that future generations might know what it means to be human in ways that cannot be quantified, optimized, or sold. In an age of digital chains, the simple act of disconnection becomes the most radical form of resistance, and the reclamation of our attention becomes the foundation of all other freedoms.

The revolution will not be digitized. It will happen in the quiet moments when we remember who we are without the mediation of machines, in the relationships we build without algorithmic assistance, in the thoughts we think without digital amplification. It will happen person by person, choice by choice, disconnection by disconnection, until we remember what it means to be free.

Chapter 13: Building Alternative Futures

Decentralized Technologies and Their Potential for Liberation

After twelve chapters documenting how digital technology has reproduced and amplified the surveillance state dynamics of Orwell's "1984," it might seem that technological determinism has trapped humanity in an irreversible slide toward digital authoritarianism. Yet this pessimistic narrative ignores a crucial reality: the same technological innovations that enable unprecedented surveillance and control also contain the seeds of genuine liberation and democratic empowerment. Decentralized technologies—systems that distribute power across networks rather than concentrating it in central authorities—offer pathways toward digital futures that could fulfill rather than betray the original promise of networked communication.

The potential for liberation through decentralized technologies lies not in their technical specifications but in their political possibilities. Unlike centralized systems that require users to trust powerful intermediaries with their data, communications, and digital lives, decentralized systems enable peer-to-peer interaction that eliminates single points of control and failure. These technologies don't just provide alternative technical architectures—they enable alternative social and economic relationships that could fundamentally transform the power dynamics underlying digital society.

However, the liberatory potential of decentralized technologies is neither automatic nor inevitable. The same technologies that could democratize power can be co-opted by existing power structures, used to create new forms of exploitation, or simply fail to achieve widespread adoption due to usability challenges and network effects. The crucial question is not whether decentralized technologies are inherently liberating, but whether they can be developed and deployed in ways that actually serve democratic values and human flourishing rather than merely providing technological alternatives that reproduce existing power relationships in new forms.

The Architecture of Digital Democracy

Decentralized technologies embody fundamentally different assumptions about power, trust, and social organization than the centralized systems that currently dominate digital life. Where centralized systems require users to trust powerful intermediaries—governments, corporations, or other institutions—decentralized systems distribute trust across networks of peers who can verify each other's actions without relying on central authorities. This shift from hierarchical trust to distributed verification creates possibilities for democratic participation that go far beyond traditional electoral politics.

The democratic potential of decentralized architectures lies in their ability to make power relationships transparent and contestable rather than opaque and imposed. In centralized systems, algorithmic decisions are typically made by private companies or government agencies without meaningful public input or oversight. Users experience these algorithmic decisions as natural features of technological systems rather than recognizing them as policy choices that could be made differently. Decentralized systems can make algorithmic decision-making processes transparent and subject to community governance, enabling genuine democratic participation in technological governance.

Perhaps most importantly, decentralized architectures can eliminate the economic incentives that drive surveillance capitalism by removing the need for centralized data collection and analysis. When users can interact directly with each other without intermediaries, there is no natural point for comprehensive data collection and behavioral analysis. This doesn't eliminate surveillance entirely—determined surveillance actors can still monitor decentralized networks—but it removes the automatic surveillance that emerges from centralized architectures and business models.

Blockchain and Distributed Consensus

Blockchain technologies represent the most visible example of decentralized systems that enable coordination without central authority. By creating distributed ledgers that record transactions across networks of computers, blockchain systems eliminate the need for trusted intermediaries in economic transactions, data storage, and identity verification. This technological capability has profound political implications because it enables economic and social coordination that doesn't depend on existing power structures.

The liberatory potential of blockchain technologies lies not in their current applications—which often reproduce existing economic relationships in digital form—but in their capacity to enable new forms of economic organization that could challenge surveillance capitalism and centralized control. Blockchain systems can enable peer-to-peer economic transactions without intermediaries, creating possibilities for economic relationships that don't depend on surveillance-based business models. They can enable decentralized identity systems that give users control over their personal information rather than requiring them to surrender identity management to centralized authorities.

However, blockchain technologies also demonstrate how decentralized systems can be co-opted by existing power structures or used to create new forms of exploitation. Many blockchain applications simply digitize existing financial relationships rather than creating genuinely alternative economic arrangements. Cryptocurrency systems often reproduce existing wealth inequalities in digital form. The energy consumption required for some blockchain systems creates environmental costs that may outweigh their democratic benefits. The key challenge is developing blockchain applications that actually serve democratic values rather than merely providing technological novelty.

Mesh Networks and Communication Freedom

Mesh networking technologies offer another pathway toward decentralized communication that could break the stranglehold of centralized internet service providers and communication platforms. In mesh networks, each device serves as both a communication endpoint and a relay point for other devices, creating resilient communication networks that can function without centralized infrastructure. This technological capability has obvious applications for communities that lack reliable internet access, but it also has profound implications for communication freedom and resistance to censorship.

The democratic potential of mesh networking lies in its capacity to enable communication that doesn't depend on centralized infrastructure controlled by governments or corporations. Mesh networks can provide internet access in areas where traditional infrastructure is unavailable or unreliable. They can enable communication during emergencies when centralized infrastructure fails. Most importantly, they can provide communication capabilities that are resistant to censorship and surveillance because they don't depend on centralized control points that can be monitored or shut down.

Mesh networking also enables community-controlled communication infrastructure that operates according to community values rather than corporate or government priorities. Communities can develop mesh networks that prioritize privacy protection, democratic governance, and local economic development rather than data extraction and behavioral manipulation. These community networks can serve as testing grounds for alternative models of technological governance that could eventually scale to larger populations.

Distributed Storage and Information Freedom

Centralized data storage creates single points of control that enable comprehensive surveillance and information manipulation. Distributed storage systems—where information is stored across networks of computers rather than in centralized data centers—offer alternatives that could preserve information freedom while maintaining the benefits of digital information sharing. These systems don't just provide technical alternatives to centralized storage—they enable fundamentally different relationships between users and their information.

Distributed storage systems can give users genuine control over their personal information by eliminating the need to trust centralized storage providers with sensitive data. Users can store encrypted information across networks of computers while maintaining the keys necessary to access that information, ensuring that no single entity can access their data without permission. This technological capability could eliminate the surveillance business models that depend on centralized data collection and analysis.

Perhaps most importantly, distributed storage systems can preserve information against censorship and historical manipulation by making it impossible for any single entity to control or alter stored information. Distributed storage networks can preserve historical records, research data, and cultural information against attempts at censorship or revisionist history. They can enable information sharing that doesn't depend on the continued cooperation of centralized authorities who might change their policies or be pressured by governments or other powerful actors.

The Role of Open-Source Software in Preserving Freedom

Open-source software development represents one of the most successful examples of decentralized collaboration and democratic governance in digital technology. Unlike proprietary software developed by corporations for profit, open-source software is developed collaboratively by communities of programmers who share their code freely and subject it to public scrutiny. This collaborative development model doesn't just produce software—it demonstrates alternative forms of technological governance that prioritize transparency, democratic participation, and user empowerment over corporate profit and control.

The freedom-preserving potential of open-source software lies in its transparency and modifiability. Users can examine the source code of open-source software to understand exactly what it does, verify that it doesn't contain surveillance or manipulation features, and modify it to better serve their needs. This transparency eliminates the need to trust software developers with sensitive information or accept unwanted features that serve developers' interests rather than users' needs. Open-source software puts users in control of their technological environment rather than making them dependent on corporate decisions about software functionality.

However, open-source software faces significant challenges in achieving widespread adoption and maintaining its independence from corporate influence. Many users find open-source software more difficult to use than commercial alternatives, limiting its appeal to technically sophisticated users who understand its benefits. Corporate interests increasingly influence open-source development through funding, employment of key developers, and integration of open-source components into proprietary systems. The challenge is ensuring that open-source development continues to serve democratic values rather than being co-opted by the same corporate interests it was designed to circumvent.

The Philosophy of Software Freedom

The open-source software movement is grounded in a philosophy of software freedom that treats access to source code as a fundamental right rather than a commercial privilege. This philosophy, articulated most clearly by Richard Stallman and the Free Software Foundation, argues that users should have the freedom to run software for any purpose, study how it works, redistribute copies to help others, and improve the software for the benefit of the entire community. These freedoms are not just technical preferences—they are political principles that challenge the concentration of power in software development and distribution.

Software freedom represents a form of technological sovereignty that enables communities to control their own technological environment rather than depending on external authorities for essential tools and services. When communities can examine, modify, and redistribute software, they can ensure that their technology serves community values rather than external commercial or political interests. This technological sovereignty becomes increasingly important as software mediates more aspects of social, economic, and political life.

The philosophy of software freedom also challenges the artificial scarcity that underlies proprietary software business models. Software, once created, can be copied and distributed at minimal cost, making artificial restrictions on software sharing economically inefficient and ethically problematic. Open-source development harnesses the natural abundance of digital information to create shared resources that benefit entire communities rather than enriching individual corporations through artificial scarcity.

Collaborative Development Models

Open-source software development demonstrates alternative models of collaborative work that could inform broader economic and social organization. Open-source projects coordinate the efforts of thousands of volunteers and paid contributors through transparent decision-making processes, distributed version control systems, and reputation-based governance mechanisms. These collaborative models show how complex projects can be managed democratically without centralized control or hierarchical management structures.

The success of open-source collaboration challenges assumptions about motivation and incentives that underlie traditional economic theories. Open-source contributors are motivated by a complex mix of factors including technical challenge, community recognition, ideological commitment, and economic interests that don't reduce to simple profit maximization. This demonstrates that people will contribute to collective projects when they have genuine influence over project direction and when their contributions are recognized and valued by communities they respect.

Open-source development also demonstrates how distributed collaboration can produce higher quality results than centralized development by harnessing diverse perspectives and subjecting work to extensive peer review. The transparency of open-source development enables "many eyes" review that can identify bugs, security vulnerabilities, and design problems that might be missed by smaller, centralized development teams. This collaborative quality assurance process produces software that is often more reliable and secure than proprietary alternatives.

Community Governance and Meritocracy

Open-source projects have developed sophisticated governance mechanisms that balance democratic participation with technical expertise and project coherence. These governance models typically combine elements of meritocracy—where influence is based on technical contribution and community respect—with democratic decision-making processes that give community members voice in project direction. While these governance models are not perfect and often struggle with issues of inclusion and representation, they offer valuable examples of democratic technological governance.

The governance challenges faced by open-source projects provide insights into broader questions about democratic participation in technological decision-making. Open-source communities must balance the need for technical expertise with the goal of democratic participation, manage conflicts between different community factions, and maintain project coherence while accommodating diverse perspectives and use cases. The solutions developed by successful open-source projects could inform broader efforts to democratize technological governance.

Open-source governance also demonstrates how reputation-based systems can complement traditional democratic mechanisms to create more sophisticated forms of collective decision-making. In open-source communities, reputation is earned through valuable contributions and responsible behavior rather than being inherited, purchased, or imposed by external authorities. This merit-based reputation system creates incentives for positive contribution while giving community members influence proportional to their demonstrated commitment and competence.

The Economic Model Challenge

One of the greatest challenges facing open-source software development is creating sustainable economic models that can compete with well-funded proprietary alternatives while maintaining the freedom and community governance that define open-source development. Many open-source projects struggle with funding, developer burnout, and the challenge of maintaining quality while relying primarily on volunteer labor. These economic challenges limit the ability of open-source software to provide genuine alternatives to corporate-controlled proprietary software.

However, innovative economic models are emerging that could provide sustainable funding for open-source development while preserving its democratic character. These models include government funding for open-source infrastructure projects, cooperative ownership of open-source projects by user communities, and hybrid models that combine commercial services with open-source software development. The key challenge is ensuring that these economic models strengthen rather than undermine the democratic governance and user freedom that make open-source development valuable.

The economic sustainability of open-source development is crucial for its broader political potential. If open-source software cannot compete effectively with proprietary alternatives, it will remain a niche alternative used primarily by technically sophisticated users rather than providing genuine technological sovereignty for broader communities. Developing sustainable economic models for open-source development is therefore not just a technical challenge but a political necessity for preserving technological freedom.

Community-Driven Alternatives to Big Tech Platforms

The concentration of digital life on a handful of centralized platforms controlled by massive technology corporations represents one of the greatest threats to digital freedom and democratic governance. Facebook, Google, Amazon, Apple, and Microsoft exercise unprecedented control over human communication, information access, and economic activity, creating single points of failure that can be exploited by authoritarian governments, commercial interests, or the platforms themselves. Community-driven alternatives to these centralized platforms offer pathways toward digital ecosystems that serve community values rather than corporate profits.

Community-driven platform development faces enormous challenges because it must compete with well-funded corporate alternatives that benefit from network effects, economies of scale, and sophisticated manipulation techniques designed to maximize user engagement. However, community platforms also have significant advantages including democratic governance, privacy protection, and alignment with user interests that could make them superior alternatives if they can achieve sufficient scale and usability. The key question is whether community-driven development can overcome the structural advantages of corporate platforms.

The Fediverse and Distributed Social Media

The Fediverse—a network of interconnected social media platforms that can communicate with each other while maintaining independent governance—represents the most promising current example of community-driven alternatives to centralized social media. Platforms like Mastodon, Diaspora, and PeerTube demonstrate how social media can operate through distributed networks of community-controlled servers rather than centralized corporate platforms. These platforms enable social media interaction while giving communities control over their own governance policies, content moderation, and data management.

The democratic potential of federated social media lies in its ability to combine the network effects that make social media valuable with the community governance that can make it accountable to user interests. Users can choose to join communities that reflect their values and governance preferences while still being able to communicate with users on other platforms. This enables diverse approaches to content moderation, privacy protection, and community governance that can evolve through experimentation rather than being imposed by corporate policy.

However, federated social media faces significant challenges in achieving mainstream adoption because it requires users to make complex decisions about server selection and governance that most users would prefer to avoid. The technical complexity of federation also creates barriers for non-technical users who want simple, reliable social media experiences. Overcoming these usability challenges while preserving the democratic governance benefits of federation represents a crucial challenge for community-driven social media development.

Cooperative Platform Development

Platform cooperatives represent another approach to community-driven alternatives that combines the benefits of platform technology with cooperative ownership and governance structures. Instead of being owned by investors and operated for profit, platform cooperatives are owned and controlled by the users, workers, or communities that depend on them. This cooperative ownership structure aligns platform governance with user interests rather than investor returns, creating possibilities for platforms that prioritize user welfare over engagement maximization and data extraction.

Successful platform cooperatives like Stocksy (stock photography), Resonate (music streaming), and CoopCycle (delivery services) demonstrate that cooperative ownership can work for digital platforms while providing better working conditions, user control, and community benefit than traditional corporate platforms. These cooperatives show how platform technology can be used to strengthen community economic development rather than extracting wealth from communities for the benefit of distant investors.

The challenge for platform cooperatives is achieving sufficient scale to compete with well-funded corporate alternatives while maintaining democratic governance and cooperative values. Cooperative development typically requires more time and resources than corporate development because it must balance diverse stakeholder interests and maintain democratic decision-making processes. However, cooperatives can also draw on community loyalty and commitment that corporate platforms cannot match, potentially providing sustainable competitive advantages if they can overcome initial scaling challenges.

Decentralized Content Creation and Distribution

Centralized content platforms like YouTube, Netflix, and Spotify control access to audiences and extract significant value from content creators while providing limited creator control over content distribution and monetization. Decentralized content platforms offer alternatives that could give creators direct relationships with audiences while eliminating platform intermediaries that extract value without adding proportional benefits. These platforms could transform content creation from a form of digital sharecropping into genuine creative entrepreneurship.

Blockchain-based content platforms like LBRY and DTube demonstrate how decentralized technology can enable content creators to distribute their work directly to audiences while maintaining control over monetization and content policies. These platforms eliminate the censorship and demonetization risks that creators face on centralized platforms while providing more equitable revenue sharing arrangements. However, they currently lack the audience scale and content discovery features that make centralized platforms attractive to both creators and audiences.

The development of effective decentralized content platforms requires solving complex technical challenges around content discovery, quality control, and sustainable monetization that centralized platforms address through algorithmic recommendation systems and advertising-based business models. Community-driven alternatives must develop different solutions that serve creator and audience interests while maintaining the discoverability and quality that make content platforms valuable.

Local Digital Infrastructure

Community-driven platform development increasingly includes efforts to create local digital infrastructure that serves specific geographic communities rather than attempting to compete globally with corporate platforms. Community broadband networks, local social media platforms, and community-controlled digital services offer pathways toward technological sovereignty that doesn't depend on scaling to compete with global corporations but instead focuses on serving local community needs effectively.

Local digital infrastructure development recognizes that communities have different values, priorities, and governance preferences that may not be well-served by global platforms designed to maximize engagement and data extraction across diverse populations. Community-controlled digital infrastructure can be designed to strengthen local economic development, support local democratic institutions, and preserve local cultural values rather than homogenizing communities according to corporate platform policies.

The success of local digital infrastructure projects like community broadband networks and local platform cooperatives demonstrates that communities can develop technological capacity to meet their own digital needs rather than depending entirely on corporate-controlled alternatives. These projects also provide testing grounds for democratic technological governance that could inform broader efforts to democratize digital infrastructure.

Policy Recommendations for Democratic Digital Governance

Creating genuinely democratic alternatives to surveillance capitalism and centralized platform control requires not just technological innovation but comprehensive policy reform that addresses the structural factors that concentrate digital power and undermine democratic governance of technology. Current policy frameworks typically treat digital technology as a private market activity that should be regulated minimally, if at all. This laissez-faire approach ignores the public utility character of digital infrastructure and the democratic governance implications of concentrated technological power.

Democratic digital governance requires policy frameworks that recognize digital infrastructure as a public good that should serve democratic values rather than just commercial interests. This means treating internet access as a human right, ensuring that digital platforms are accountable to democratic oversight, protecting user rights to privacy and digital autonomy, and promoting technological development that serves community interests rather than just corporate profits. These policy goals require fundamental changes to current regulatory approaches that prioritize corporate freedom over democratic governance.

Universal Digital Rights Framework

The foundation of democratic digital governance must be a comprehensive framework of digital rights that protects individual autonomy and democratic participation in digital environments. These rights should include privacy protection, freedom from manipulation, access to information, and genuine control over personal data. Digital rights frameworks should be understood not as limitations on technological development but as essential foundations for technological systems that serve human flourishing rather than corporate extraction and social control.

Digital rights must go beyond traditional civil liberties frameworks to address the unique challenges posed by algorithmic decision-making, comprehensive surveillance, and behavioral manipulation. Citizens should have rights to understand how algorithmic systems affect their lives, to contest algorithmic decisions that impact them, and to opt out of behavioral manipulation systems even when such systems are integrated into essential services. These rights require active protection through regulatory enforcement rather than relying on corporate self-regulation or market mechanisms.

The implementation of digital rights requires international cooperation because digital platforms operate across national boundaries and can exploit jurisdictional arbitrage to avoid accountability. International frameworks like the European Union's General Data Protection Regulation provide models for rights-based approaches to technology governance, but more comprehensive international cooperation is needed to create effective global standards for digital rights protection that cannot be circumvented by platform forum shopping.

Antitrust and Platform Regulation

The concentration of digital power in a handful of technology corporations requires aggressive antitrust enforcement and new regulatory frameworks specifically designed to address the unique characteristics of digital platforms. Traditional antitrust approaches that focus on consumer prices and market efficiency are inadequate for addressing platforms that provide "free" services while extracting value through data collection and behavioral manipulation. New antitrust frameworks must address the democratic implications of concentrated digital power rather than just economic efficiency.

Platform regulation should include structural separations that prevent platforms from competing with their own users, requirements for interoperability that prevent platforms from using network effects to maintain monopoly positions, and public utility regulation for platforms that provide essential communication or information services. These regulatory approaches should be designed to promote genuine competition and user choice rather than just limiting the most obvious abuses of platform power.

Effective platform regulation also requires addressing the global character of digital platforms through international regulatory cooperation. Platforms that can relocate operations to avoid regulatory accountability pose fundamental challenges to democratic governance that require coordinated international responses. International agreements on platform regulation could create regulatory standards that platforms cannot avoid through jurisdictional arbitrage while ensuring that regulation serves democratic values rather than authoritarian control.

Public Digital Infrastructure Investment

Democratic digital governance requires public investment in digital infrastructure that serves community interests rather than just commercial profits. This includes public broadband networks that provide universal access to high-speed internet, public cloud computing services that give communities alternatives to corporate-controlled data storage, and public platform development that provides community-controlled alternatives to corporate social media and communication platforms.

Public digital infrastructure investment should prioritize democratic governance, privacy protection, and community control rather than just economic efficiency or technological innovation. Public broadband networks should be designed to serve community development goals rather than just providing market alternatives to private internet service providers. Public platform development should prioritize user control and democratic governance rather than competing with corporate platforms on engagement metrics or advertising revenue.

The development of public digital infrastructure requires significant public investment and technical capacity building that may face political opposition from corporate interests that benefit from the current system of private platform control. However, the democratic benefits of public digital infrastructure—including greater community control, better privacy protection, and alignment with public rather than private interests—justify public investment even when such infrastructure cannot achieve the same scale or efficiency as corporate alternatives.

Digital Literacy and Democratic Education

Democratic digital governance requires citizens who understand how digital systems work and can participate meaningfully in technological decision-making. This requires comprehensive digital literacy education that goes beyond basic technical skills to include critical analysis of technological systems, understanding of digital rights and responsibilities, and skills for democratic participation in technological governance. Digital literacy education should be understood as essential civic education for technological societies rather than just vocational training for digital economy participation.

Digital literacy education must address the political economy of digital systems, helping citizens understand how surveillance capitalism works, how algorithmic systems shape their experiences, and how they can protect their autonomy and participate in democratic technology governance. This education should include practical skills for privacy protection, critical evaluation of digital information, and collective action for technological change. Citizens who understand digital systems are better positioned to make informed decisions about technology adoption and participate effectively in democratic technology governance.

The development of comprehensive digital literacy education requires significant changes to educational curricula and teacher training that may face resistance from institutions that benefit from digital illiteracy. However, democratic societies cannot function effectively when citizens lack the knowledge necessary to understand and govern the technological systems that increasingly mediate social, economic, and political life. Digital literacy education is therefore not just an individual benefit but a democratic necessity.

Community Technology Sovereignty

Policy frameworks for democratic digital governance should recognize and support community rights to technological sovereignty—the ability of communities to make their own decisions about technology adoption, governance, and development rather than having technological systems imposed by external authorities. This includes supporting community broadband development, community platform cooperatives, and community-controlled digital infrastructure that serves local values and priorities.

Community technology sovereignty requires policy frameworks that remove barriers to community technology development while providing support for communities that lack technical and financial resources for independent technological development. This includes regulatory reforms that make community technology development easier, funding programs that support community technology projects, and technical assistance programs that help communities develop their own technological capacity.

The recognition of community technology sovereignty also requires addressing the ways that current policy frameworks favor large-scale, corporate-controlled technological development over community-controlled alternatives. Regulatory frameworks that assume large-scale deployment and corporate ownership create barriers for community technology projects that operate at smaller scales and prioritize democratic governance over economic efficiency. Policy reforms should create space for diverse approaches to technological development that serve different community values and priorities.

Conclusion: The Possibility of Technological Liberation

After examining the ways that digital technology has reproduced and amplified the surveillance state dynamics of Orwell's dystopian vision, it would be easy to conclude that technological liberation is impossible—that the same systems that promise freedom inevitably become instruments of control and manipulation. However, this technological pessimism ignores the genuine alternatives that exist within current technological possibilities and the policy reforms that could redirect technological development toward democratic ends rather than authoritarian control.

The examples explored in this chapter—decentralized technologies, open-source software, community-driven platforms, and democratic technology governance—demonstrate that alternative technological futures are not utopian fantasies but practical possibilities that are already being developed by communities around the world. These alternatives face significant challenges in competing with well-funded corporate platforms and overcoming the network effects and usability advantages of centralized systems. However, they also offer genuine benefits including democratic governance, privacy protection, and community control that could make them superior alternatives if they can achieve sufficient scale and support.

The crucial insight is that technological liberation requires not just technological innovation but political transformation that addresses the structural factors that concentrate technological power and undermine democratic governance. The most sophisticated decentralized technologies will not create democratic societies if they are developed within economic and political systems that prioritize corporate profit over community welfare. Similarly, the most democratic policy frameworks will not be effective if they lack the technological infrastructure necessary to provide genuine alternatives to corporate-controlled systems.

Creating democratic technological futures therefore requires coordinated efforts that combine technological innovation with political organizing, policy reform with community development, and individual behavior change with structural transformation. Citizens must develop digital literacy skills that enable them to recognize and resist technological manipulation while also supporting policy reforms that create structural alternatives to surveillance capitalism. Communities must invest in local technological infrastructure while also participating in global networks that can provide alternatives to corporate-controlled platforms.

Perhaps most importantly, creating democratic technological futures requires rejecting technological determinism—the belief that technological development follows natural laws that cannot be influenced by human choice and political action. Current technological systems reflect specific values and power relationships that were created by human decisions and can be changed through different human decisions. The concentration of digital power in a few technology corporations is not a natural result of technological efficiency but a consequence of policy choices, economic structures, and social arrangements that prioritize some interests over others.

The window for creating democratic technological alternatives may be closing as current systems become more entrenched and develop more sophisticated techniques for maintaining user engagement and preventing alternatives from achieving competitive scale. However, the same digital technologies that enable unprecedented surveillance and manipulation also provide tools for democratic organization, decentralized coordination, and community empowerment that were not available to previous generations of democratic activists.

The choice between technological liberation and technological subjugation remains open, but it requires active effort to choose liberation over the default trajectory toward greater corporate control and social manipulation. This choice cannot be made by individuals alone—it requires collective action that combines personal behavior change with political organizing, technological innovation with policy reform, and local community development with global solidarity. The alternative technological futures described in this chapter provide roadmaps for such collective action, but they require sustained commitment and broad participation to become reality.

The question is not whether technological liberation is possible—the examples in this chapter demonstrate that it is. The question is whether societies will make the political choices necessary to prioritize democratic technological development over corporate profit and authoritarian control.

The technologies exist, the policy frameworks have been developed, and the community examples have been demonstrated. What remains is the political will to choose technological liberation over technological subjugation, and the collective action necessary to make that choice effective.

In the end, the possibility of technological liberation depends not on technological determinism but on human agency and political choice. We are not condemned to live in Orwell's dystopia simply because we have created some of its technological infrastructure. We retain the capacity to build alternative futures that use the same digital technologies to enhance rather than undermine human freedom, democratic participation, and community flourishing. The question is whether we will exercise that capacity or allow the default trajectory of technological development to foreclose democratic possibilities that remain within our reach.

Chapter 14: Lessons from Room 101

What Orwell got right and what he missed about technology

George Orwell's prophetic vision in "1984" demonstrated a remarkable understanding of how technology could be weaponized for social control, yet even his dystopian imagination could not fully anticipate the sophistication and subtlety of the digital surveillance and manipulation systems that would emerge in the 21st century. Orwell correctly foresaw the potential for comprehensive surveillance, thought control, and behavioral modification through technological means, but he envisioned these capabilities being deployed through explicit government coercion rather than voluntary participation in commercial systems that provide convenience and entertainment while extracting compliance and control.

The telescreens of Orwell's Oceania represent perhaps his most prescient technological prediction, anticipating devices that could simultaneously monitor behavior and deliver propaganda directly into private spaces. However, Orwell imagined these devices as obviously intrusive government surveillance tools that citizens would recognize as oppressive and resist if possible. He could not have anticipated that people would eagerly purchase and install multiple surveillance devices in their homes, carry tracking devices in their pockets, and voluntarily share intimate details of their lives through social media platforms that monitor and manipulate their behavior more comprehensively than any government surveillance system he could imagine.

Orwell's concept of the Memory Hole, where inconvenient information disappears from the historical record, accurately predicted the digital manipulation of information and the systematic alteration of historical narratives. However, he envisioned this manipulation being conducted by obvious government propaganda departments rather than search algorithms and social media platforms that subtly adjust what information billions of people can access while maintaining the illusion of comprehensive and neutral information availability. The digital Memory Hole operates through algorithmic filtering and search result manipulation that is far more sophisticated and less detectable than the crude censorship mechanisms Orwell imagined.

The Two Minutes Hate sessions that Orwell described as ritualized expressions of collective anger and conformity have found their digital equivalent in viral social media campaigns, trending topics, and algorithmic amplification of emotionally arousing content designed to generate engagement and behavioral compliance. However, these digital hate sessions operate continuously rather than at scheduled times, are personalized to individual psychological profiles, and feel voluntary and enjoyable rather than mandatory and oppressive. The psychological manipulation achieved through social media engagement exceeds Orwell's conception while feeling like entertainment and social connection rather than political indoctrination.

The Underestimation of Voluntary Compliance

Perhaps Orwell's most significant oversight was his failure to anticipate how effectively authoritarian control could be achieved through voluntary participation in systems that provide genuine benefits while extracting compliance and behavioral modification. He imagined totalitarian control requiring obvious coercion, state violence, and explicit oppression that would generate natural resistance from oppressed populations. He could not foresee that people would voluntarily surrender privacy, autonomy, and critical thinking capabilities in exchange for convenience, entertainment, and social connection provided by commercial platforms designed to exploit rather than serve their users.

Orwell's vision of resistance focused on individuals maintaining independent thought and authentic relationships in opposition to state control systems. However, he did not anticipate how algorithmic systems could manipulate the formation of thoughts and relationships themselves, making resistance not just dangerous but psychologically difficult to conceive. When people's preferences, beliefs, and social connections are shaped by recommendation algorithms designed to maximize engagement and behavioral compliance, the foundation for independent thought and authentic resistance becomes systematically eroded without obvious coercion or violence.

The psychological sophistication of modern control systems exceeds Orwell's imagination in their ability to create genuine satisfaction and positive experiences while simultaneously extracting compliance and behavioral modification. Social media platforms provide real social connection and entertainment while harvesting data and manipulating behavior. Search engines provide access to vast amounts of information while filtering and biasing what information is actually accessible. E-commerce platforms provide convenience and choice while creating dependencies and compulsive consumption behaviors. These systems generate authentic positive experiences that make their manipulative aspects difficult to recognize or resist.

The Evolution Beyond Binary Control

Orwell's dystopia operated through binary systems of control where individuals were either compliant Party members or rebellious enemies of the state. He envisioned clear distinctions between freedom and oppression, truth and falsehood, resistance and compliance. However, modern digital control systems operate through gradations and spectrums that make binary categories obsolete. People exist on continuums of surveillance, manipulation, and behavioral control rather than simply being free or oppressed, making their situation more difficult to recognize and address.

The graduated nature of modern control systems creates what researchers call "surveillance creep," where invasive monitoring and behavioral manipulation expand gradually through small increments that individually seem reasonable and acceptable. Users accept each new level of data collection, behavioral tracking, or algorithmic manipulation because it represents only a small change from the previous level of surveillance they had already accepted. This gradual expansion makes it difficult to identify clear moments of resistance or obvious boundaries that have been crossed.

The personalization capabilities of modern systems create individualized experiences of control and manipulation that make collective resistance more difficult to organize. While Orwell's citizens of Oceania all experienced the same propaganda and surveillance systems, modern digital platforms provide personalized experiences that make it difficult for users to understand how their experiences compare to others or to identify systematic patterns of manipulation and control. This individualization of oppression prevents the formation of collective consciousness necessary for effective resistance movements.

The Sophistication of Modern Newspeak

Orwell's concept of Newspeak, a language designed to limit thought by eliminating words and concepts that might enable dissent, has found sophisticated implementation in the content moderation systems and algorithmic filtering that govern digital communication. However, modern Newspeak operates through dynamic content filtering rather than static language restrictions, making it more adaptable and harder to detect than Orwell's version. Words and concepts are not permanently eliminated but are temporarily or selectively suppressed based on context, user profiles, and changing political priorities.

The algorithmic implementation of Newspeak operates through search result manipulation, social media content filtering, and recommendation system bias that limits exposure to certain ideas and perspectives without explicitly prohibiting them. Users experience the illusion of access to comprehensive information while actually receiving filtered and biased content that shapes their understanding of reality in ways that serve the interests of platform operators and their commercial or political allies. This creates more effective thought control than explicit censorship because users don't recognize that their access to information is being manipulated.

The dynamic and personalized nature of modern Newspeak makes it far more sophisticated than Orwell's static language restrictions. Different users receive different versions of reality based on their psychological profiles, political leanings, and behavioral patterns, creating fragmented information environments where people cannot easily communicate about shared reality because they are not actually experiencing the same information landscape. This fragmentation of truth makes collective resistance more difficult while making systematic manipulation less detectable.

The psychology of freedom vs. security in the digital age

The fundamental tension between freedom and security that has characterized human societies throughout history has been transformed and complicated by digital technologies in ways that make traditional frameworks for understanding this balance inadequate for contemporary challenges. The digital age has created new categories of security threats and new forms of freedom that don't fit neatly into historical precedents, while simultaneously making the trade-offs between liberty and safety more subtle, complex, and difficult to evaluate. The result is a psychological and political environment where people struggle to make informed decisions about acceptable levels of surveillance and control because they cannot fully understand the implications of their choices or the true nature of the systems they are choosing to accept or reject.

Traditional conceptions of the freedom versus security balance assumed that increased security measures would involve obvious restrictions on liberty that individuals and societies could evaluate and accept or reject through democratic processes. However, digital security systems often provide increased convenience and functionality while implementing comprehensive surveillance and control systems that operate below the threshold of conscious awareness. People may experience enhanced security and improved services while unknowingly accepting unprecedented levels of behavioral monitoring and manipulation that would have been rejected if presented explicitly as security measures.

The psychological challenge of evaluating digital freedom versus security trade-offs is complicated by the technical complexity of modern systems that makes it difficult for ordinary citizens to understand what they are accepting or rejecting. The privacy policies and terms of service that govern digital platforms contain thousands of pages of legal language that most users cannot understand, while the actual surveillance and control capabilities of these systems are often not disclosed in accessible language. This creates situations where people cannot make informed decisions about security trade-offs because they don't have access to accurate information about what they are trading away or what they are receiving in return.

The temporal dimension of digital security trade-offs also creates psychological challenges that differ from traditional security decisions. Historical security measures typically involved immediate and obvious restrictions on freedom in exchange for immediate security benefits. However, digital surveillance systems collect data and create behavioral profiles that may not be used for control or manipulation until years later, making it difficult to evaluate the long-term implications of current decisions. People may accept surveillance systems that seem benign in their current political and social context without considering how these capabilities might be used under different circumstances or by different actors.

The Illusion of Digital Security

One of the most significant psychological challenges in evaluating digital freedom versus security trade-offs is the prevalence of security theater that provides the appearance of increased safety without meaningful security improvements. Many digital surveillance and control systems are marketed as security measures while actually serving commercial or political control objectives that have little relationship to genuine security needs. Airport security measures that require comprehensive behavioral monitoring and invasive searches may provide minimal security benefits while normalizing surveillance and compliance behaviors that extend beyond transportation contexts.

The complexity of digital security systems makes it difficult for citizens to evaluate their effectiveness or necessity, creating opportunities for security theater that exploits fear and anxiety to justify surveillance and control measures that serve other purposes. Cyber security threats are often presented in language that makes them seem more severe and imminent than they actually are, while the proposed security solutions often involve comprehensive surveillance and behavioral control that exceeds what would be necessary to address the actual security concerns.

The psychological impact of security theater extends beyond immediate surveillance acceptance to include the normalization of comprehensive monitoring and control as necessary features of modern life. People who accept invasive security measures in specific contexts like airports or government buildings may become psychologically conditioned to accept similar measures in other contexts where the security justifications are less compelling. This creates gradual expansion of surveillance and control systems that leverages fear and security anxiety to achieve objectives that have little relationship to actual security needs.

The Commodification of Privacy and Freedom

The digital economy has transformed privacy and freedom from fundamental rights into consumer products that can be purchased, sold, and traded in commercial markets. This commodification fundamentally changes the psychological dynamics of freedom versus security decisions by introducing economic considerations that may override principled positions about rights and liberty. People may accept surveillance and control systems not because they believe the security benefits justify the privacy costs, but because they cannot afford to purchase privacy protection or because the economic benefits of surveillance acceptance outweigh their privacy concerns.

The creation of privacy and freedom markets enables systematic discrimination where wealthy individuals and organizations can purchase protection from surveillance and manipulation while less affluent populations are subjected to comprehensive monitoring and control. This creates tiered systems of rights and freedoms that undermine the universal principles that traditionally governed freedom versus security balances. The result is the emergence of digital class systems where privacy and autonomy become luxury goods rather than fundamental rights.

The commercialization of privacy also creates perverse incentives for companies to manufacture security threats and privacy violations that can then be solved through additional product purchases. Security software companies may exaggerate threats to drive sales of protection products. Social media platforms may create privacy problems through data sharing and then offer premium privacy protection services. This creates economic incentives for the artificial manufacture of security and privacy problems that serve commercial rather than genuine security or privacy interests.

The Psychology of Learned Helplessness

The complexity and pervasiveness of digital surveillance and control systems has created widespread psychological conditions resembling learned helplessness, where people believe they have no meaningful choices about their digital privacy and security and therefore stop attempting to protect themselves or resist invasive systems. This learned helplessness is reinforced by the technical complexity of privacy protection measures, the pervasiveness of surveillance systems, and the economic and social costs of opting out of digital platforms that have become essential for modern life.

The learned helplessness response to digital surveillance is often accompanied by rationalization processes where people convince themselves that privacy is not important, that they have nothing to hide, or that the benefits of surveillance systems outweigh the costs. These rationalizations serve psychological defense functions by reducing anxiety about loss of privacy and control, but they also make people more vulnerable to manipulation and less likely to resist expanding surveillance systems.

The social normalization of comprehensive surveillance contributes to learned helplessness by making privacy protection seem unusual, antisocial, or indicative of criminal intent. When most people accept comprehensive digital monitoring as normal and necessary, those who attempt to maintain privacy may face social pressure to conform and participate in surveillance systems. This social pressure can be more effective than legal or economic coercion in encouraging acceptance of invasive monitoring and control systems.

The Paradox of Digital Convenience

One of the most psychologically challenging aspects of digital freedom versus security decisions is the genuine convenience and functionality provided by systems that also implement comprehensive surveillance and behavioral control. Unlike traditional authoritarian systems that provided few benefits to their subjects, digital surveillance systems often enhance productivity, social connection, and life convenience while extracting privacy and autonomy. This creates psychological conflicts where people must choose between genuine benefits they value and abstract principles about privacy and freedom.

The convenience benefits of digital surveillance systems are often immediate and obvious, while the privacy and autonomy costs are delayed, abstract, and difficult to perceive. People experience real improvements in their daily lives from location tracking, personalized recommendations, and automated services, while the surveillance and manipulation implications of these systems may not become apparent until much later. This temporal mismatch between benefits and costs makes it psychologically difficult to make rational decisions about surveillance acceptance even when people understand the privacy implications.

The integration of surveillance systems into essential life activities makes the convenience versus privacy trade-off increasingly coercive rather than voluntary. When digital surveillance systems become necessary for employment, education, healthcare, financial services, and social participation, the choice to reject surveillance becomes a choice to accept significant life disadvantages rather than a simple preference between convenience and privacy. This coercive aspect of digital surveillance systems undermines the psychological foundations for voluntary consent and informed decision-making about privacy trade-offs.

Why voluntary submission is more dangerous than forced compliance

The most insidious and dangerous aspect of modern digital authoritarianism lies not in its ability to compel obedience through force and coercion, but in its capacity to generate genuine enthusiasm and voluntary participation from those it seeks to control. Voluntary submission to comprehensive surveillance and behavioral manipulation systems represents a far greater threat to human freedom and dignity than traditional forms of authoritarian control because it operates through psychological conditioning and genuine satisfaction rather than fear and coercion. When people eagerly embrace systems that monitor their behavior, manipulate their thoughts, and constrain their choices, the foundations for resistance and liberation become systematically eroded in ways that make recovery of freedom extremely difficult.

Forced compliance with authoritarian systems maintains psychological distance between the individual and the oppressive system, preserving internal spaces of resistance and authentic identity that can serve as foundations for eventual liberation. People who are compelled to comply with surveillance and control systems through threats of violence or punishment may maintain awareness of their oppression and resentment toward their oppressors that can motivate resistance activities and liberation movements. However, voluntary submission creates psychological identification with surveillance and control systems that makes resistance feel like self-betrayal rather than legitimate defense of freedom.

The psychological mechanisms underlying voluntary submission operate through the gradual modification of preferences, values, and identity in ways that make surveillance and control feel natural, beneficial, and desirable rather than imposed and oppressive. People who voluntarily embrace comprehensive monitoring and behavioral modification systems may experience genuine satisfaction and positive outcomes that reinforce their commitment to these systems while making alternatives seem inadequate or undesirable. This creates self-reinforcing cycles of participation that become increasingly difficult to break as psychological and practical dependencies deepen over time.

The social dynamics of voluntary submission also create peer pressure and community expectations that make resistance more difficult than under systems of forced compliance. When most people enthusiastically participate in surveillance and control systems, those who attempt to maintain privacy or autonomy may face social isolation and professional disadvantages that make resistance costly and difficult to sustain. The voluntary nature of participation makes resistance seem antisocial and paranoid rather than principled and necessary, reducing social support for privacy protection and freedom preservation efforts.

The Addiction Model of Digital Control

Modern digital platforms operate using psychological techniques derived from addiction research and gambling psychology to create compulsive usage patterns that make voluntary participation feel inevitable rather than chosen. These systems deploy variable ratio reinforcement schedules, social validation mechanisms, and reward optimization algorithms designed to create psychological dependencies that override rational decision-making about privacy and autonomy. The result is voluntary submission that feels involuntary because it operates through psychological compulsion rather than conscious choice.

The addiction-based model of digital control is particularly dangerous because it exploits fundamental aspects of human psychology that evolved for beneficial purposes but can be artificially triggered and manipulated for control objectives. Social validation needs that originally served community cohesion and cooperation are exploited through social media metrics and peer approval systems. Curiosity and information-seeking behaviors that originally aided survival and learning are exploited through infinite scroll mechanisms and algorithmic content recommendation. These natural psychological processes are weaponized against users in ways that make resistance feel like fighting against their own psychological needs and desires.

The gradual escalation of addictive digital systems mirrors the progression of substance addiction, with users requiring increasing levels of stimulation and engagement to achieve the same psychological satisfaction. Social media platforms gradually increase the frequency and intensity of notifications, content recommendations, and social validation mechanisms to maintain user engagement as tolerance develops. This escalation process makes users increasingly dependent on digital platforms while making alternative activities feel boring, unfulfilling, or inadequate by comparison.

The Internalization of Surveillance Values

Perhaps the most dangerous aspect of voluntary submission to digital surveillance systems is the gradual internalization of surveillance values and monitoring behaviors that transform individuals into agents of their own oppression. People who become accustomed to comprehensive self-monitoring through fitness trackers, productivity applications, and social media platforms may internalize the assumption that all behavior should be tracked, measured, and optimized according to external standards. This internalization transforms surveillance from an external imposition into an internal psychological requirement that feels necessary for self-improvement and social acceptance.

The internalization process operates through the gradual adoption of surveillance logic and optimization thinking that reduces human experience to metrics and data points that can be measured and improved. People begin evaluating their own lives according to algorithmic assessments of their productivity, health, social engagement, and other quantifiable aspects of human experience while losing appreciation for non-quantifiable aspects of life like creativity, contemplation, spontaneity, and authentic relationship. This metric fixation makes individuals psychologically dependent on external monitoring and validation systems while undermining internal sources of meaning and satisfaction.

The social transmission of internalized surveillance values creates communities and cultures where comprehensive self-monitoring becomes normalized and expected rather than optional. Parents teach children to track and optimize their behavior through digital applications. Employers expect workers to monitor their productivity and optimize their performance through technological systems. Social groups pressure members to share personal data and participate in collective monitoring activities. This social normalization makes surveillance values seem natural and beneficial rather than imposed and controlling, making resistance appear antisocial and self-defeating.

The Erosion of Counter-Surveillance Consciousness

Voluntary submission to digital surveillance systems systematically erodes the cognitive and emotional capabilities necessary for recognizing and resisting invasive monitoring and control. People who become accustomed to comprehensive surveillance may lose the ability to recognize privacy violations or appreciate the value of personal autonomy because they have been conditioned to experience monitoring as beneficial and protective rather than invasive and controlling. This erosion of counter-surveillance consciousness makes individuals psychologically unable to resist even obviously problematic expansions of monitoring and control systems.

The loss of privacy intuition and autonomy appreciation operates through habituation processes that make previously unacceptable levels of surveillance feel normal and reasonable through gradual exposure and positive reinforcement. People who initially felt uncomfortable with location tracking or behavioral monitoring may gradually accept and even embrace these systems as they experience their convenience benefits and social normalization. This habituation process makes it difficult for individuals to maintain consistent privacy standards or recognize when surveillance systems have expanded beyond acceptable boundaries.

The cognitive frameworks necessary for understanding and resisting surveillance also atrophy through disuse as people become dependent on algorithmic systems for decision-making and behavior guidance. Critical thinking skills related to privacy protection, risk assessment, and autonomy preservation may deteriorate when they are not regularly practiced and reinforced through actual privacy protection activities. This cognitive atrophy makes individuals less capable of understanding surveillance threats or developing effective resistance strategies even if they become motivated to protect their privacy.

The Democratic Deficit of Voluntary Oppression

The voluntary nature of modern digital surveillance and control systems creates what can be called a "democratic deficit" where traditional democratic mechanisms for resisting and reforming oppressive systems become inadequate because the oppression operates through voluntary participation rather than governmental coercion. Democratic institutions and constitutional protections were designed to address government overreach and protect individuals from state power, but they are less effective at protecting people from commercial surveillance and manipulation systems that operate through voluntary contracts and market mechanisms.

The voluntary participation in oppressive systems also undermines the moral and political foundations for resistance by making oppression appear to be the result of individual choices rather than systemic imposition. When people voluntarily surrender privacy and autonomy through commercial transactions and service agreements, the resulting surveillance and control may appear to be legitimate and democratically chosen rather than imposed and oppressive. This appearance of legitimacy makes collective resistance more difficult to organize and justify even when the actual effects of voluntary oppression exceed those of traditional authoritarian systems.

The global nature of voluntary digital surveillance systems also creates challenges for democratic resistance because these systems operate across national boundaries and may be subject to different regulatory frameworks in different jurisdictions. People may have little democratic influence over the surveillance and control systems that most affect their lives because these systems are operated by multinational corporations or foreign governments that are not accountable to local democratic institutions. This creates situations where voluntary participation in global digital systems effectively removes individuals from democratic governance and constitutional protection while making them subject to unaccountable private or foreign power.

The path forward: conscious choice in an unconscious digital world

The challenge of maintaining human freedom and dignity in an increasingly unconscious digital world requires the development of new forms of consciousness, resistance, and social organization that can operate effectively within technological systems designed to exploit and manipulate human psychology. The path forward cannot rely simply on individual awareness or consumer choices because the scale and sophistication of modern digital manipulation systems exceed what individuals can effectively resist through personal action alone. Instead, conscious choice in the digital age requires collective action, institutional innovation, and cultural transformation that can create alternative systems and protective frameworks capable of preserving human autonomy within technological environments designed to erode it.

The foundation for conscious choice in the digital world begins with the development of technological literacy and critical consciousness that enables individuals to understand how digital systems actually operate and how their behavior is being monitored, analyzed, and manipulated. This technological literacy must extend beyond basic computer skills to include understanding of data collection methods, algorithmic manipulation techniques, psychological influence mechanisms, and the economic incentives driving surveillance and behavioral modification systems. Without this foundational understanding, people cannot make informed decisions about their digital participation or recognize when they are being manipulated.

However, technological literacy alone is insufficient for creating conscious choice in digital environments because the systems involved are too complex and pervasive for individual understanding and resistance to be fully effective. Conscious digital choice requires collective action and institutional support that can provide alternatives to manipulative systems while creating regulatory and legal frameworks that protect individual autonomy from systematic exploitation. This may require new forms of digital rights legislation, alternative platform development, and economic models that prioritize human well-being over engagement optimization and data extraction.

The development of conscious choice capabilities also requires cultural transformation that can restore appreciation for privacy, autonomy, contemplation, and non-digital forms of human experience that are being systematically devalued by digital engagement systems. This cultural work involves creating social norms and institutions that support digital minimalism, privacy protection, and authentic human relationship while resisting the social pressures toward comprehensive digital participation and constant technological engagement that serve commercial rather than human interests.

Building Alternative Digital Ecosystems

One of the most promising approaches to creating conscious choice in the digital world involves the development of alternative digital ecosystems that prioritize human well-being, privacy, and autonomy over engagement optimization and data extraction. These alternative systems would operate according to different economic models and design principles that serve user interests rather than exploiting user psychology for commercial gain. The creation of such alternatives requires significant technical expertise, financial resources, and social coordination, but represents one of the few paths toward genuine choice in digital environments dominated by manipulative commercial platforms.

Alternative digital ecosystems would need to address the fundamental economic incentives that drive surveillance and manipulation in current digital platforms by developing sustainable business models that do not depend on advertising revenue generated through behavioral data collection and targeted psychological manipulation. This might involve subscription-based services, public funding models, cooperative ownership structures, or other economic arrangements that align platform incentives with user well-being rather than engagement maximization and behavioral control.

The technical design of alternative digital systems would need to incorporate privacy-by-design principles, user control mechanisms, and transparency features that enable users to understand and control how their data is collected and used. This would require significant departures from current platform design practices that prioritize data extraction and user engagement over user control and understanding. The development of such systems requires not just technical innovation but also new design philosophies and ethical frameworks that prioritize human autonomy and well-being.

Developing Digital Rights and Regulatory Frameworks

The creation of conscious choice in digital environments requires regulatory and legal frameworks that can protect individual autonomy from systematic exploitation by digital platforms while preserving the benefits of technological innovation and global connectivity. Current regulatory approaches that focus primarily on data protection and privacy rights may be inadequate for addressing the psychological manipulation and behavioral modification capabilities of modern digital systems that can influence human behavior even when users are aware of data collection practices.

Effective digital rights frameworks would need to address not just data collection and privacy protection, but also psychological manipulation, behavioral modification, addiction-by-design, and other techniques that exploit human psychology for commercial gain. This might require new categories of rights related to cognitive liberty, psychological autonomy, and freedom from manipulation that extend beyond traditional privacy concepts to encompass protection of human consciousness and decision-making capabilities.

The global nature of digital platforms creates additional challenges for regulatory approaches because these systems operate across national boundaries and may be subject to regulatory arbitrage where companies relocate to jurisdictions with weaker protection standards. Effective digital rights protection may require international cooperation and harmonization of regulatory standards that can prevent companies from avoiding accountability by operating in jurisdictions with inadequate protection frameworks.

Cultivating Counter-Surveillance Culture

The development of conscious choice in digital environments requires cultural transformation that can restore appreciation for privacy, autonomy, and non-digital forms of human experience while creating social support for resistance to invasive digital systems. This cultural work involves challenging the normalization of comprehensive surveillance and constant digital engagement while creating alternative cultural narratives that value privacy protection, contemplation, authentic relationship, and other aspects of human experience that are being systematically devalued by digital engagement systems.

Counter-surveillance culture would need to address the social pressures and professional requirements that make digital surveillance participation seem necessary for social and economic participation. This might involve creating alternative social networks and professional communities that do not require comprehensive digital surveillance, developing privacy-protecting alternatives for essential services, and creating social norms that respect and support privacy protection choices rather than treating them as antisocial or paranoid.

The educational aspects of counter-surveillance culture would need to include not just technical training in privacy protection tools, but also psychological education about manipulation techniques, addiction mechanisms, and the importance of maintaining cognitive autonomy in digital environments. This education would need to be accessible to people with varying levels of technical expertise while providing practical guidance for reducing exposure to manipulative digital systems.

Creating Spaces for Genuine Human Connection

Perhaps the most important aspect of developing conscious choice in the digital world involves creating and protecting spaces for genuine human connection and authentic experience that exist outside the surveillance and manipulation systems of commercial digital platforms. These spaces might include physical communities, non-digital social activities, contemplative practices, creative pursuits, and other forms of human engagement that do not depend on technological mediation or commercial platform participation.

The creation of genuine connection spaces requires intentional effort to resist the social and economic pressures toward comprehensive digitalization of human experience and relationship. This might involve defending physical spaces from digital surveillance integration, supporting non-digital cultural activities and institutions, and creating community resources that enable people to meet essential needs without participating in comprehensive digital surveillance systems.

The psychological and spiritual dimensions of creating genuine connection spaces involve developing practices and perspectives that can maintain human consciousness and authentic identity within technological environments designed to manipulate and exploit human psychology. This might include contemplative practices, artistic expression, philosophical inquiry, and other activities that cultivate internal awareness and resistance to external manipulation while providing sources of meaning and satisfaction that do not depend on technological systems or commercial validation.

The Role of Conscious Technology Development

The path toward conscious choice in digital environments also requires the participation of technology developers, designers, and entrepreneurs who can create digital systems that serve human well-being rather than exploiting human psychology. This involves developing new approaches to technology design that prioritize user autonomy, psychological well-being, and authentic choice over engagement maximization and behavioral manipulation.

Conscious technology development would need to incorporate ethical design principles, user empowerment features, and transparency mechanisms that enable users to understand and control their digital experiences rather than being subjected to manipulation and exploitation. This requires not just technical innovation but also ethical reflection and value clarification among technology developers about their responsibilities toward users and society.

The economic and social incentives surrounding conscious technology development present significant challenges because systems designed to serve user well-being may be less profitable than systems designed to exploit user psychology, and may face competitive disadvantages in markets dominated by manipulative platforms. Creating sustainable business models and market conditions for conscious technology development may require regulatory intervention, public funding, and cultural change that can support technologies designed to serve human flourishing rather than maximize engagement and data extraction.

Conclusion

The lessons learned from examining Orwell's prophetic vision through the lens of contemporary digital reality reveal both the remarkable prescience of his warnings and the ways in which actual technological authoritarianism has exceeded even his dystopian imagination. Orwell correctly anticipated the potential for technology to enable comprehensive surveillance and thought control, but he could not foresee how these capabilities would be implemented through voluntary participation in commercial systems that provide genuine benefits while extracting compliance and behavioral modification. The reality of digital authoritarianism has proven more sophisticated and insidious than Orwell imagined, operating through psychological manipulation and voluntary submission rather than obvious coercion and state violence.

The psychology of freedom versus security in the digital age has revealed fundamental challenges to traditional frameworks for understanding liberty and safety that make informed democratic decision-making about technology governance extremely difficult. The complexity and opacity of modern digital systems, combined with the temporal displacement between benefits and costs, create psychological and political environments where people cannot effectively evaluate the trade-offs they are making between convenience and autonomy. The commodification of privacy and freedom has further complicated these decisions by introducing economic factors that may override principled positions about rights and liberty.

The analysis of voluntary submission versus forced compliance has demonstrated that willing participation in oppressive systems represents a far greater threat to human freedom than traditional forms of authoritarian control. Voluntary submission operates through psychological conditioning and authentic satisfaction that makes resistance feel like self-betrayal rather than legitimate defense of freedom, while creating social pressures that make privacy protection seem antisocial and paranoid rather than necessary and principled. The addiction-based models of digital control exploit fundamental aspects of human psychology to create dependencies that override rational decision-making about autonomy and privacy.

The path forward toward conscious choice in an unconscious digital world requires comprehensive approaches that combine individual awareness with collective action, technological innovation, regulatory reform, and cultural transformation. No single approach is sufficient to address the scale and sophistication of modern digital manipulation systems, but coordinated efforts across multiple domains may be able to create alternative systems and protective frameworks that preserve human autonomy within technological environments designed to erode it.

The development of alternative digital ecosystems represents one of the most promising avenues for creating genuine choice in digital environments, but requires significant resources and coordination to develop sustainable business models and technical systems that serve user well-being rather than commercial exploitation. The creation of regulatory frameworks that can protect cognitive liberty and psychological autonomy presents additional challenges due to the global nature of digital platforms and the technical complexity of modern manipulation systems.

Perhaps most importantly, the cultivation of counter-surveillance culture and the creation of spaces for genuine human connection offer pathways for maintaining authentic human identity and relationship within technological systems designed to manipulate and commodify human experience. These efforts require intentional resistance to the social and economic pressures toward comprehensive digitalization while creating alternative sources of meaning and satisfaction that do not depend on technological mediation or commercial validation.

The stakes of this challenge extend beyond individual privacy concerns to fundamental questions about the future of human consciousness and social organization. If comprehensive digital surveillance and behavioral manipulation systems become normalized aspects of human life, future generations may lose the cognitive and emotional capabilities necessary for autonomous decision-making, authentic relationship, and democratic participation. The preservation of human freedom and dignity in the digital age requires conscious effort to resist technological systems designed to exploit human psychology while creating alternatives that serve genuine human flourishing.

The window of opportunity for developing conscious choice in digital environments may be narrowing as the infrastructure of surveillance and manipulation becomes embedded in essential systems and social relationships. The economic advantages gained by organizations that effectively exploit human psychology create competitive pressures that may make psychological manipulation a requirement for commercial survival rather than a choice. The development of resistance to these systems requires urgent action to create alternatives and protections before the technological and social momentum toward comprehensive surveillance and control becomes irreversible.

The ultimate lesson from Room 101 is that the greatest threats to human freedom and dignity often come disguised as benefits and conveniences that people eagerly embrace rather than obviously oppressive systems that generate natural resistance. The conscious recognition of this dynamic, combined with the development of individual and collective capabilities for resisting psychological manipulation, may offer the best hope for preserving human autonomy and authentic choice in an age of algorithmic control and behavioral modification. The challenge is not merely technological or political, but fundamentally psychological and cultural, requiring the development of new forms of consciousness and resistance appropriate to the digital age while preserving the essential human capacities that make freedom and dignity possible.

CONCLUSION: Switching Off the Telescreen

In the final pages of *1984*, Winston Smith sits in the Chestnut Tree Café, his rebellion crushed, his love for Julia transformed into love for Big Brother, his capacity for independent thought permanently destroyed. Orwell's telescreen flickers above him, broadcasting the Party's endless stream of propaganda and surveillance, but Winston no longer needs to be watched—he has internalized his oppressor so completely that external monitoring has become redundant. This chilling image of total psychological surrender represents Orwell's ultimate warning: that the greatest threat to human freedom lies not in the technology of oppression but in our willingness to embrace it, to internalize it, and ultimately to love it.

Today, we face a remarkably similar choice, though the stakes and circumstances have evolved beyond anything Orwell could have imagined. The telescreens of our age are not imposed upon us by totalitarian decree but invited into our homes, carried in our pockets, and integrated so thoroughly into our daily lives that we can barely imagine existence without them. The surveillance they enable is not crude and obvious but sophisticated and seductive, designed not to terrify us into submission but to make submission feel like empowerment, monitoring feel like service, and manipulation feel like personalization.

Yet unlike Winston Smith in his final defeat, we still possess the power to choose. The telescreen can still be switched off—not permanently, not completely, but consciously, deliberately, and with full awareness of both what we gain and what we lose in the process. This conclusion is not a call for Luddite rejection of all digital technology, but an invitation to conscious engagement with tools that can genuinely serve human flourishing rather than undermine it. The question before us is not whether we can escape the digital age, but whether we can navigate it as autonomous human beings rather than as products in a surveillance economy.

THE SYNTHESIS: WHERE WE STAND TODAY

The Convergence of Orwellian Warnings and Digital Reality

The journey through the preceding chapters has revealed how Orwell's dystopian imagination has materialized in forms more subtle and pervasive than anything he envisioned. The Party's crude telescreens have evolved into smartphones that provide genuine value while enabling comprehensive surveillance. The Ministry of Truth's obvious propaganda has been replaced by algorithmic news feeds that create personalized realities tailored to individual psychological profiles. Room 101's physical torture has given way to psychological manipulation so sophisticated that victims experience their exploitation as entertainment and empowerment.

This convergence between Orwellian prophecy and digital reality is not coincidental but structural. The technologies that enable mass surveillance also enable mass convenience. The systems that commodify human attention also provide genuine connection and communication. The platforms that manipulate behavior also offer authentic opportunities for creativity and self-expression. This duality—the simultaneous potential for liberation and oppression within the same technological systems—represents the central challenge of our digital age.

The sophistication of contemporary surveillance and manipulation systems has surpassed Orwell's darkest imaginings while maintaining the appearance of voluntary participation and individual choice. We are not forced to carry tracking devices—we pay premium prices for the latest models. We are not compelled to share our personal information—we compete to create more engaging content. We are not coerced into accepting surveillance—we demand better personalization and more relevant advertising. This transformation of oppression into desire, of monitoring into service, represents a form of soft totalitarianism that may be more complete and enduring than any system based on fear and coercion.

The Paradox of Technological Progress and Human Regression

One of the most striking patterns emerging from our analysis is the paradox of unprecedented technological capability coinciding with apparent regression in human autonomy, attention span, social cohesion, and democratic discourse. We live in an age of miraculous technological achievement—artificial intelligence that can compose poetry, communication networks that connect billions of people instantaneously, computational power that exceeds the wildest dreams of previous generations—yet rates of anxiety, depression, social isolation, and political polarization have reached crisis levels.

This paradox suggests that technological progress, as currently implemented and commercialized, may be fundamentally misaligned with human psychological needs and social requirements. The same technologies that promise to solve human problems often create new forms of suffering and social dysfunction that may be more severe than the original challenges they sought to address. Social media promises connection but delivers isolation. Smartphones promise productivity but fragment attention. Algorithmic systems promise efficiency but eliminate human agency and judgment.

The resolution of this paradox requires recognizing that technology is not neutral but embodies particular values, assumptions, and power relationships. The surveillance capitalism model that dominates contemporary technology development prioritizes engagement and data collection over user wellbeing, short-term profit over long-term social health, and platform growth over human flourishing. Alternative approaches to technology development and implementation are possible but require conscious choice and deliberate resistance to the economic and social forces that drive current patterns of technological deployment.

The Spectrum of Digital Adaptation and Resistance

The analysis of contemporary responses to digital surveillance and manipulation reveals a broad spectrum of adaptation strategies ranging from complete embrace to total rejection, with most individuals and communities occupying various positions along this continuum. Understanding this spectrum provides insight into the range of possible responses and the factors that influence individual and collective choices about technology adoption and use.

At one extreme, digital maximalists embrace comprehensive technological integration, accepting surveillance and manipulation as acceptable costs for convenience, connectivity, and access to digital services. This position reflects rational calculation for individuals whose lives and livelihoods depend on digital participation, as well as genuine appreciation for the benefits that digital technologies provide. However, maximalist approaches often involve unconscious surrender of autonomy and privacy that may have long-term consequences for individual wellbeing and democratic society.

At the other extreme, digital minimalists and technology rejecters seek to limit or eliminate their participation in surveillance capitalism and digital manipulation systems. This approach can provide significant benefits for mental health, productivity, and authentic relationship building, but may also create social isolation, economic disadvantage, and reduced access to beneficial digital services. Pure rejection strategies may be sustainable for some individuals but are not viable for entire populations or societies.

Between these extremes lies a range of approaches that might be characterized as "conscious engagement"—strategies that seek to capture the benefits of digital technology while minimizing the costs and risks associated with surveillance and manipulation. These approaches require ongoing attention, technical sophistication, and social support that may not be available to all individuals, but they demonstrate the possibility of more balanced and autonomous relationships with digital technology.

The Role of Individual Agency in Systemic Change

One of the persistent tensions throughout this analysis has been the relationship between individual choices and systemic change in addressing the challenges of surveillance capitalism and digital manipulation. Individual actions—digital detox practices, privacy protection measures, conscious consumption choices—can provide genuine benefits for those who implement them but may have limited impact on the broader systems that shape technological development and deployment.

This limitation does not diminish the importance of individual action but highlights the need for collective responses that address the structural and institutional factors driving surveillance capitalism and digital authoritarianism. Personal digital minimalism practices can provide foundation for broader cultural and political movements, while legal and regulatory reforms can create frameworks that support individual choice and protect vulnerable populations from exploitation.

The relationship between individual and collective action is particularly important in addressing the addictive design and psychological manipulation that characterize many digital technologies. While individuals can develop strategies for resisting manipulation and protecting their attention, the systematic deployment of persuasive design and behavioral modification techniques requires collective responses that address the business models and regulatory frameworks that enable and incentivize these practices.

The development of individual agency and critical consciousness about digital technology serves as foundation for broader social movements and political reforms, while systemic changes create conditions that make individual resistance and conscious choice more feasible and effective. This reciprocal relationship suggests that sustainable solutions to digital authoritarianism require both personal transformation and collective action.

THE ROADMAP: PRACTICAL STEPS FOR DIGITAL AUTONOMY

Immediate Actions: The Digital Detox Starter Kit

For individuals beginning the journey toward digital autonomy, certain immediate actions can provide quick wins and build momentum for deeper changes in technological relationship and consumption patterns. These starter strategies require minimal technical knowledge or resources while providing noticeable improvements in digital wellbeing and autonomy.

The first category of immediate actions involves what might be called "friction engineering"—deliberately introducing obstacles and delays that interrupt automatic digital consumption patterns and create space for conscious choice. This includes removing social media applications from smartphones while maintaining access through web browsers, implementing app time limits and notification restrictions, and creating device-free zones and times in personal living spaces. These changes don't prevent digital engagement but make it more intentional and less compulsive.

Privacy protection represents another category of immediate actions that individuals can implement without significant technical expertise or cost. Basic privacy measures include using privacy-focused web browsers and search engines, implementing ad blockers and tracker blocking extensions, reviewing and restricting social media privacy settings, and being more conscious about the personal information shared with websites and applications. While these measures don't provide complete protection from surveillance, they significantly reduce data collection and behavioral tracking.

Digital consumption auditing provides crucial foundation for more substantial changes by creating awareness of current technology use patterns and their impact on time, attention, and wellbeing. This involves tracking screen time and app usage, identifying triggers and patterns in compulsive device use, and evaluating which digital activities provide genuine value versus those that primarily serve platform engagement and advertising goals. This awareness often motivates deeper changes in digital consumption patterns.

The implementation of regular digital sabbaths—periods of complete disconnection from digital devices and online services—provides immediate experience of unmediated reality and often reveals the extent to which digital consumption has colonized attention and consciousness. Starting with short periods of disconnection and gradually extending to longer sabbaths allows individuals to rediscover non-digital forms of entertainment, productivity, and social connection.

Intermediate Strategies: Building Digital Literacy and Technical Capability

As individuals develop greater awareness of their digital consumption patterns and begin implementing basic privacy and attention protection measures, intermediate strategies can provide deeper protection and more sophisticated approaches to technological autonomy. These strategies require greater technical knowledge and ongoing attention but provide more comprehensive protection and control over digital experience.

Advanced privacy protection involves implementing more sophisticated tools and techniques for protecting personal data and communications from surveillance and interception. This includes using virtual private networks (VPNs) to encrypt internet traffic and obscure browsing locations, employing encrypted messaging applications for sensitive communications, and learning to use anonymous networks like Tor for activities requiring strong privacy protection. These tools require technical learning and careful implementation but provide significantly enhanced privacy protection.

Digital literacy development involves building understanding of how digital technologies and business models actually operate, enabling more informed choices about technology adoption and use. This includes learning about surveillance capitalism and advertising-based business models, understanding how algorithmic systems shape information exposure and behavior, and developing critical thinking skills for evaluating the claims and promises made by technology companies. This knowledge provides foundation for making autonomous choices about digital engagement rather than simply following platform design and marketing guidance.

Alternative platform adoption represents another intermediate strategy that involves seeking out and using technology services and applications that prioritize user privacy and wellbeing over engagement and data collection. This might include using privacy-focused email providers, social media alternatives, and productivity applications that don't track user behavior or sell user data to third parties. While these alternatives often have smaller user bases and fewer features than mainstream platforms, they demonstrate the possibility of different approaches to technology design and business model development.

Community building and social support development are crucial intermediate strategies for sustaining digital minimalism and autonomous technology use in social environments that assume constant digital connectivity and availability. This involves finding and connecting with others who share similar values around technology use, creating social activities and relationships that don't depend on digital mediation, and developing communication strategies for managing others' expectations about digital availability and responsiveness.

Advanced Approaches: Technical Sovereignty and Systemic Engagement

For individuals who develop significant digital literacy and become committed to technological autonomy, advanced approaches can provide even greater independence from surveillance capitalism and digital manipulation while contributing to broader movements for technological accountability and democratic control over digital systems. These approaches require substantial technical knowledge and ongoing commitment but can provide leadership for broader social and political movements.

Technical sovereignty involves developing personal and community control over digital infrastructure and systems rather than depending entirely on corporate-controlled platforms and services. This might include running personal email servers, participating in mesh networking and decentralized communication systems, using cryptocurrency and blockchain systems for financial transactions, and contributing to open-source software development and maintenance. These activities require significant technical expertise but provide genuine independence from corporate surveillance and control systems.

Political engagement and advocacy represent another advanced approach that involves working to change the legal, regulatory, and cultural frameworks that enable surveillance capitalism and digital authoritarianism. This might include supporting privacy rights organizations, advocating for stronger digital rights legislation, participating in campaigns for antitrust enforcement against technology monopolies, and educating others about the social and political implications of digital surveillance and manipulation.

Economic resistance involves making consumption and investment choices that withdraw support from surveillance capitalism while providing resources for alternative approaches to technology development and deployment. This includes choosing to pay for privacy-respecting services rather than using "free" advertising-supported platforms, supporting businesses and organizations that prioritize user privacy and wellbeing, and divesting from companies that profit from surveillance and behavioral manipulation.

Community organizing and education involves building local and regional networks of individuals and organizations committed to technological autonomy and digital rights. This might include organizing digital literacy workshops, creating tool libraries for privacy protection technologies, establishing community broadband networks, and developing mutual aid networks for supporting individuals and families seeking to reduce their dependence on surveillance capitalism systems.

Long-term Vision: Technological Democracy and Human Flourishing

The ultimate goal of individual digital autonomy efforts should be the creation of technological systems and social institutions that genuinely serve human flourishing rather than exploit human psychology and behavior for corporate profit and political control. This long-term vision requires imagining and working toward alternative approaches to technology development, deployment, and governance that prioritize human wellbeing and democratic participation.

Technological democracy involves creating systems for democratic participation in decisions about technology development and deployment that affect entire communities and societies. Rather than allowing technology companies and government agencies to make unilateral decisions about surveillance capabilities, artificial intelligence deployment, and platform governance, democratic approaches would create mechanisms for public participation in technology policy and oversight.

Human-centered design represents an alternative approach to technology development that prioritizes user wellbeing and autonomy over engagement and data collection. This approach would involve designing technologies to support human capabilities and social relationships rather than exploit psychological vulnerabilities and create dependency. While some examples of human-centered design exist, systematic implementation would require fundamental changes in business models and regulatory frameworks.

Decentralized infrastructure development involves creating technological systems that operate independently of corporate and government control while providing the connectivity and functionality that contemporary life requires. This includes mesh networking, blockchain systems, and peer-to-peer technologies that enable communication, commerce, and coordination without depending on centralized platforms and services that enable surveillance and manipulation.

Educational and cultural transformation involves developing new forms of digital literacy and technological wisdom that enable individuals and communities to make informed choices about technology adoption and use. This requires educational systems that teach critical thinking about technology rather than simply technical skills, cultural narratives that emphasize human agency rather than technological determinism, and social norms that support conscious technology use rather than compulsive consumption.

ACKNOWLEDGING THE GENUINE BENEFITS OF DIGITAL TECHNOLOGY

The Double-Edged Nature of Digital Innovation

Any honest assessment of contemporary digital technology must acknowledge that the same systems that enable surveillance and manipulation also provide genuine benefits that have improved human life in measurable and meaningful ways. This recognition does not diminish the validity of concerns about surveillance capitalism and digital authoritarianism, but it does require nuanced thinking about how to preserve beneficial capabilities while addressing harmful practices and business models.

Digital communication technologies have genuinely revolutionized human connection and collaboration, enabling relationships and communities that would be impossible without technological mediation. Long-distance relationships, international collaboration, diaspora communities, and support networks for marginalized populations all depend on digital communication technologies that provide real value for human connection and mutual aid. The challenge is preserving these capabilities while eliminating the surveillance and manipulation that currently accompanies most digital communication platforms.

Information access and educational resources available through digital technologies represent another category of genuine benefit that has democratized learning and knowledge sharing in unprecedented ways. Online education, digital libraries, research databases, and instructional content have made high-quality educational resources available to populations that would otherwise lack access to such materials. The manipulation of information systems for political and commercial purposes doesn't negate the fundamental value of democratic access to information and knowledge.

Creative tools and platforms have enabled new forms of artistic expression and creative collaboration while providing economic opportunities for artists, writers, musicians, and other creative professionals who might not have access to traditional publishing and distribution systems. Digital creativity tools have lowered barriers to entry for many forms of creative expression while enabling global audiences for creative work. The commodification and surveillance of creative platforms doesn't eliminate the genuine creative possibilities that digital technologies enable.

Medical and scientific applications of digital technology have provided crucial tools for research, diagnosis, treatment, and public health monitoring that have saved countless lives and improved health outcomes for millions of people. Telemedicine, electronic health records, research databases, and diagnostic technologies represent genuine advances in human capability that would be difficult to replicate through non-digital means.

The Potential for Ethical Technology Development

The existence of harmful practices in contemporary technology development doesn't preclude the possibility of ethical approaches that prioritize human wellbeing and social benefit over profit maximization and behavioral manipulation. Examples of ethical technology development demonstrate that alternative approaches are feasible and can provide both technological capability and respect for human autonomy and privacy.

Open-source software development represents one model for ethical technology creation that prioritizes community benefit and user control over corporate profit and surveillance. Projects like Linux, Wikipedia, and various privacy-focused applications demonstrate that high-quality technological tools can be developed and maintained through collaborative, non-commercial approaches that serve user interests rather than exploit them.

Public interest technology organizations and projects demonstrate another approach to ethical technology development that explicitly prioritizes social benefit and democratic values. Organizations working on election security, digital rights advocacy, and community technology development show that technological capability can be directed toward strengthening democratic institutions and community resilience rather than undermining them.

Cooperative and community-owned technology platforms provide examples of alternative governance and ownership models that align platform incentives with user wellbeing rather than creating conflicts between profit maximization and user interests. While still experimental and limited in scope, these alternatives demonstrate the feasibility of different approaches to platform governance and business model development.

Research and development in human-centered design, privacy-preserving technologies, and wellbeing-focused applications shows that technical innovation can be directed toward solving surveillance and manipulation problems rather than creating them. Privacy-preserving machine learning, decentralized networking protocols, and attention-supporting interface design represent technical approaches that could enable beneficial digital capabilities while protecting human autonomy and privacy.

Navigating Technological Nuance and Complexity

The challenge of conscious engagement with digital technology requires developing sophisticated judgment about which specific technologies, platforms, and practices provide genuine benefit versus those that primarily serve surveillance and manipulation purposes. This judgment cannot be based on simple rejection or acceptance of entire categories of technology but requires ongoing evaluation of specific tools and their impact on individual and social wellbeing.

Platform evaluation frameworks can help individuals make informed choices about which digital services and applications align with their values and priorities. Factors to consider include business models and revenue sources, privacy policies and data collection practices, user interface design and attention impact, community standards and content moderation approaches, and the availability of alternatives and platform switching options.

Use case analysis involves carefully considering which specific applications of digital technology provide genuine value versus those that primarily serve as entertainment or distraction. This might involve maintaining digital tools for essential communication and productivity while eliminating recreational social media use, or using navigation and information applications while avoiding addictive gaming and entertainment platforms.

Harm reduction approaches recognize that complete elimination of potentially problematic technologies may not be feasible or desirable for many individuals, but that conscious modification of usage patterns can significantly reduce negative impacts while preserving beneficial capabilities. This might involve implementing time limits and usage restrictions, modifying notification settings and platform algorithms, or using technical tools to limit exposure to manipulative design features.

Regular reassessment and adjustment of technology use patterns acknowledges that the landscape of digital technology continues to evolve rapidly, requiring ongoing attention to how specific tools and platforms affect individual wellbeing and social relationships. What works for one person or situation may not work for another, and what provides benefit at one time may become problematic as circumstances or platform practices change.

THE CHOICE BEFORE US: CONSCIOUS PARTICIPATION OR DIGITAL SERVITUDE

The Window of Opportunity

The current moment represents a unique window of opportunity for making conscious choices about humanity's relationship with digital technology. Unlike previous eras of technological change, we have the benefit of several decades of experience with digital systems, growing awareness of their psychological and social impacts, and emerging alternatives that demonstrate different possibilities for technological development and deployment.

The current awareness of surveillance capitalism and digital manipulation represents a significant shift from the early enthusiasm for digital technology that characterized previous decades. Public consciousness of privacy violations, mental health impacts, and democratic threats has created political and cultural space for challenging the assumptions and practices that have dominated technology development. This awareness creates opportunities for individual and collective choices that could alter the trajectory of technological development.

The emergence of alternative technologies and business models demonstrates that the current approach to digital technology is not inevitable or unchangeable. Privacy-focused platforms, human-centered design principles, cooperative ownership models, and decentralized technologies show that different approaches to technology development are technically feasible and economically viable. The existence of these alternatives creates options for individuals and communities seeking to reduce their dependence on surveillance capitalism.

However, this window of opportunity may not remain open indefinitely. As digital surveillance systems become more sophisticated and integrated into essential services, as artificial intelligence capabilities advance, and as digital native generations accept surveillance and manipulation as normal aspects of technological interaction, the possibilities for resistance and alternative development may diminish. The choices made in the next decade may determine whether future generations experience technology as liberation or as an inescapable system of control.

The Stakes: What We Stand to Lose and Gain

The choices we make about digital technology over the next decade will have profound implications for fundamental questions of human freedom, social organization, and individual flourishing that extend far beyond personal convenience or even privacy protection. Understanding these stakes provides context for the importance of conscious engagement with technological choices that might otherwise seem like minor lifestyle preferences.

At stake is the future of human attention and consciousness as autonomous resources that individuals control and direct according to their own values and purposes. The attention economy's systematic capture and manipulation of human awareness represents a form of cognitive colonization that could permanently alter human psychological development and social relationships. Preserving the capacity for sustained attention, contemplative thought, and unmediated experience requires conscious resistance to systems designed to fragment and commodify consciousness.

The future of democratic governance and collective decision-making depends partly on citizens' capacity for independent thought, critical evaluation of information, and meaningful participation in public discourse. When information environments are manipulated by algorithmic systems optimized for engagement and profit rather than truth and democratic participation, the foundations of democratic society are undermined. Protecting democratic institutions requires preserving citizens' capacity for autonomous thought and genuine dialogue.

The development of artificial intelligence and automated decision-making systems raises questions about human agency and autonomy that will affect every aspect of social organization. If these systems are developed and deployed primarily to maximize corporate profit and state control rather than to support human capabilities and democratic values, they could create forms of technological authoritarianism that make resistance increasingly difficult. Ensuring that artificial intelligence serves human flourishing requires conscious participation in its development and deployment.

The implications for future generations are particularly profound, as children growing up in comprehensively surveilled and manipulated digital environments may never develop the psychological capacities and social skills necessary for autonomous thought and democratic participation. The normalization of surveillance and manipulation for digital natives could create permanent changes in human consciousness and social organization that would be extremely difficult to reverse.

The Path Forward: Neither Luddite Rejection nor Uncritical Acceptance

The path toward conscious engagement with digital technology requires avoiding both the extreme of complete technological rejection and the opposite extreme of uncritical acceptance of whatever technologies and practices dominate the marketplace. This middle path demands ongoing attention, critical thinking, and conscious choice about which technologies genuinely serve human purposes and which primarily exploit human psychology for corporate and political gain.

Conscious engagement requires developing what might be called "technological wisdom"—the capacity to distinguish between beneficial and harmful applications of digital technology while remaining open to genuine innovation and improvement. This wisdom cannot be achieved through simple rules or universal principles but requires ongoing evaluation of specific technologies, platforms, and practices in relation to their impact on individual wellbeing and social health.

The development of technological wisdom requires both individual reflection and collective dialogue about values, priorities, and the kind of society we want to create and inhabit. These conversations must involve not only technical experts and technology industry leaders but also ordinary citizens, community leaders, educators, health professionals, and others who understand human needs and social requirements that may not be reflected in technology design and business model development.

Building sustainable alternatives to surveillance capitalism and digital authoritarianism requires coordinated action across multiple levels—individual lifestyle choices, community organizing, legal and regulatory reform, and cultural transformation that changes social norms and expectations around technology use. No single approach is sufficient, but the combination of individual and collective action can create momentum for systemic change.

The goal is not to eliminate digital technology from human life but to ensure that technological capabilities serve human flourishing rather than exploit human psychology and behavior for profit and control. This requires vigilance, ongoing effort, and willingness to make choices that may sometimes be inconvenient or socially challenging but that preserve human autonomy and democratic possibilities for future generations.

Making the Choice: Personal Responsibility in a Systemic Challenge

While the challenges of surveillance capitalism and digital authoritarianism are systemic and require collective responses, they also demand personal responsibility and individual action from each person who recognizes the stakes involved. The choices that individuals make about their own digital consumption and engagement create the cultural and economic conditions that either support or undermine broader movements for technological accountability and democratic control over digital systems.

Personal responsibility in this context does not mean blaming individuals for systemic problems or expecting individual action to solve structural issues. Rather, it means recognizing that personal choices about technology use contribute to larger patterns of demand, cultural norms, and economic incentives that shape technological development and deployment. Every person who chooses conscious engagement over compulsive consumption, privacy protection over convenient surveillance, and authentic relationship over digital performance contributes to creating conditions that support alternative approaches to technology.

The development of personal practices for digital autonomy serves not only individual wellbeing but also collective resistance to technological authoritarianism. Individuals who successfully limit their digital consumption, protect their privacy, and maintain capacity for independent thought provide examples and resources for others seeking to develop similar capabilities. Personal transformation and collective change reinforce each other in ways that make both more sustainable and effective.

However, personal responsibility must be balanced with recognition of the structural constraints and pressures that limit individual choice and make resistance difficult or impossible for many people. Economic necessity, social isolation, educational limitations, and other factors can make digital minimalism and privacy protection challenging or unfeasible for individuals who nonetheless share concerns about surveillance and manipulation. Effective responses to digital authoritarianism must address both individual agency and structural constraints.

The choice before each individual is whether to remain unconscious consumers of whatever digital technologies and practices achieve market dominance, or to become conscious participants in determining how technology affects their own lives and the broader society. This choice requires ongoing attention and effort, but it also provides opportunities for meaningful agency and contribution to creating a more human-centered and democratic approach to technological development.

THE FINAL CHOICE: LOVE OR REBELLION

Learning from Winston's Defeat

Winston Smith's ultimate defeat in *1984* provides crucial insight into the nature of totalitarian control and the conditions necessary for preserving human freedom. Winston's rebellion failed not because of inadequate technique or insufficient commitment, but because he ultimately faced his opposition alone, without genuine community, sustainable resources, or realistic prospects for success. His isolation made him vulnerable to the psychological manipulation that eventually broke his will and transformed his resistance into love for his oppressor.

The lesson of Winston's defeat is not that resistance is futile, but that sustainable resistance requires community, mutual support, and realistic strategies that can persist over time despite setbacks and repression. Individual acts of defiance, while important for maintaining human dignity and moral clarity, are insufficient for challenging systemic oppression that operates through comprehensive control over information, social relationships, and economic resources.

Contemporary digital resistance faces similar challenges to those that defeated Winston Smith. The isolation inherent in digital communication, the fragmentation of attention that prevents sustained political engagement, and the economic dependency on systems that exploit and manipulate users create conditions that favor surrender over resistance. However, unlike Winston's analog world, digital technologies also provide tools for coordination, communication, and mutual aid that could support more effective and sustainable resistance strategies.

The key difference between Winston's situation and our own lies in the timing and scope of our response. Winston began his resistance after totalitarian control was already complete and unopposed. We still have opportunities to shape technological development and deployment before comprehensive digital authoritarianism becomes entrenched and irreversible. The choices we make now determine whether future generations will face Winston's impossible situation or will have genuine alternatives and opportunities for human freedom.

The Power of Collective Consciousness

The most hopeful aspect of contemporary resistance to digital authoritarianism is the growing collective consciousness of surveillance capitalism's harms and the possibilities for alternative approaches to technology. This awareness creates opportunities for coordinated action that could alter the trajectory of technological development in ways that serve human flourishing rather than corporate profit and state control.

Collective consciousness manifests in various forms—from individual digital detox movements to legal and regulatory reforms, from academic research on technology's social impacts to grassroots organizing for digital rights. While these efforts may seem scattered and insufficient compared to the scale of digital surveillance and manipulation systems, they represent the early stages of broader social movements that could achieve significant changes in how technology is developed, deployed, and governed.

The development of collective consciousness about digital technology parallels earlier social movements that challenged other forms of systemic exploitation and control. Environmental, civil rights, labor, and feminist movements all began with growing awareness of structural problems, developed into organized efforts for change, and eventually achieved significant legal, cultural, and institutional reforms. Digital rights and technological accountability movements are following similar patterns of development and may achieve comparable results if sustained over time.

The global nature of digital technology creates opportunities for international cooperation and mutual support among digital resistance movements that could be more effective than purely national or local efforts. Privacy advocates, digital rights organizations, and technology accountability movements in different countries can share resources, strategies, and support in ways that transcend the jurisdictional limitations that often constrain domestic political action.

The Technology of Liberation

Perhaps the most remarkable aspect of contemporary resistance to digital authoritarianism is the extent to which the same technological capabilities that enable surveillance and manipulation also provide tools for resistance and liberation. Cryptographic systems can protect communication from government and corporate surveillance. Decentralized networks can enable coordination without central control or monitoring. Anonymous systems can protect dissidents and whistleblowers from identification and retaliation.

This technological paradox means that the future of human freedom depends partly on technical developments and the communities of developers, researchers, and activists who create and maintain privacy-preserving and liberation-supporting technologies. Unlike previous forms of resistance that required primarily political and social organization, contemporary resistance to digital authoritarianism also requires technical expertise and ongoing innovation to stay ahead of surveillance and manipulation systems.

The democratization of privacy and resistance technologies through open-source development, educational initiatives, and user-friendly interface design makes these tools accessible to broader populations rather than limiting them to technical elites. This democratization is crucial for building sustainable resistance movements that can include ordinary citizens rather than depending entirely on specialized knowledge and capabilities.

However, the technical arms race between surveillance and privacy technologies creates ongoing vulnerabilities and risks for resistance movements that depend on technological tools for protection. The constant need for technical updating, operational security awareness, and adaptation to new threats requires resources and attention that may not be available to all resistance participants, creating persistent challenges for democratic participation in technologically mediated resistance.

The Moment of Decision

We stand at a historical moment that parallels the choice faced by Winston Smith when he first wrote "DOWN WITH BIG BROTHER" in his diary—the moment of deciding whether to accept the reality being imposed upon us or to assert our human capacity for independent thought and autonomous action. The difference is that our choice is collective rather than individual, and the consequences will affect not only our own lives but the future of human freedom for generations to come.

The decision before us is whether to sleepwalk into digital dystopia or to wake up and make conscious choices about how technology affects our lives and societies. This decision cannot be postponed indefinitely—each day of unconscious consumption and passive acceptance makes resistance more difficult and alternatives less viable. The systems of surveillance and manipulation become more sophisticated and comprehensive over time, while human capacities for sustained attention, independent thought, and autonomous action may atrophy without conscious cultivation and protection.

Yet the choice remains ours to make. Unlike Winston Smith, we are not isolated individuals facing an already-complete totalitarian system. We are part of a global community of people who share concerns about surveillance capitalism and digital authoritarianism and who are developing tools, strategies, and alternatives that could preserve human freedom and democratic possibilities.

The moment of decision is not a single dramatic choice but an ongoing series of daily decisions about how to engage with digital technology, what values to prioritize, and what kind of society to work toward creating. Each choice to disconnect, to protect privacy, to seek authentic relationship, to support alternative technologies, and to resist manipulation contributes to collective outcomes that will determine the future of human freedom.

This is our generation's defining challenge—not climate change or economic inequality or political polarization, though digital technology affects all of these issues, but the fundamental question of whether human consciousness and social organization will be shaped by our own values and choices or by algorithmic systems designed to maximize profit and control.

The telescreen can still be switched off. The question is whether we will choose to switch it off, or whether we will follow Winston Smith into the Chestnut Tree Café, learning to love our surveillance and celebrating our own surrender.

The choice is ours. The time is now.

The revolution will not be digitized—it will be human, conscious, and free. It begins the moment we remember who we are without the mediation of machines, and it continues every time we choose authentic connection over digital performance, present-moment awareness over algorithmic distraction, and human values over technological imperatives.

In the end, Orwell's warning was not about the inevitability of totalitarian control but about the importance of conscious resistance to forces that would reduce human beings to mere objects of manipulation and control. We still have the power to choose consciousness over compulsion, freedom over convenience, and love over submission.

The screen is watching, but we are still here, still human, still capable of looking away.

The future remains unwritten.

Also by David G. Stone

BEYOND THE VEIL: The Uncompromising Life of James Baldwin
James Baldwin: A Life in Four Acts: Volume 1: "Harlem's Son" (1924-1948)
James Baldwin: A Life in Four Acts: Volume 2: "The Paris Years" (1948-1957)
James Baldwin: A Life in Four Acts: Volume 3: "The Fire This Time" (1957-1968)
James Baldwin: A Life in Four Act Volume 4: "The Final Years" (1968-1987)

THE CELESTIAL BONDS SAGA
The Phoenix And The Shadow: A warrior bound to fire.
The Dragon's Claim: She swore she'd never surrender.
The Qilin's Reckoning
The Jade Throne
The Crimson Eclipse

The Covenant Keeper Saga
The Siren's Covenant: A Dark Fantasy Novel of Ocean Magic, Blood Bonds, and the War Between Worlds
The Abyssal Throne: A Dark Fantasy of Ancient Powers and Forbidden Depths
The Drowned Crown: A Dark Fantasy of Ancient Oaths and Ocean Magic

The Leviathan's Pact: A Dark Fantasy of Ancient Bargains and Oceanic War
The Abyssal Verdict: How Love Changed the Pattern

The Oscarville Chronicles

The Promised Land: The Rise Of Oscarville America's Forgotten Black Paradise
The Reckoning Comes: How Oscarville became a target
Waters of Betrayal: The Government Conspiracy That Drowned Oscarville Forever
Beneath The Surface: The Drowning Of Oscarville
Legacy Of The Depths: How Oscarville's Ghosts Haunt Lake Lanier Today

THE YASUKE CHRONICLES

The Forgotten Warrior: From the Shores of Mozambique to the Gates of Kyoto
The Rise Of The Black Samurai
The Last Stand

Standalone

African Darkness: The continent where vampire legends began
Atomic Grit: Tiny Habits That Build Unstoppable Willpower
The Piper's Curse: A Song For The Damned
The Billion Dollar Heist: How Hackers Nearly Stole from Bangladesh Bank
Death's Gentleman: The Baron Samedi Chronicles
Chasing Outlaws: Bass Reeves and the Taming of the Territory
The Ecstasy Chronicles: John Fletcher and the Golden Age of Hip-Hop: How Whodini's Visionary Shaped Rap Culture and Defined a Generation
Blood in the Bay: The DNA Hunt for Charles Jackson and the Untold Story of Oakland's Most Elusive Killer

Children of the Night: Louisiana's Living Vampires: True Stories from the Shadow World of New Orleans
The Patent Warriors: Untold Stories of Black Innovators Who Fought the System and Won From Courtroom Battles to Breakthrough Inventions That Shaped American Industry (1865-1965)
Caught: The Ashley Madison Data Breach and the Unmasking of America's Secret Lives From Josh Duggar to Washington Insiders
The Stolen Gift: When Science Took What Wasn't Theirs
Badge of Honor
Thunder on the Frontier
The Last Socialite: Ghislaine Maxwell's Journey from Billionaire Parties to a Brooklyn Cell
The Socialite's Secret: Inside Ghislaine Maxwell's Web of Power, Privilege, and Predation
Ted Bundy: The Charismatic Predator
Aileen Wuornos: America's Female Serial Killer
Jeffrey Dahmer: The Milwaukee Monster
John Wayne Gacy: The Killer Clown
The Zodiac Killer: The Unsolved Enigma
The Butcher of Congo: How King Leopold II's Greed Created History's Most Brutal Colonial Nightmare
The Idaho Student Murders: Inside The Bryan Kohberger Case
The Quiet Accomplice: A Gripping Psychological Crime Thriller
Fangs of the French Quarter: Real Vampire Encounters in New Orleans
Exploit: The Rise Of Mara Voss
The Idaho Student Murders: Inside the Bryan Kohberger Case
Steel Dreams: The Forgotten Genius Behind America's Most Iconic Chopper
Survive The Season: California
Survive The Season Florida
Andrei Chikatilo: The Soviet Monster
The Werewolf's Shadow: Inside the Mind of Russia's Most Prolific Serial Killer
Survive the Season: Gulf States
Survive The Season: MidWest USA

Survive the Season: NorthEast USA
Survive The Season: Pacific NorthWest
Survive the Season: Texas
The 300 Million Yen Affair: Japan's Vanishing Cash Case
Cambridge Five: Britain's Most Notorious Spy Ring
Markus Wolf: The Stasi's Master of Disguise
Virginia Hall: The Limping Lady Who Outwitted the Nazis
Room 101 Has WI-FI: How Digital Technology Turned Orwell's Warning Into Today's World

Watch for more at https://www.elcpublishing.com.

About the Author

Passionate about educating others, David G. Stone has now turned their expertise into an easy-to-follow guide designed to help remote workers, freelancers, and businesses safeguard their online accounts. Through The Remote Worker's Guide to Password Management, they provide practical, real-world strategies to enhance digital security and prevent cyber risks.

Read more at https://www.elcpublishing.com.

www.ingramcontent.com/pod-product-compliance
Lightning Source LLC
LaVergne TN
LVHW050747061126
851857LV00026B/637